HIDDEN
HISTORY

HIDDEN

*African American Cemeteries
in Central Virginia*

HISTORY

Lynn Rainville

University of Virginia Press   *Charlottesville and London*

University of Virginia Press
© 2014 by the Rector and Visitors of the University of Virginia
All rights reserved
Printed in the United States of America on acid-free paper

First published 2014
First paperback edition published 2016
ISBN 978-0-8139-3891-2 (paper)

1 3 5 7 9 8 6 4 2

LIBRARY OF CONGRESS CATALOGING-IN-PUBLICATION DATA

Rainville, Lynn.
    Hidden history : African American cemeteries in central Virginia / Lynn Rainville.
        pages   cm
    Includes bibliographical references and index.
    ISBN 978-0-8139-3534-8 (cloth : alk. paper) — ISBN 978-0-8139-3535-5 (e-book)
    1. African American cemeteries—Virginia—Albemarle County—History. 2. African American
cemeteries—Virginia—Amherst County—History. 3. African Americans—Funeral customs
and rites—Virginia—Albemarle County—History. 4. African Americans—Funeral customs and
rites—Virginia—Amherst County—History. I. Title.
    F232.A3R35 2014
    393.93089'960730755482—dc23

                                                                                          2013017583

For my parents,
who instilled in me the
desire to explore

Contents

Illustrations

Maps

Preface

In the spring of 2008 I received a series of phone calls and e-mails from an archaeologist who has spent dozens of hours mapping Virginia cemeteries with me. Leah and her husband, Joey, first noticed the damage when they witnessed a crew from the electric company driving machinery across the small cemetery located near their house in Crimora, Virginia. Apparently, while pruning tree limbs along some existing power lines near her house, a cleaning crew with a tractor and Bush Hog had severely damaged a historic black cemetery. Such an event is all too common, but it highlights the precarious nature of unmarked historic cemeteries.

This unnamed cemetery near Rock Mountain Lane was originally associated with the now demolished Wesley/Belvedere Chapel, a late nineteenth-century African American church once surrounded by a black neighborhood. Many of the original residents have long since moved on, leaving behind white newcomers such as Leah and Joey, and an elderly caretaker who felt powerless to defend the cemetery against the cleaning crew. Longtime neighbors remember the cemetery before the construction of Rock Mountain Lane. They believe that the road cuts right through it and that some of the graves must be under the asphalt.

The remaining monuments range from carved marble to metal funeral-home markers. The few inscribed stones date from the early twentieth century, with birth dates from the 1840s to the 1880s. One of these marked headstones belonged to a free black man, Napoleon Vena, who was registered in Augusta County in the 1850s. Freed African Americans were required to register annually with local authorities—a means of monitoring and restricting them, even when they were not in bondage.[1]

When Leah noticed the Bush Hog parked among the markers, it had already damaged several stones and created deep ruts in the middle of the cemetery. Nearby stood the line of utility poles that had prompted the destruction. The electrical cooperative was focused on keeping the lines free of debris; the workers were just doing their job. Unfortunately, the gravestones were casualties of the operation.

In an effort to prevent more destruction, Leah and Joey planted dozens of pink flags to highlight the rows of graves, both marked and unmarked. Then they began their public relations campaign. Initially they hoped to convince the power company to pay for the damage done to the stones and clean up the site. Instead, they met resistance at every level, everything from a lack of acknowledgment of culpability to a flat-out denial of the cemetery's existence. They spent a week placing unreturned phone calls to an employee of the power company. When they first observed the desecration, they contacted the Augusta County sheriff's office (in Virginia, the destruction of funerary monuments is a crime). A deputy arrived at the cemetery and sent a message to a supervisor at the Shenandoah Valley Electric Cooperative (SVEC), who said that something would be done immediately. But the next workday saw the return of a pair of crew members, neither of whom had been told to cease their work. One of the men admitted to having seen the headstones they were running over; the other maintained that he'd never run over a cemetery in twenty years.

Leah called the power company again. This time she spoke with the manager of district operations. He repeatedly insisted that Leah was mistaken about the presence of a burial ground at any site where his crew would be working. She asked him what the procedure would be for getting the cemetery marked on the SVEC maps and was told that the company had no maps of the lines or poles that they maintain—contradicting Leah's sighting of a nearby telephone pole tagged with a yellow label presumably indicating that the location had been designated as a cemetery.

Finally, Leah called 911 and reported a crime in progress, pursuant to the Code of Virginia, section 18.2-127. Her call was returned by a second sheriff's deputy, who said that he would "slip up there sometime." He called her back about forty-five minutes later to say that he'd talked to the crew on the scene and that while the tractor was still parked on top of the gravesites, they had promised him they would move it later.

A week after her original e-mail, Leah left a message on my answering machine, sounding very frustrated and worn down. While she and her husband had spent dozens of hours trying to rally support to protect the cemetery, only a handful of groups expressed an interest in her mission. Her last sentence was "I'm not sure why I should care about this cemetery any longer." Leah's concern is valid. Why should nondescendants or even the descendants themselves care about an abandoned, century-old graveyard? In today's age of rising cremations, would it be better to use the land for something more practical and remove skeletal remains into European-style crypts, thereby reclaiming even more land from the dead?

Despite their initial discouragement, Leah and Joey persevered, and several other community members joined them in the battle to protect the site. Their e-mail campaign—distributed to the power company, the sheriff's office, a local historical and genealogical society, an Augusta County district supervisor, the State Corporation Commission, U.S. Representative Bob Goodlatte's office, some of the SVEC board members, three local archaeologists, two newspaper publishers, and an employee at the Department of Historic Resources in Richmond—in combination with repeated phone calls, finally prompted a response from the power company. The electric company agreed to clean up the cut brush they left behind from their initial clear-cutting efforts. The second step was to add the site to their maps so that it wouldn't happen again. To improve community relations in the future, a supervisor looked into the breakdowns in communication among employees and contractors. Finally, the Virginia Department of Transportation placed "no mowing" signs and bollards along the road's edge to discourage intrusion by cars, Bush Hogs, or snowplows. And a local poultry farmer started spraying herbicide under the utility lines to decrease the need for SVEC crews to bring in heavy equipment.

In the end, Leah and Joey's efforts paid off and helped prevent further destruction of the site. But it is unfortunate that they had to fight so hard to protect the funerary monuments in this small cemetery. Moreover, the lackluster response from the sheriff's office and the initial stonewalling from the power company demonstrate just how difficult it can be to ensure a modicum of consideration and respect for these sacred sites.

My own study of historic African American cemeteries began by coincidence. As an undergraduate at Dartmouth College, I needed a paper topic for a class on gender and anthropology, and I wanted an excuse to collect data outside so I could enjoy the beautiful New England fall. Having just read the classic article by Edwin Dethlefsen and James Deetz on colonial-era death's heads and grinning cherubs, I decided to study gender relations as evidenced by pronouns carved into gravestones.[2] I found that colonial New England husbands referred to their wives as "consorts" and that women were almost always memorialized in reference to their relation to men (e.g., "wife of" or "daughter of").[3] The social identities of men were commemorated by reference to their occupations (e.g., "Dr." or "Professor"). Their identity was defined independently of their marital status; they were almost never referred to as the "husband of" their wives.

I enjoyed writing the paper but did not return to the topic until my senior year, when I decided to study gravestone variability for my honors thesis in anthropology. Borrowing one of the earliest Mac PowerBooks, I collected information from twenty-five hundred stones in the public cemeteries within one New Hampshire township. The thesis, titled "Hanover Deathscapes: Attitudes toward Death and Community as Reflected in Cemeteries and Gravestones; An Archaeological Investigation of Mortuary Variability in Hanover Township, 1770–1920," demonstrated that gravestones illustrate cultural themes, such as ideas about the family, religion, society, and attitudes toward death.

I went on to earn my Ph.D. in Mesopotamian archaeology, but when I was hired to teach at Sweet Briar College (one hour south of Charlottesville, Virginia), my interest in historic cemeteries was renewed. I was surprised to learn that the college was founded by the daughter of a slave owner and that the three thousand acres of the campus were once plantation fields. Several structures remained from the antebellum period, including a standing slave cabin. By the end of my first semester, I was beginning to ask questions. What was known of the antebellum African American community? Where were the other slave cabins that housed the dozens of enslaved people? Were there any artifacts remaining from their daily lives? And, of course, who was buried in the recently discovered slave cemetery?

As it turned out, my research into the Sweet Briar Slave Cemetery was the beginning of an ongoing project. More than ten years and dozens of cemeteries later, I have created a website to disseminate the genealogical and historical importance of these sites to the public and the academy and have written several articles in locally accessible journals, such as the local historical society magazine and the college alumnae magazine.[4] My research includes archaeological investigations of cemetery sites (mapping and recording the aboveground features), recording all of the legible inscriptions from gravestones, conducting oral interviews with descendants, and archival research into enslaved and postbellum African American communities. Although my academic training is in archaeology, I do not excavate or disturb any human remains in my research; all of the information that I collect from Virginia cemeteries comes from aboveground artifacts.

I have come to view this work as an opportunity to bring the past lives of ordinary and exceptional African Americans into public and scholarly discourse. We cannot fully understand nineteenth-century Virginia history if we do not account for these people, who often made up more than 50 percent of a Piedmont county's population between about 1830 and 1860. Their achievements and disappointments must be incorporated into local histories, and in turn they will help us to assess the impact of these families and communities on broader trends in American history.

Cemetery sites preserve the voices of the past, telling of family intrigue, neighborhood relations, community history—even artistic skills.

This book presents more than a decade of research into more than 150 historic African American cemeteries in central Virginia, primarily focused on Albemarle and Amherst Counties, but also containing examples from a dozen other Virginia counties. It provides an overview of the rich mortuary and funerary traditions of African Americans between the late eighteenth and mid-twentieth centuries, using cemetery landscapes, gravestones, obituaries, wills, deeds, letters, family Bibles, and oral histories. It discusses how to locate these cemeteries, methods for recording cemetery features, and the challenges of preserving them.

In this book, I try to answer my friend Leah's fundamental questions: Why are historic cemeteries important, and why should we care about them?

Notes

1. In the antebellum period, a small portion of Africans and African Americans avoided or escaped enslavement. In nineteenth-century records, these individuals were referred to as "Free Persons of Color," "Free Negros," or "Free Blacks." The last term will be used in this book.

2. Dethlefsen and Deetz, "Death's Heads, Cherubs, and Willow Trees."

3. A widowed woman was called a "relict."

4. Rainville, "An Investigation of an Enslaved Community"; Rainville, "Saving the Remains of the Day"; Rainville, "African American History at the Sweet Briar Plantation"; Rainville, "Social Memory." For the past two hundred years, various terms have been used to identify people of African descent living in America. In the archival records used in this study, those terms range from "negro" to "colored," "Afro-American," "black," and today's preferred terminology, "African American." This book follows the *Chicago Manual of Style* in printing the phrase without a hyphen even when used as an adjective.

Acknowledgments

I have been fortunate to receive advice and support on this project from numerous individuals. These enthusiasts ranged from descendents of individuals buried within the cemeteries that I studied to professional historians and archaeologists and from landowners to hikers. Since my work on historic African American cemeteries has spanned more than a decade, I cannot possibly list the hundreds of individuals who helped me along the way, but the following lists give a small sense of the community effort that went into the research behind this book.

I received generous financial support from the Virginia Foundation for the Humanities, the National Endowment for the Humanities, and Sweet Briar College. These grants enabled me to hire assistants to help with the recording of gravestones and mapping of cemeteries. Some of these assistants include Derek Wheeler, Celine Beauchamp, Julie Solometo, Steve Burdin, Don Gaylord, Nathaniel Schwartz, Grace Miller, Laquisha Banks, and several Sweet Briar students, including Mandi Ponton, Dana Ripperton, Anne Mathias, Sasha Levine, Katharina Fritzler, Karli Sakas, Wendy Harder, Jodie Weber, Tiffany Meadows, Crystal Collins, Katie Miller, and Ashleigh Hawkins. Many other local residents volunteered their time to help read inscriptions and take photographs of gravestones.

I have had the pleasure of working with many descendent communities. These families generously shared family stories and photographs and helped me locate and identify historic black cemeteries. I spoke with descendents at most of the sites where I worked, but a few individuals took additional time to work with me in the subsequent research phases. These skilled family genealogists include Shirley Parrish, Shelley Murphy, Edwina St. Rose, Lenora McQueen, Sheila Rogers, Linda Johnson, Jackie Johnson, Jasper "Eddie" Fletcher, Crystal Rosson, William "Billy" Hearns, Liz Cherry Jones, Mary Reaves, Virginia Burton, Gene Burton, Jada Golden Sherman, Vickie Dean, and Bettie Fitch. I also owe a debt of gratitude to Julian Burke (now deceased) for the work that he led on transcribing African

American death records and Martin Burks III for sharing information about area cemeteries and burial practices.

Many of the historic African American cemeteries discussed in this book lie on private land (often no longer owned by the families interred at the site). Thus I often relied on the hospitality of current landowners to get access to these sites. I am very grateful for the opportunity to visit sites located on land owned by the Hart family, the Carter family, the Douglass family, the Pflug family, Wilson Steppe, the Innisfree community, Wiley Martin, Alison and Mark Trimpe, Mario diValmarana, Jim Murray, Phyllis Ripper, and Peter Agelesto. In other cases, the descendants of white families who once owned plantations in the region shared with me their research, which helped me locate antebellum cemeteries, most notably Kevin Brown and Jeanne Brown.

The Charlottesville region is rich in historians and archaeologists. Many of these experts helped me track down archival leads and locate historic cemeteries, especially K. Edward Lay, Leah Stearns, Joey Combs, Ted Delaney, Mieka Brand Polanco, Alice and Jon Cannon, Sara Lee Barnes, Robert Vernon, Scot French, Sam Towler, Ben Ford, Steve Thompson, Margaret O'Bryant, Cinder Stanton, Gayle Schulman, Leni Sorensen, Fraser Neiman, Sara Bon-Harper, Jerome S. Handler, Reginald Butler, Steven Meeks, and Dede Smith.

In some cases I reached out to specialists to answer questions about specific topics. I am very grateful for the insights provided by Dr. Rebecca Ambers (associate professor of environmental science at Sweet Briar College, who helped me identify gravestone material), Rick Barton (for providing statistical assistance), Laura Knott (for giving me references about historic cemetery landscaping), and Tamara Northern (curator emeritus, Dartmouth College, for images of African obelisks). The staff at the Albemarle Charlottesville Historical Society, the Amherst Historical Society and Museum, and the University of Virginia Special Collections Library were extremely helpful.

Any remaining errors in the book are my changes to the professional and much-appreciated editing assistance from Jessica Mesman Griffith, Carrie Brown, Alice Cannon, Kathleen Placidi, Carolyn Cades, George Roupe, Jane and Roger Rainville, and Ian Freedman. I also very much appreciate the insight and suggestions provided by Lorena Walsh and two anonymous reviewers.

My husband, Baron, provided support and honest assessments of the various versions of the manuscript. My twin daughters were born during the editorial stages of this research and are rapidly proving adept at locating small stones sticking out from the ground. I hope to instill a love of graveyards and their histories in this next generation.

HIDDEN
HISTORY

1

FINDING ZION

On a crisp fall Saturday in 2008, following a lead in attempting to locate a "Burton Family Cemetery," I traveled down a rural Virginia lane to an African American church cemetery. When I arrived, I found the churchyard deserted, with only silent stone sentinels to note my approach.

The gravestones mark each life, often clustered into families, illustrating untold histories. I document each stone, one person at a time. Later, I will upload the photos and inscriptions to a website where I have collected six thousand other memorials from historic African American cemeteries in central Virginia.

I have visited over 150 such cemeteries in a multicounty area; of these, I have documented 118 with maps, photographs, and additional research. This includes more than six thousand individual stones, dating between 1800 and 2000. But many more unmarked or forgotten burials remain to be photographed and recorded. There is no good way to estimate the number of African American burials in Virginia between the nineteenth and twentieth centuries, but we can review the census figures for one Virginia county and estimate the number of deaths per one thousand individuals per year. The U.S. Slave Census for Albemarle County, Virginia, illustrates that the enslaved population more than doubled between 1790 and 1860, from 5,579 individuals to 13,916;[1] the number of deaths would have paralleled this increase in births if it were a closed population with no out-migration. To the contrary, Albemarle County would have experienced in-migration from the Tidewater and out-migration to other southern states (especially Kentucky and Tennessee). Not knowing those migration figures precisely, we can crudely estimate that at least six thousand individuals (or approximately eighty-six per year) died in Albemarle County prior to emancipation while enslaved on a plantation or a small family farm. Only a fraction of their graves have been located.[2]

Another way to calculate the number of African American burials for a given time period is to search death certificates for the county and add up the number of reported deaths. In Virginia, death certificates were not officially collected until 1912. In Albemarle County, the Charlottesville African American Genealogy Group transcribed 8,088 death certificates for burials that occurred between 1917 and 2001. As a crude estimate of mortality, that translates to ninety-six burials per year over an eighty-four-year period. Hundreds of these individuals lie buried on family land in small, sometimes forgotten graveyards. Sometimes these bodies reemerge in surprising ways, as when an old cemetery is discovered because of a modern construction project. In other instances, remains are lost, forever buried under unmarked ground. We lose important pieces of local and family history when we allow these sacred sites to go unrecorded and disappear.

Origins

In 2001, I was hired to teach at Sweet Briar College, the site of a former plantation willed by its nineteenth-century owner to become a school for women. The college has retained much of its original agricultural land. Hundreds of historic and archaeological sites remain on the three-thousand-acre campus. The plantation owners' cemetery was well known to the campus community. Every year students and faculty would march up to the plantation graveyard and lay flowers at the grave of the founder and her daughter, in whose honor the school was founded. Situated atop a high hill, containing tall obelisks and surrounded by a stone wall, this cemetery was hard to miss. But the resting place of the enslaved individuals who worked on the plantation had been lost to modern memory.

Fortuitously, a riding instructor at the college had spent years exploring the fields and, just before his retirement, announced the discovery of an unmarked cemetery, overgrown with brush. He had located the plantation's slave burial ground. As the college proceeded with plans to erect a memorial, I mapped the cemetery and began researching the individuals who were anonymously buried under the gravestones; as is often the case in slave cemeteries, none of the markers were inscribed.

In my research of three dozen antebellum cemeteries, which include 406 individual slave gravestones, I've found less than 5 percent of the markers to be inscribed. There are a few explanations for this. A law was passed in Virginia in 1831 that made it illegal to teach "free Negroes" or slaves how to read and write.[3] We know from many sources that this law was not always followed, but if you were black and literate, carving a tombstone would be damning evidence to anyone who wanted to make trouble. The urge to carve gravestones is closely tied to a sense of individualism and the desire to know where each individual is buried. Yet within many enslaved communities, kin were forcibly separated through sales, inheritance, or death. Given the fragility of their family structure, these communities developed extended and multigenerational kinship connections to safeguard domestic ties. In antebellum slave graveyards we see this focus on family units rather than individuals in unmarked but uniform stones. These individual yet unmonogrammed grave markers of African Americans would not interfere with mourning practices that were aimed at remembering families. Moreover, this preemancipation tradition of uninscribed stones puts more importance on oral histories, which, among other details, pass down the location of burials from generation to generation. Native and African American communities are known for their centuries-long oral traditions. Our difficulty is in finding a living informant who has preserved such knowledge generations later.

While mapping the cemetery at Sweet Briar, I realized how easily it might have remained buried under leaves and fallen trees, forever lost to the living whose ancestors were buried there. Thankfully, the college realized that it, too, was close to losing a significant part of its history. When I began my investigation of the Sweet Briar site, I could find no existing studies of aboveground remains from slave cemeteries in America, so I attempted to locate another cemetery in Albemarle County, hoping to document what sorts of variations existed from plantation to plantation.[4] I had no idea what to expect. Would there be any inscribed graves? Did descendants continue to visit the gravesites? Would it be easy to locate these 150-year-old sites on the modern, often modified landscapes of antebellum plantations?

I concentrated my search for African American cemeteries in central Virginia. Between 2001 and 2011, I visited burial sites, mapping and recording all the aboveground features; collected oral interviews from descendants; conducted archival research of the surrounding communities; and recorded all legible inscriptions from the gravestones. Though often brief and cryptic, these inscriptions can point the way to a wealth of information about the community in which a person lived and died.

Most gravestones compress a life story into a name and date of birth and death, but with additional archival research, an individual's passage becomes part of a larger story—a story of families and neighborhoods, successes and failures. Sometimes the impact of a single life is still felt today, far beyond the grave site.

Burton Family Cemetery

Some of my methods are necessarily more intuitive than scientific. Small family cemeteries in particular are rarely noted on topographic maps. In 2008, on that fall day when I went in search of the Burton Family Cemetery I'd seen mentioned in several funeral records, I used a method that works about half the time: I checked a map for roads named after the family. These roads often correlate with homesteads and thus with family burial grounds.

In this case, by researching the death certificates for the Burtons, I knew they had died in Albemarle County, so I'd already narrowed my geographic search. I quickly found a road named "Burton Lane" in the county atlas and began driving up and down the road, searching for any signs of a graveyard: a fence, markers, or even a sign.

After driving back and forth for about thirty minutes, I noticed a two-foot-long sign that read "Burton" in the front yard of a modest yellow 1950s ranch house. I could not believe my luck: how many people signpost their surnames in the front yard? For all I knew, the Burtons had moved out decades ago and the current owner had simply neglected to take down the sign, but it was the only lead I had, so I pulled into the driveway. Fortunately, the elderly woman who came to the door was indeed a Burton—Virginia Burton—and she'd lived in this rural neighborhood for fifty-three years. Her husband of forty-five years, Curtis, had died in 1998.

As Mrs. Burton recounted a brief family history, my eyes scanned her crowded living room. If gravestones provide permanent family memorials, the material culture within our houses provides an ephemeral one. I saw dozens of family photos—on the walls, stuck under glass on side tables—and knickknacks of all sorts. On every available horizontal surface sat a glass menagerie of animals, from domestic to exotic. Virginia's faith was also clearly on display, in objects ranging from a prominently placed Bible and a pair of black angels to religious inscriptions and wall hangings that encouraged the viewer, "Don't Quit."

Zion Baptist Church

While she wasn't aware of a nearby cemetery, Mrs. Burton pointed me to her church, Zion Baptist Church, a mile down the road in North Garden, where many of her family members lay at rest. She counted off the relatives buried there: her husband, sister, three uncles, and mother and father. I noticed on her wall a folksy painting of an oddly proportioned church, with many more than four sides. When I commented on it, she revealed that she was the artist. The "ten-cornered church" was the original Zion Church, built in 1871 (fig. 1). Mrs. Burton theorized that the younger members wanted a more modern building. In particular they were not happy with the lack of indoor plumbing for the congregation. So they built a modern, concrete church and, in 1975, tore down the one-hundred-year-old structure. Only later did they find out that it had been recorded in the *Historic American Buildings Survey* as a rare example of a decahedral American church.[5]

Today, any number of preservation groups would have jumped to help Mrs. Burton preserve the Zion Church. But in the 1970s, the preservation movement was still an elite, predominantly white group, and African American history was undervalued in federal programs. At the time, the National Register of Historic Places

FIG. 1 Original Zion Baptist Church, decahedron-shaped building built in 1871, Albemarle County. Photograph taken shortly before its demolition. (Photograph courtesy of K. Edward Lay, May 1975)

listed homes associated with notable white men. In fact, the entire American preservation movement had started in the nineteenth century, when a group of women banded together to save George Washington's Mount Vernon. Fortunately, times have changed, and the register has broadened its scope to include historic black schools, old barns, rural cemeteries, and Native American archaeological sites. But it was too late to save the unique and beautiful ten-sided church.

Further destruction of the Zion Church grounds resulted from the enlargement of the nearby rural throughway, Route 29. Mrs. Burton recalled that many gravestones were moved or destroyed during the road expansion. "It was so bad to disturb those old people," Mrs. Burton lamented. When I arrived at the cemetery, I found a small group of older stones adjacent to the road, while the majority of the stones lay safe, a greater distance away. It's possible that many burials lie under the current roadway, their markers discarded during the construction.

I was able to guess the age of the cemetery by a quick perusal of the stone types. Among the surviving headstones are those crafted from older materials, such as marble and fieldstones, as well as newer granite markers that did not become popular in America until the late nineteenth century. It was also important to realize what might be missing: the wooden stakes that undoubtedly once marked the numerous depressions. I guessed which floral plantings might have originally been used to mark burials. What stood before me in 2008 suggested that the cemetery had been in use for a century or more. Like many black cemeteries in the South, it was probably founded after emancipation, in parallel with the first free black churches. This guess is supported by records that date the founding of the Zion Baptist Church to 1871.[6]

In the new portion of the cemetery, I saw a series of orderly rows with evenly spaced markers of all shapes and sizes. I wondered if I would find the deceased family members that Mrs. Burton had mentioned during our visit. I took out my digital camera, a sheet of graph paper, a measuring tape, and a mirror to redirect sunlight onto particularly dark or hard-to-read stones. With my measuring appara-tus I created a sketch of the markers, roughly to scale. I often bring a paper spread-sheet to label each stone as I photograph it, recording any available information. With inscribed stones, it's most efficient to methodically photograph each stone beginning at one end of a row rather than transcribing the information in the field. Later, at home, I transcribe the information from the photographs into an Excel spreadsheet that records two dozen categories of information. This rapid recording method is particularly advantageous during the hot summer months, when ticks take advantage of organisms that stand too long in one place, or on cold winter days when equipment, pens, and surveyors tend to freeze up if you stand still. That day, the temperature was a comfortable sixty degrees, but the good light would only last for another hour, so I moved quickly from stone to stone.

Having spent two decades recording gravestone inscriptions, I immediately noticed that the Zion Church Cemetery contained a high percentage of "love" inscriptions: "In Loving Memory," "Beloved Husband," "I Love You—Miss You," and "Always Loving, Always Loved." Other inscriptions focused on a subtheme: "Always In Our Hearts" and the variation "Forever In Our Hearts." A remarkable number, 33 percent of its inscribed stones, used this adage. The "loving" theme was an intriguing deviation from the standard, more prosaic inscriptions such as "In Memory of" and "Rest in Peace." I made a note to research any possible connection with a nearby "Loving Road"—probably just a coincidence, but you never know.

Beyond the unique inscription variations at the Zion Cemetery, I uncovered many typical structural forms and motifs. Two common styles are the standardized white marble stones provided by the government for veterans and the short metal markers provided by funeral homes. Most graves (70 percent or more) bore plain markers, often carved from marble or granite, with only the name of the deceased and birth and death dates (or, in some cases, a death date and age). But the cem-etery also had a surprising number of inscribed and decorated graves: fifty-four stones had some inscription, and seventy-one were decorated with a design, some containing multiple motifs. One was inscribed "Sending Up My Timber," the title of a popular gospel song of the era.

The congregation selected typical late nineteenth- and twentieth-century mo-tifs: the majority, about 65 percent, expressed religious themes (such as crosses, praying hands, Bibles, and rays of sunlight from heaven), while the remaining designs focused on floral themes (mostly roses and ivy, associated with mourning and immortality, respectively). Each of these motifs was used indiscriminately for men and women, the old and the young. Other motifs are specific to certain identities: an infant is commemorated with a ribbon tied into a bow at the top of the stone or a pair of baby shoes (all inscribed into granite). On another, a carved dove, carrying a piece of ivy in its beak, flies through an elaborate curtain. The stone commemorates Angieline Walker, who died at age thirty-four in 1920. A more contemporary stone, from 2004, is a three-dimensional double heart. Each heart represents half of a married couple, with a ribbon inscribed with the family name connecting the two.

Some church members expressed their aesthetic preferences by combining two otherwise common styles into an unusual stone type. In one example, a carver pasted a metal funeral-home marker in the center of a piece of whitewashed concrete. The metal markers usually stand alone, stuck into the ground on a rod. An even more unusual variant in the Zion Church Cemetery is a concrete stone with small pieces of quartz affixed to the front (fig. 2). A three-foot-high concrete cross with pieces of crystal set into the mortar marks another cluster of graves. These styles show the ingenuity and creativity of the community, which adopted popular styles but added their own signatures to these funerary markers.

Near this same cluster of crosses lie Mrs. Burton's relatives: her parents, the Carters, and her husband, Curtis. Later I used census data to supplement the family tree that Mrs. Burton shared with me. Virginia Burton is only two generations removed from slavery. Since less than 5 percent of Albemarle's African American population was free, it is likely that her ancestors were enslaved.[7]

At the Zion Church Cemetery, the earliest recorded burial was in 1908, but there were probably earlier burials marked with impermanent memorials, given that the

FIG. 2 Decorated concrete gravestone in the Zion Baptist Church Cemetery, Albemarle County. (Photograph by Lynn Rainville, 2012)

church itself was founded twenty years before that date. The earliest preserved headstone, a marble one for Louise Walker, has fallen over, but it is legible—for now. In another five or ten years, the grass will cover it completely, and leaf decay will bury it. This is a common fate for stones that have tipped over, making it important to prop up fallen stones. Moreover, a headstone lying on the ground face up will erode much more quickly, as it is directly exposed to rain and snow.

Among the approximately 140 burials, two dozen were unmarked depressions or illegible markers, leaving only 118 individual burials with legible markers. Among these, the average age at death was sixty-six, which is consistent with the life expectancy of a mid-nineteenth- to twentieth-century population. The cemetery residents had been born as early as 1858, seven years prior to emancipation.

Forty different families are buried there, but just three represent the majority of the burials: the Burtons (sixteen burials), the Carters (nine burials), and the Walkers (seventeen burials). As in much of pre–World War II rural America, the multigenerational memorials point to the close-knit character of these communities. Southern African American communities were restricted in their schooling and employment options. Prior to the civil rights movement of the 1950s and 1960s, African American children attended supposedly "separate but equal" black schools, often miles from their homes, passing white public schools each way. In urban areas, there would be segregated elementary, middle, and high schools. In rural communities, more basic facilities often meant just a one-room schoolhouse for black youth, serving all ages of children. Most of these schools went only to the seventh or eighth grade. If parents wanted their children to get more education, they would have to send them to one of a handful of black high schools in Virginia. Most rural families could not afford this expense. Gravestones, of course, do not indicate the amount of schooling that the deceased had, but cross-checking census data does reveal whether someone could read or write. My research revealed that many of the deceased at Zion were illiterate, despite a small school located adjacent to the church. Their occupations did not require literacy as much as hands-on training, reminiscent of the feudal age guilds and apprentice system. They were farmers, blacksmiths, cooks, carpenters, and cobblers. Several of the men worked on the railroad that ran through this rural community.[8]

The Continued Search for the Burton Family Cemetery

My Albemarle County cemetery research received a major boost from the fortunate discovery of the Zion Baptist Church grounds, though my windshield survey of Burton Lane had failed. Fortunately, weeks later at a local historical society meeting, the society's president heard me asking about the Burton Cemetery. He knew of the church cemetery and was friendly with another Burton family member. He sent me Gene Burton's phone number.

I can only imagine how strange my questions sound to families when I call, unannounced, asking where relatives are buried. But they are usually surprisingly gracious. I introduced myself to Gene Burton and asked him if he knew where the Burton Family Cemetery was on Burton Lane, recounting my visit with his cousin Virginia, and my fruitless expedition. Gene was stumped; he'd never heard of a family cemetery along that road. "But several of the North Garden Burtons are buried at the Zion Church," he said.

Disappointed, I thanked him for his time. However, still thinking aloud, he said, "Nope, no family cemetery there at the church. We have our cemetery here in South Garden." The Burton Cemetery wasn't on Burton Lane at all; it was about one hundred feet from his house, a fortunate breakthrough for my research.

Later Gene invited me into his living room on a bitterly cold morning a week before Christmas. We reviewed his immediate family ties so that I could place him in relationship to the North Garden Burtons. Three other families shared his family cemetery, and he ticked off a half dozen more neighboring burial grounds off the top of his head. His ties to nearby black communities provided a wealth of knowledge of deceased family members and their final resting places.

When we walked up to his own family cemetery, Gene, a treasure trove of African American history, was able to recount some of the tragedies behind the younger deaths: a girl strangled by her own mother at age six, a teenager shot by mistake in Charlottesville while trying to pay his rent, an infant girl who died in 1979. From there we walked to his former neighbor's house, now an abandoned ruin, where a second family cemetery lay, covered by weeds. It contained only five burials, but they illustrated a range of gravestone styles: a flat piece of soapstone carved into a pointed rectangle, small fieldstones, and even a metal and a granite marker. Stylistically these markers ranged over a one-hundred-year period, showing a remarkable diversity for a very small family cemetery. An eight-foot-high berm protects the site from the road, and the rolling landscape includes planted yucca bushes.

Black Cemeteries in North and South Garden

On the same day as my visit with Gene Burton, I visited the larger church cemeteries at the nearby Rising Sun Baptist Church and South Garden Baptist Church. The density of black churches and cemeteries within a three-mile radius illustrates the interconnected communities of the living and the dead.

The Rising Sun Baptist Church Cemetery contained several dozen stones of all shapes and materials, roughly aligned into rows and located about one hundred feet from the church. Some markers were illegible; others were granite with multiple motifs and inscriptions. The earliest inscribed markers denoted individuals who were born in the 1890s, around the time the church was founded. But the most recent were surrounded by flowers, with dirt still mounded above the grave shaft.

The South Garden Baptist Church Cemetery was far more recent than the other two church burial grounds. The earliest grave dated to only 1989, though the church itself was founded in 1871. The stones were lined in perfect order along an asphalt road behind the church. I had actually visited this same location a year earlier but noted "no cemetery" because I had not driven far enough down the driveway.

Now, as I walked down the rows taking photos, I noticed the graves were lined up in chronological order. This was the first time I had seen this practice in a black cemetery. In other parts of America the Moravian religion organizes its cemeteries in this manner to encourage egalitarianism. But here in rural Virginia it was not clear why these African American churches had selected this manner of burial. Later, it occurred to me that the burials may have been relocated to this site and organized chronologically after the move. The graves at another nearby African American church, the Covesville First Baptist Church, were also arranged in orderly rows. Most cemeteries encourage families to cluster relatives together, and the result over time is irregular groupings of stones. But if you are trying to fit the greatest number of people into a limited amount of space, then a chronological and orderly line of graves makes sense. However, chronological organization is more difficult for families. When I asked Gene Burton if he had any relatives buried here, he replied that an uncle was buried there "somewhere," but he couldn't recall exactly where. This efficient spatial system can dissolve physical associations among family stones.

The last location that I visited was the hardest to find, the original Covesville First Baptist Church Cemetery, established around 1890. The precise founding date of this church is not recorded, but as early as 1890 a black newspaper reported that "Friday [after Easter] being a day of fasting and praying several persons went to Covesville where we feasted upon the Country pies, cakes, and chickens, and preyed much food."[9] In those days, it was a several-hour trip in a wagon to reach Covesville from Charlottesville, the hometown of the reporter quoted above. Apparently, urban black churches sometimes offered field trips to their rural neighbors, reinforcing the ties among dispersed communities, and most likely reuniting multigenerational family members.

The original Covesville cemetery was located near the church. But the 1960s expansion of Route 29—the main north-south thoroughfare in Albemarle County—from a two-lane to a four-lane divided highway confiscated some of the church land. The congregation moved to the other side of the new road, about a mile away. The original cemetery was thus left behind. Today the cemetery is overgrown with dozens of yucca plants. These plants do not normally multiply so prolifically, and the result of their uncontrolled growth, combined with the burgeoning tall wild grasses, is an almost hidden area that makes it difficult to see any of the stones from the road. If Mr. Burton hadn't guided me to the site, I would never have seen them. Only a quarter of the burials were marked; the others were depressions, with an odd row of four white crosses made from PVC tubing complete with plastic caps at each of the three visible ends. There were no names, only crosses. Laid out in a line, they most likely represent unknown but recent burials, given the materials used. It is important to locate these poorly preserved and marked cemeteries before land changes hands or the character of the rural neighborhood changes. And although twenty-first-century online maps and atlases attempt to mark the location of cemeteries, less than a third of the 150 cemeteries that I visited were indicated in these sources.

The Hidden History of Cemeteries

Though the living Burtons knew where their cemeteries—and apparently, many others—were located, the information may not have been passed down to the next generation. With so much oral history preserved only in memory, many of these burial grounds will undoubtedly be forgotten. Would it matter if they were? In this book I suggest many reasons for preserving these outdoor museums of African American culture. One pressing reason to document this hidden history is the value that descendants have always placed on their family history.

Since 2005, I've received dozens of e-mails resulting from the website I created to list the more than six thousand individuals I've surveyed. As a result, I've had the privilege of recording numerous family stories that illustrate the important role of African American families in the growth of central Virginian businesses, agricultural productivity, and cultural innovations in cookery, music, dance, religious worship, and other pursuits. Preserving those stories—and all the information contained in historic graveyards—is important, not just for these families but for our historical record. A cemetery is often the only record we have of the lost community it memorializes.

The Burtons hadn't come to me for help, but many descendants do. For example, I met with a couple who had seen the husband's great-grandmother listed on my website in one of the cemeteries I surveyed. They lived in Santa Fe but were visiting Charlottesville. I took them on a tour of the cemetery, and while we walked, the wife shared her background, which included a wealthy white family who owned several antebellum plantations. Ironically, after researching both their families, I found that the wife's ancestors very likely owned Chestnut Farm, where her husband's family had been enslaved. This often obscure history provides the context for our shared heritage.

2

LOCATING AND
RECORDING THE DEAD

Before recording gravestones, you have to know the location of the cemetery. Unfortunately, there is no master database for American cemeteries. There are dozens of websites that purport to list all local cemeteries by county or township, but these sites rarely include historic nineteenth-century burial grounds. The methods for locating a cemetery vary with its age. For example, slave cemeteries are often located on former plantation land, while free black cemeteries are often in the backyards of old homes. The first half of this chapter describes how to locate these historic cemeteries. Although some techniques are useful for locating any cemetery — white or black, historic or modern — comments are organized in three sections for locating (1) antebellum free black cemeteries, (2) slave cemeteries, and (3) twentieth-century cemeteries.

The second half of the chapter addresses techniques for gathering and recording the information contained within a cemetery. There are several ways to map and record historic African American cemeteries, ranging from detailed investigations to more superficial but still useful recording techniques. I have selected one of the first cemeteries I studied to demonstrate these methods, choosing this example to show that you don't need a background in mapping, geometry, or history in order to accomplish this work. A methodical approach to each stone or depression within a cemetery will help preserve the information for future generations. The appendixes to this book include templates for collecting information from historic burial grounds. The first template is focused on the marker, while the second asks for information about the individual buried under the marker. There are two separate forms because one marker might commemorate multiple individuals, and each person requires a separate form.

Locating Historic Nineteenth-Century Cemeteries

Free black burials are usually the most difficult to find, since these individuals were most often buried on their own land. The term *free black* refers to African Americans during the antebellum period who were manumitted or never enslaved. As free blacks comprised only 3 to 5 percent of Albemarle County's antebellum population[1] and were often interred in small family burial grounds, I learned of only two free black graveyards in Albemarle County (both located in the yards of the deceaseds' homes). Because these rural graves often lack inscriptions, it is difficult to differentiate a free black grave from one belonging to a postbellum African American. Some of the rural graveyards I located may contain the burials of free blacks, but currently I have no proof of this.

In order to locate this type of cemetery you first need to identify free black neighborhoods. There are two leads to follow: old maps that sometimes label these neighborhoods with telling names (such as "Canada"[2] or "Free State") or property records that enable you to locate the houses of free blacks and any possible attendant graveyards. For example, a mid-nineteenth-century free black laundress, Catherine "Kitty" Foster (ca. 1790–1863), who lived just east of the University of Virginia in a community then called "Canada," buried her family in her backyard. The two dozen graves were found by accident in the 1980s, when the university expanded a parking lot. Fortunately, the grave shafts were identified, and special care was taken to protect the burials during additional construction projects (chapter 9 tells more of this story). Graves of free blacks are also found in segregated areas of public cemeteries, but unless you know the names you are looking for, there may not be anything to distinguish the graves of free blacks. For example, a free African American mother and daughter, Agnes (1789–1874) and Lizzle Langley (1833–1891), are buried under a marble obelisk in the Lynchburg city cemetery. Their wealth earnings from a men's "sporting house" afforded them a typical Victorian marker indistinguishable from their wealthy, white grave-plot neighbors, the Cabells.[3]

Locating Slave Cemeteries

Slave cemeteries are rarely indicated on modern maps. So where to begin? There are three primary types of interment for enslaved populations: (1) burial within the cemetery of the plantation owner, sometimes segregated in a corner of the grounds, sometimes not; (2) burial just outside of a white cemetery, whether a churchyard or a family burial ground; (3) burial in a separate cemetery set aside for African Americans. In order to locate any of these three burial site types, you must find the historic plantation associated with the enslaved community. There are two main ways to do this: (1) familiarize yourself with the names of these communities and look for them on a modern map (in urban areas they have often been transformed into subdivisions; in rural areas they are more likely to be partially intact as part of a large homestead); and (2) locate a nineteenth-century map that includes the names of wealthy owners (for Albemarle County there are two options, a Civil War–era map and an 1875 map).

Once you have located a former plantation, look up the white property owner in the 1850 or 1860 slave census.[4] If he or she owned only a handful of slaves, it is more likely that the enslaved community was buried in or near the plantation cemetery (the white cemetery where the owner and his or her family are buried). If there was a large enslaved community on the property, they were probably provided a separate plot of land for burying their dead. In either case, the best way to begin is by locating the white cemetery. This is usually a straightforward task because most plantation cemeteries are located within sight of the owners' house. If the enslaved individuals are not buried within or adjacent to this cemetery, then you need to look for a separate burial ground. In my study of three dozen slave cemeteries in Virginia, the largest ones ranged from one-quarter to one mile away from the main house. There was one outlier, a slave cemetery at the Redlands Plantation that was located more than a mile away. Presumably there were once cabins for field hands located at this distance from the main house.

As you search the countryside, look for several features: high elevations, rings of trees, and old fence lines.[5] The preferred location for a cemetery is on land that lies above the water table. This does not mean that cemeteries can't be located near water. In fact, religious beliefs sometimes encourage people to bury their dead near rivers. The River Jordan is mentioned in the Bible as a source of fertility, for example (Genesis 13:10), and many mourners appear to prefer to bury bodies near rivers. But when remains are buried near a river, an effort is made to find high ground to keep the bodies—at least initially—above water. These hilltop locations are desirable because they are that much closer to the heavens and symbolize the "city on a hill," a biblical reference to Jerusalem and its nearby mountains.

A ring of trees can also signal an old burial ground. While enslaved individuals did not often have the opportunity to do extensive landscaping, a circle of trees can occur for two reasons: deliberate planting or removal of trees within the burial ground. Nineteenth-century descriptions of slave cemeteries support the conclusion that either enslaved people deliberately chose wooded areas or their owners limited them to these areas because they were not ideal for crops. For example, a formerly enslaved individual recalled a "fine smooth slope covered with tall trees" where the plantation community was buried.[6]

Most slave cemeteries were located in agriculturally unproductive areas of a plantation such as in rocky soil or on steep slopes so as not to compete with economically productive land. Because most active nineteenth-century plantations in Virginia used a majority of their land for crops or livestock, much of the area was denuded of trees. Accordingly, the ring of trees around a slave cemetery would stand out on an otherwise clear field. Sometimes slave cemeteries were located at the edge of fields, along fence lines. The arboreal topography today is made up of second- or third-generation trees, so the rings may be less clear and most of the former fields overgrown. But careful observation reveals the remnants of the historic landscape.

While searching for topographic features, consider the surrounding vegetation. Periwinkle, or vinca, often indicates a historic cemetery (black or white). Most of the cemeteries in my study, whether from the nineteenth or twentieth century, contained this plant. It is easiest to locate in the spring, when in bloom with purple flowers.

The following example from my research in central Virginia serves to illustrate recommended steps for locating a slave cemetery. The northwest region of Albemarle County is referred to as Brown's Cove. The Browns were a large white family who emigrated from Hanover County, Virginia, in the 1740s. The patriarch, Benjamin Brown Sr., built a house called Walnut Level, and his sons built or inherited half a dozen additional homes in the Cove. The example of the Brightberry Plantation[7] can illustrate how to determine whether a site included a slave cemetery and, if so, how to locate it. First, it is necessary to determine whether the landowners owned slaves. Brightberry Plantation was built for Captain Brightberry Brown around 1818.[8] The U.S. Census reveals that he had twenty-five slaves in 1810 and twenty-three in 1830.[9] With a living population of two dozen people over at least one generation, one could expect that the enslaved community was provided with a separate burial ground to accommodate its dead. Next, the Brightberry house had to be located on a modern map. Brightberry can be identified as a site on a "VA Home Town Locator" online map.[10] I began this research at the beginning of the online geospatial boom, using topographic maps to locate features; one such map shows "Browns Cove" listed as a map quadrant, but the site of the Brightberry house is not shown. I was fortunate to have the guidance of local residents to help identify the correct house. Once oriented, I consulted the U.S. Geological Survey map and located three associated structures (indicated by squares) and a cemetery (indicated by "Cem"). When I checked the map coordinates at the site, one of the three dots corresponded to the historic house called Brightberry. Upon inspection of the gravestone inscriptions, the cemetery proved to be the white family's burial ground.[11]

Having located two antebellum features, the "big house" and the associated white cemetery, I turned to an aerial photograph. In some cases, the outline of cemetery walls or vegetative enclosures can be seen from the air. At Brightberry, the white cemetery is enclosed by a rectangular fence; beyond a second fence there is a very distinct line of trees (following an old fence line) and a circular enclosure of trees and shrubs. Investigating the site in person, I easily located the raised area that contained the slave burials, which lay about three hundred feet behind the big house on a small hill. The location adhered to each of the attributes discussed above: a hilltop site, ringed by trees, located at the edge of an old field, along a fence line. The ring of trees was supplemented in part by an old wooden fence (not antebellum, but perhaps fifty years old). Overgrown with summer grasses, the low-lying gravestones would have been almost impossible to locate without the other landscape clues. Chapter 8 discusses the connections between individuals buried in this cemetery and those in surrounding plantation cemeteries. The majority of the thirty-six slave cemeteries in my study were located by consulting a combination of human resources, topographic maps, aerial photographs, and, occasionally, archival documents.[12]

Locating Twentieth-Century Cemeteries

In the postbellum period we find three types of black cemeteries: the graveyards of newly founded churches, neighborhood cemeteries (sometimes maintained by burial or fraternal societies), and traditional small family cemeteries located on private property. For each type, hilltop locations were preferred, but landowners had to make do with whatever was available. By the beginning of the twentieth century, public cemeteries became available for African Americans, although blacks were buried in segregated sections into the 1960s. A clear example of this segregation policy is found in Charlottesville's Oakwood Cemetery, whose historic plats explicitly designated a "colored" section; oral history maintains that there was once a fence that separated the white section from the burials of African Americans.[13]

Many twentieth-century cemeteries are relatively easy to find. Churchyards are usually indicated in atlases and online maps. One exception is small rural black churches, whose graveyards do not always appear in these sources. Secular neighborhood cemeteries are also sometimes missed by surveyors. In other cases I have come across, a historic white cemetery was indicated on maps, but it was only upon visiting that I learned there was a segregated section for African Americans (e.g., the Wild Rose Cemetery in Batesville and the adjacent historic black burial ground associated with the Mountain View Baptist Church).

In Albemarle County the largest concentration of contemporary African American burials is in the large public cemetery in Charlottesville and in a newer "memorial park" on the outskirts of the city limits. Burials also occur in churchyards, but it is increasingly uncommon for individuals to use backyard plots. Another, less direct way to locate modern burials is to locate the death certificate of the person you are seeking. Since 1912, the Virginia Bureau of Vital Statistics has required a certificate for every death. These forms include a space for "place of burial." Unfortunately, there is no requirement for an address, and sometimes the forms read simply "family cemetery." However, as related in the previous chapter's discussion of the search for the Burton Family Cemetery, there are ways to proceed if you are looking for a family cemetery and all you have is a surname.

Visiting a Historic Cemetery

At the start of my field research, following a lead from a colleague at Monticello, I visited a former University of Virginia professor of architecture who lived in a rural community called Free Union. The professor had recently called an archaeologist at Monticello with a fairly common question: "What should I do if I have a cemetery on my property?"

When the question was passed on to me, I decided to conduct a field investigation. On the drive west of Charlottesville, I passed the sites of former plantations: Stillfield, Ivy, Ingleside. The buildings and contiguous land holdings are long gone, replaced by modern developments that often include densely packed apartment complexes.

Similar plantations exist throughout Albemarle County, and many of them contained family cemeteries used by both white and black residents. In a few cases, the burials are cordoned off within the new construction. But most of the nineteenth-century cemeteries used by African Americans contain only simple inscribed stones and have been buried by modern construction or are long forgotten in the surrounding overgrowth.

When I reached Free Union, the professor shared the little he knew. The only living member of the former community was an old man who lived in a trailer just beyond the edge of his property. The man wasn't directly related to any of the deceased, but he was sure there were black families buried there. He suggested that they were "Thompsons," so I used that nomenclature for my note taking.

At first I thought I was in the wrong place. All I could see was vegetation and young trees. Then I began to notice what looked like small metal picture frames sticking out of the overgrowth. This was only the second African American cemetery I had examined, and I was not yet familiar with these markers, which in the 1900s were provided by funeral homes with the price of burial. All but one of the pieces of paper that had once been included within the frames to identify the deceased had rotted away long ago. The surviving piece of paper read "Allen Douglas . . . ," but years of rain had erased any other words that had described the burial.

Since the "Thompson Cemetery" was one of my first investigations, I wanted to be as accurate and scientific as possible. I measured each metal marker (sixteen inches by five inches), just in case the size was relevant; it wasn't. Gradually, I realized there was a pattern to the burials. There was a line of four metal markers with

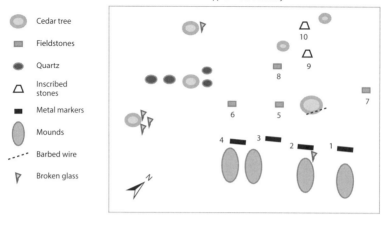

Cedar tree

Fieldstones

Quartz

Inscribed stones

Metal markers

Mounds

Barbed wire

Broken glass

MAP 1 Thompson Family Cemetery. Gravestones 1, 2, and 4 are illegible metal funeral-home markers; 3 is a metal funeral marker for "Allen Douglas, died 1948"; 5 through 8 are uninscribed fieldstones; 9 is a concrete stone with an illegible inscription that begins "Fee . . ."; 10 is a hand-carved concrete stone that reads "Annie Thompson and J. F. Thompson died 16 1916." (Map by Lynn Rainville)

vaguely visible depressions. Nearby lay a roughly linear group of fieldstones and quartz, placed between several pine trees (map 1). These ten stones did not contain inscriptions, but it was clear that they had been placed deliberately. In the back corner of this small family cemetery, an eroded concrete marker had undergone a surgery of sorts. It had long since lost one-third of its mass—the pieces were nowhere to be found, probably buried under the leaf litter over the decades. The remaining two-thirds contained cracks and were set within two bands of metal to help stabilize the edges. At first, the top half of the inscription was obscure: "At . . . Me . . . Robe . . . So." The second half was more informative: "Annie. Thomps . . . J. E. Thompson. Born. January . . . died 16 1917." I assumed the stone commemorated either Annie or J. E., but I could not explain the top half of the stone.

When I returned home, I thought about patterns of inscriptions and eventually realized the first line probably read "At Rest," a very common early twentieth-century inscription. The "Me" could be part of "In Memory." After conducting more research, I realized the individual buried under the stone was probably "Robert," the "Son of" the two people listed at the bottom of the stone. Robert, not his parents, died in 1917. Later census research demonstrated that J. E. and Annie Thompson had had at least six children born after 1918, suggesting that Robert may have been their first child and died in infancy. The eroded marker was matched by a smaller, equally illegible concrete marker, located roughly four feet away. This marker is very likely the matching footstone.

Given the paucity of inscribed markers, I turned to an online database that the Charlottesville African American Genealogy Group created in 1998.[14] Their invaluable effort transcribed more than eight thousand African American death certificates that date to between 1917 and the 1980s. In the case of the Thompson Cemetery, this online database provided many links between individuals listed under the "Thompson Fam. Cem."[15] For example, two known individuals who did not have preserved or legible stones—Annie Bettie Thompson (1892–1983) and Emmett Edgar Thompson (1898–1990)—were recorded in the funeral database. Annie was the mother of Robert; Emmett was probably a cousin of her husband, James E. Thompson. James is listed in the funeral records, which simply mention a "Family Cemetery." I assumed that all three individuals rested in this cemetery, under uninscribed stones, eroded metal markers, or possibly in unmarked graves. However, six years later I discovered that my assumptions concerning the burial place of Anne and James E. were incorrect.

Of the ten stones in the Thompson Family Cemetery, some are paired head- and footstones (as at Robert's grave), so there were a total of eight different burials. The burial ground includes two family lines: the Thompsons and the Douglases. Both families are large, with dozens of descendants who died between 1917 (the earliest recorded burial) and 1990 (the most recent burial, according to death certificate records). The records suggest that the deceased ranged in age from infancy to ninety-two and included burials in the 1910s, 1920s, 1940s, 1950s, 1980s, and 1990s.

Perhaps the individuals buried here could not afford to pay for a plot within a church or public cemetery, so they used some of their own land for a cemetery. But why hadn't anyone been buried here since 1990? One possible explanation was the sale of the land—both in the 1980s and again in the 1990s. Laws protect family access to historic cemeteries, but descendants can be pressured to bury elsewhere. Or perhaps the family simply moved away from Free Union.

In the course of researching census records to document the Thompson family tree, I was able to uncover fragments of their family history, hidden within dry census tallies. Several late nineteenth-century Thompsons were shoemakers, and several of their neighbors were blacksmiths. Another discovery was a woman who began her large family late in life by nineteenth-century standards: Celia Thompson was forty-one years old in 1860 when she had her first child, Wise. Over the next eighteen years she had seven more children. Her last child, Terry, was born in 1878 when she was fifty-nine.[16] Her resting place might well be another of the unmarked graves in the Thompson Family Cemetery.

Six years after I documented the burials in the Thompson Family Cemetery, I received a call from Vickie Dean, a granddaughter of James E. Thompson. She wanted to add another family burial to my online list: her mother, Mary Maria Williams, who died in 1958 at only twenty-eight years old. As Ms. Dean described the cemetery, I realized we were not talking about the same spot. We eventually understood that the cemetery where her mother and grandparents were buried was a couple of miles down the road, on property still owned by a granddaughter of J. E. Thompson. The cemetery I had called the Thompson Cemetery, based on one of the inscribed stones, was referred to by the surviving descendants as the "Douglas Family Cemetery."[17] In her own, more recent genealogical queries, Ms. Dean had never been told of the infant Robert who died in 1917.

Fortunately, Ms. Dean did know a lot about her family history, including the fact that a cousin had recently completed DNA testing and received results that suggest the family descended from the Mendinka and Igbo tribes in West Africa. James Edward Thompson (her grandfather) purchased land in Albemarle County in the early 1900s and built a two-story house near the site of the original Thompson Family Cemetery. He worked for the Southern Railway Company, necessitating months away from home, until he lost a leg in a railroad accident. After our initial conversation I did a bit more research and was able to uncover James's World War I draft card. When I sent it to Ms. Dean, she replied:

January 9, 2009

Lynn,

I could not believe my eyes when I opened your e-mail. Tears came to my eyes. Imagine the Draft Card of my late grandfather. It feels like I have stepped back in time. This person who I never knew is now more real.

I shared this information a few minutes ago with Edward Perry (Cousin Nellie's son). He was very happy to get this information. Edward has been trying to find out about our family too. I told him about how I had been working with you.

I'm on my way to Washington, DC, now with JOY in my heart. It feels like the whole Thompson family are with me in spirit to witness the election of our forty-fourth president.

Lynn, thank you so much for the knowledge gained.

Vickie D.

While it is not feasible to research each of the thousands of individuals in my database of African American cemeteries, the combined efforts of families and historians can help preserve many of the stories from local communities. It is especially important to collect and verify African American family stories because blacks were so often omitted from written county histories. To this day, African American family cemeteries are often left out of written documentation.

Virtual Genealogy

The Internet has changed the face of genealogical research and public history. With the rise of blogs, wikis, and online services that send e-mails if someone has contributed to your virtual family tree, it is far easier to connect with relatives and learn more about the thousands of American families that are not discussed in history textbooks. In the case of my cemetery project, the Internet has been an invaluable way to post the information collected and to receive feedback from descendants and interested members of the public.

Traditionally, the raw data collected for historic research remained in the files of the researcher. In a handful of cases it was published as appendixes in academic books. Neither of these types of resource is readily accessible to the public. When beginning this project, I was committed to a two-tiered research agenda: one for academic publications and the other to share everything that I learned with descendant communities and the public to educate them about these important resources. In 2002, I designed a simple website titled African-American Cemeteries in Albemarle County, later expanding the project to central Virginia and changing the name accordingly. I also upgraded the technology behind it to make it easier to use.

Initially, I programmed the website using Dreamweaver, creating a simple framework to provide information about the handful of cemeteries I had studied up until that point. By 2005 I had mapped and photographed several dozen cemeteries, but the website was not designed to handle that much information, nor was it flexible enough to easily add content or search for individuals. I hired a database designer to create a central online repository for the thousands of photographs and transcribed inscriptions that I had collected. Using the open source program MySQL enables me to keep track of an almost infinite amount of data by storing information in tables. For example, there is a table that stores "surname," "date of birth," "date of death," "inscription," and two dozen other categories of information. The tables are correlated through a unique number that is assigned to each person; thus the data are organized around individuals, not gravestones. Some stones commemorate two or more people. If I had used the gravestone as a unique identifier, there would be an overlap if more than one person was named on a stone.

Each cemetery I document is presented to the public with four web pages: (1) a brief, two-paragraph introduction to the cemetery and its history; (2) a page entitled "burial details" that provides a photograph and the transcribed information from the stone for each grave within the cemetery; (3) a map of the cemetery, usually created by recording points with an electronic mapping device called a

Total Station and editing the map in Adobe Illustrator; and (4) a separate page that contains information about any veterans buried in the cemetery. The last page was added early in the project, inspired by the Veterans History Project at the Library of Congress, which encourages volunteers to collect stories and information on veterans of military service.[18] Veterans' gravestones provide useful information on the deceased's name, death date, wars served in, and regiment.

My African American cemetery website catalogs dozens of cemeteries, documented with photographs and burial information. To keep a search simple for individuals looking for their relatives, I added an "ancestor search" button on the front page of the website, allowing the user to choose whether to search by cemetery or by individual.

Short essays on the website discuss a variety of topics ranging from gravestone variability within black cemeteries to the types of landscaping and mortuary rituals used. Also included is a separate section on preserving these sacred sites: how to document them, the legal precedents for protecting them, and links to other preservation resources. A final section encourages local residents to get involved and submit information about a family or neighborhood cemetery. I have received hundreds of e-mails since first posting the site, which have led to dozens of newly discovered cemeteries. The e-mails have also included information from relatives, providing important biographical information about the deceased. Interactive websites are an invaluable way to reach new audiences and solicit feedback from local communities.

Finally, in February 2012, I created a Facebook page, African American Cemeteries in Virginia, to connect with more descendants and attempt to reach a younger audience.[19]

3

THE ACCIDENTAL MUSEUM
Gravestone Designs

Gravestones can be read like books; each stone contains the abbreviated story of a life. The information that can be gleaned from gravestones includes birth and death dates, names, gender, age at death, and on occasion, hints regarding the occupation or social class of the deceased. But if we "read" more broadly and study the design and shape of the stone, more can be learned. Here I will explore five additional levels of interpretation: the material of the stone and its shape, the motif, the inscription, and the context of the stone within the cemetery.

Discussing only black motifs and markers would isolate them from broader American funerary traditions. This chapter will reference both white and black mortuary traditions in order to contextualize those of African Americans. In central Virginia, these were heavily influenced by the mortuary fashions popular in the white community. This stands in contrast to other regions of the country where African American gravestones sometimes retained more unique features, such as African scripts and designs.[1] To understand black gravestones in central Virginia, we must consider the differences from and similarities to contemporary white gravestones. After reviewing the features of grave memorials, I will discuss the statistical differences between black and white gravestone designs in my study.

Markers within a Cemetery

While there is tremendous variation in gravestone designs, only four main types of markers are found within most American cemeteries. The first is the headstone. This term was originally used to differentiate it from the footstone, which was placed at the feet of the deceased. The use of the term *headstone* is a little misleading, because only about a quarter of the stones in this study contained both head and footstones. Therefore I use the terms *headstone* and *gravestone* interchangeably, to signify the marker at the head of the deceased. In many cases it is the only marker.

Footstones are almost always miniature versions of the headstone, sharing the same material and form. In many cases they contain the initials of the deceased. This is a useful way for a modern observer to know which two stones should be paired together.

In addition to the markers that indicate the locations of individuals, there are also plot markers. These can take a variety of forms, including poles, rectangular posts, and link fences. Not all graves are surrounded by enclosures, but when they are, a family plot is usually indicated. In modern cemeteries they might have numbered row markers, low-lying stones, or pieces of metal that label the lines of burials. This makes it easy to locate a relative among the thousands of markers. This feature is more common in fee-based or private cemeteries that need to keep careful track of their plots as part of their business model.

The fourth type of marker is a family memorial, usually larger and more three-dimensional than the headstone style. These became popular in the late nineteenth century and are often carved from granite. Multiple generations may be listed on these stones, and often the family name is prominently featured.

Gravestone Materials

While there is an almost infinite number of materials that could be used for a grave marker, most of the markers in this study fall into four broad categories: stone, metal, wood, and other organic materials. A fifth category is the absence of a marker, which could either be the result of an intentional lack of commemoration or indicate the use of a wooden or other organic marker that did not survive into the present.

The most commonly preserved markers in both African American and white cemeteries are stone. These range from naturally occurring fieldstones to machine-carved granite memorials. As many authors have demonstrated, much of the change in stone carving over the last two hundred years corresponds to changing technologies. Slate and soapstone are two of the earliest materials used in American graveyards, dating back to the seventeenth and eighteenth centuries. These soft stones are relatively easy to carve with simple carpenter's tools. Beginning in the mid-eighteenth century, Americans began selecting bright white marble stones, and this material remained popular through the century. By the late nineteenth century, a quick perusal of these old stones—slate, soapstone, or marble—would reveal fading and erosion, the double-edged sword of the easily carved surface. In response, many twentieth-century Americans chose granite—a hard stone that was most often designed into large family memorials—for their final markers. The use of granite became feasible as carving tools improved; sharper tools allowed for more precise cuts in the hard igneous rock. However, up until World War I, granite markers were rare in central Virginia's African American cemeteries because of their high cost.

Since World War II, a new type of cemetery, the "memorial park," has flourished. Within the manicured lawns of these cemeteries, the preferred material is bronze or stone, shaped into a flat, horizontal marker. Another common use of metal is the small picture frame included in the cost of funeral-home services. These markers come in a variety of styles: metal letters mounted on a small metal frame, metal picture frames designed for a piece of paper to be inserted under glass, and embossed metal letters. Only the latter survives the test of time. The mounted letters tend to fall out over time, and the pieces of paper rarely survive more than a couple of decades. Ironically, the part of the marker that most often survives is the stamp of the funeral parlor, which is often painted in black ink directly onto the metal.

In addition to mass-produced stone and metal markers, other stone types include white and pink quartz, carved river cobbles, and unusually shaped fieldstones. Some of these stones are modified into distinct shapes, indicating a folk carving tradition. Because many stones in this category lack inscriptions and use locally available materials, they often go unnoticed and are occasionally removed or inadvertently destroyed by property owners.

The second-most common material in African American cemeteries is wood. Unfortunately, these markers rarely preserve the name of the deceased and many have long since disappeared. But if we turn to firsthand accounts, we read about "wooden posts" and "billets of wood . . . and . . . pieces of plank, cut in the ordinary form of tomb-stones" (noted in the 1850s).[2] The prominent landscape designer Frederick Law Olmsted observed "wooden posts" at the head of "each recent grave" in a slave cemetery that he visited during the 1850s.[3]

African American cemeteries contain a third type of marker: organic and impermanent memorials, either floral or arboreal. In some cases yuccas are planted at the heads of graves. One African American Albemarle County resident planted a dogwood tree at the head of the spot where he would like to be buried. Such memorials are difficult to identify if oral traditions are not preserved. Hundreds of bushes and trees stand in older cemeteries, and it is no longer clear whether they mark burials or are simply landscaping.

Gravestone Morphologies

Gravestones appear in many different shapes and sizes. These morphological differences tend to vary by time period and sometimes by the cultural background of the mourners. For example, Quaker cemeteries are characterized by nearly identical white markers with little or no decoration—emblematic of the egalitarian religion.[4]

FIG. 3 Unusual concrete marker and memorial. Chestnut Grove Baptist Church Cemetery, Albemarle County. (Photograph by Lynn Rainville, 2007)

In contrast, urban public cemeteries from the late nineteenth century contain a mixture of marble and granite memorials and the occasional metal marker.

In African American cemeteries, gravestones range from the standardized markers most often found in contemporary urban cemeteries to the unmodified fieldstones often found in slave cemeteries and often feature hand-crafted and un-usual designs (fig. 3). These markers were made of a wide variety of materials from granite slabs to impermanent wooden posts and include mass-produced markers (such as inscribed marble, metal picture frames, and soapstone "boards") and hand-carved markers (worked from soapstone, marble, and concrete).

The size of a marker can convey information beyond that conveyed by style. Large markers can correlate with wealth. In almost all cases, the more material is involved, the more expensive the marker. But a large marble marker cannot be com-pared to a granite one because granite is much more expensive per square foot. Sometimes size indicates the age of the deceased, as smaller markers are often used for children. This practice began in the eighteenth century, when children were considered to be adults in miniature. Context is important, however. A child's marker will be smaller than his or her adult kin's stones, but a poor family's markers may all be small, so any child deaths would be marked with something even smaller. Thus a relatively small marker for a wealthier family might be larger than the adult stones used for a poor family.

Headstones come in a variety of shapes, but in the past they were predominantly flat rectangles. The materials used in the nineteenth century often determined their

FIG. 4 Gravestone with circular puncture.
Elk Hill Plantation Cemetery, Nelson County.
(Photograph by Lynn Rainville, 2007)

stone shapes. Popular materials such as marble, soapstone, and schist were most easily carved into flat shapes. One may also see—at least in white cemeteries—figurative sculpture and crypts or vaults in the form of classical temples or other imposing architectural forms, particularly in the plots of wealthy families. Later, when improved carving tools helped popularize the use of granite, this hard stone was carved into a wider array of tombstone shapes. In central Virginia these include hearts, crosses, large blocks, and urns.

Most African Americans were poor after the end of slavery, struggling to purchase land and build homes. In the nineteenth century, poor families selected locally available stones or used cast-off carved stones that may have broken during the production process. Others appear to have been deliberately punctured (fig. 4). While none of my informants could explain this tradition, it may date back to the nineteenth century when some African Americans believed that breaking dishes or an item that once belonged to the deceased would help his or her spirit reach the afterlife.[5] Ironically, once granite became more affordable and widespread, it became fashionable to make it look like uncarved stone. One mid-twentieth-century granite marker in a Charlottesville cemetery, while smooth and polished in the front, appeared rough hewn from the back, as if it were a real boulder.

Obelisks

The obelisk is an interesting choice for a nineteenth-century American grave marker. Its origins predate Christianity, and obelisks were erected by ancient Egyptians to mark the entrance to temples, not graves.[6] In America, the nineteenth-century

romantic cemetery movement co-opted the pharaonic design. Marble obelisks were commonly used as family monuments, with each side dedicated to a different member of the family. Even earlier than the prevalence of this form in white graveyards, enslaved African Americans were erecting stone stele that resembled Egyptian obelisks. I have yet to find a stele in a Virginia graveyard that has a true benben, or pyramidal-shaped top (which symbolizes the mound associated with the origin of the world in Egyptian cosmology).[7] But I have found stone shafts with tapered tops in slave graveyards and in a handful of postbellum cemeteries in central Virginia (fig. 5). The antecedents to these forms can be found throughout the northern half of Africa, from the Ethiopian stele (dating to the twelfth and fourteenth centuries at Tiya and to the third and fourth centuries at Aksum) to nearby Eritrea (at the site of Metara), Tunisia, and further west in Gambia (the *steinkreis,* or stone circles).

None of the obelisks in Virginia was inscribed, so it is hard to say conclusively whom they commemorate. But in one black postbellum graveyard, there are clues as to who is buried underneath an uninscribed obelisk. The marker lies within the Hugh Carr family graveyard. Hugh Carr was born into slavery in the 1840s, but after emancipation he purchased land and became a successful farmer. By 1890, he had acquired 125 acres in the Hydraulic Mills neighborhood along the Rivanna River and named his farm River View (today known locally as the Ivy Creek Foundation).[8]

The Carr Family Cemetery is located behind the original farmhouse and contains over a dozen graves marked by granite headstones, two obelisk-shaped stones, and several unmarked graves indicated by depressions. The changing gravestone styles in this cemetery highlight one generation's concern for the newest mortuary fashions (granite headstones), while the oldest generation preferred a traditional marker (obelisks).

Strangely, the two obelisks are found just outside the family plot. It is not clear why they were not enclosed with the more modern markers. The enclosure is made from cinder blocks and was probably added after the obelisks. Perhaps a later descendant's more modern aesthetic led to the exclusion of the older, more traditional markers.

Surprisingly, Hugh Carr is buried under a modern granite headstone, even though he died in 1914, when granite markers were rare in black cemeteries. Also listed on the stone are his wife, Texie M. Hawkins (1865–1899), and their son, Marshall H. Carr (1886–1916). We know from land records that one of their other children, Mary, lived at the farm with her husband, Conly G. Greer, until their deaths in 1973 and 1956, respectively. Mr. and Mrs. Greer are buried under stones identical in style to that of Hugh Carr, even though he predeceased them by decades. It is not uncommon for descendants to upgrade stones many years after a death. Such a decision would explain why five people who died between 1899 and 1973 have almost identical gravestones (as opposed to the more common changes that we associate with gravestone design over time).

But who is buried under the two uninscribed obelisks? At a 2010 family funeral, a colleague of mine remembered the deceased told him years ago that Hugh's mother, Fanny, was buried under the two markers. This would make sense; the style associated with the earlier generation (born ca. 1800) was more traditional (fig. 6). Since descendants—not the deceased—select and erect grave markers, this may indicate that one of Fanny's children thought that the older-style marker was the best choice to mark her grave.

FIG. 6 Uninscribed obelisks in the Hugh Carr Family Cemetery at Ivy Creek Farm. (Photograph by Lynn Rainville, 2012)

Anomalous Markers

A small percentage of markers in Albemarle County do not fit any of the patterns described above. These include markers made from unusual materials like concrete or with unusual shapes like hourglass forms. They stand out among mass-produced markers. For example, an urban cemetery in Charlottesville contains a brick vault covered with concrete. This marker is anomalous for Charlottesville, but in other parts of the South curved tables made of brick were common among elites. The concrete was added at some point to help preserve the original, underlying brick structure of the barrel vault. Unfortunately, any identification that may have been carved into the bricks is now covered by the concrete matrix. As a result, this unusual vault is an anonymous, albeit substantial, marker.

In other cases, personal choice has combined two normally distinct styles. For example, at the previously mentioned Zion Church Cemetery, a piece of concrete was combined with a metal funeral marker. Perhaps the stone carver did this to elevate the usually low-to-the-ground metal marker. Or maybe the metal marker did not strike the grieving family members as permanent enough in appearance.

Gravestone Motifs

One might imagine that any one gravestone is as distinctive as a snowflake, that each one is a unique marker for a person's life and death. If you've gone shopping for a marker recently, you might be familiar with modern offerings, carved by lasers with a wide variety of motifs: indications of hobbies (fishing is a popular one), colorized scenes, and photographic images transferred to the stone. But during the period of this study, circa 1800 to 2000, less than a dozen motifs are used repeatedly. These popular themes include crosses, flowers, praying hands, rays of light, ivy, roses, hearts, birds, scrolls, and Bibles. Unusual motifs are not popular because survivors memorialize their loved ones according to prevailing religious and cultural standards, choosing designs with which they feel comfortable. This does not mean that all markers look the same. Mourners combine popular motifs with distinct raw material types, shapes, and hand-carved geometric symbols. Each style is restricted by technological constraints in any given generation. The selection of a gravestone design reveals personal choices, but these decisions occur within a broader social milieu that makes certain imagery acceptable or popular.

During this two-century period in Albemarle County, variations on floral designs are by far the most popular in both white and black cemeteries. Most floral designs are nondescript petaled leaves that could represent any blossom from a daisy to a petunia. Others are clearly roses or ivy. The former are, of course, associated with love, while the latter is an evergreen and, because of its clinging nature and roughly heart-shaped leaf, is associated with love and togetherness (most often in marriage), fidelity, and immortality. For the ancient Greeks, ivy symbolized remembrance, and a crown of ivy was thought to aid creative thinking (which is why it was used to crown their poets).

These floral motifs contrast with the more somber decorations of seventeenth- and early eighteenth-century monuments, which often featured a winged skull coming to take the deceased to heaven, crossbones, hourglasses with the sands running out, or skeletons.[9] But with the rise of the second religious awakening (from the 1790s through the 1820s), a more optimistic view of death emerged, resulting in euphemistic motifs such as budding roses, lambs, doves, and weeping willows.[10] We find these optimistic motifs in postbellum African American cemeteries. But toward the end of the nineteenth century, romantic themes declined in popularity across the country and were replaced by plain stones with no designs. In the first half of the twentieth century, as the use of granite markers became more widespread, one sees carved surnames and motifs such as praying hands, Bibles, and rays of sunlight. Perhaps out of economic necessity, plain markers also continued to be used.

During the period of slavery, African Americans generally did not have the option of purchasing a mass-produced stone. Instead, their markers on plantation cemeteries were most often plain, with no carvings whatsoever, either figural or textual. Although enslaved individuals were limited in their choice of markers, free blacks had more purchasing power. For example, the Old City Cemetery in Lynchburg, Virginia, contains mortuary designs selected from the prevailing popular culture. This historic cemetery contains the graves of the successful free blacks who lived in the community and worked as grocers, blacksmiths, millers, musicians, boatmen, barbers, midwives, and seamstresses.[11] Their markers are decorated with carved urns, drapery sculpted as if it were laid over the stone, and weeping angels. This wealthy urban community is not typical of the more commonly rural and middle- to lower-class free blacks who lived in central Virginia.

Postbellum and early twentieth-century African American cemeteries contain an array of handmade markers, more diverse in style and materials than those in most contemporary white graveyards. These stones include hand-carved motifs, designs constructed from concrete and cinder block, and shells impressed into stones. For example, local craftsmen experimented with the design of doves. The dozen doves in my study vary significantly in their craftsmanship and style, and the script in the associated inscriptions ranges from sloppy cursive to carefully printed block letters.

After World War I, these idiosyncratic markers in African American cemeteries gave way to mass-produced stones and designs, available by mail order from the

Sears and Roebuck or other catalogs.[12] Simultaneously, local stonemasons began to specialize in gravestone production, opening stores that focused on memorials. Earlier, stone production was unspecialized, and few made a living from carving stones. Instead, a local carpenter would build coffins and carve stones as a side job. But the twentieth-century technological revolution, coupled with the availability of ready-made goods, made premade gravestones accessible to anyone who could afford them.

These mass-produced (and mass-requested) designs are visible in many of the early twentieth-century black and white cemeteries in central Virginia. Crosses are very popular, as are praying or clasped hands. Variations on these themes include hands bathed in light and the rare "hand from above," a godly hand that reaches down to grasp the hand of the deceased.

Single books appear on some stones, often combined with the praying hands motif. These are usually Bibles. In other cases, spouses will share a granite marker, and each person's personal data are inscribed onto a book. In only one case was the book inscribed with a biblical verse. Less common motifs include lambs (usually reserved for the death of a child), wreaths evocative of Greek victory laurels, and candles. When burning, candles represent the flame of life.

When motifs are present, most fall into one of the dozen patterns discussed above. An even larger number of stones are plain, with no design whatsoever. But there is the occasional unique motif. In my study of more than six thousand stones, a handful of designs occurred only once. These include a truck, a butterfly, an image of Jesus Christ crucified, and a woman throwing herself prostrate on a cross. This stone includes an inscription that reads "Rock of Ages."[13]

The patterns and motifs discussed above change when we look at stones from the second half of the twentieth century. The number of unique stones increased dramatically during this period, primarily because of advances in technology that decreased the cost of granite carving. More recently, technologies that make transferring photos to mugs and posters a click away on the Internet enable carvers to decorate gravestones from a range of sources.

Motifs and Gender

Most gravestones have no carving other than the deceased's name; apart from the name, there is usually no way to tell a woman's grave from a man's. Even among the 28 percent of graves that are decorated, the majority feature gender-neutral symbols, such as crosses. But there are a handful of motifs, epitaphs, and inscriptions that correlate with the gender of the deceased.

The most obvious difference between the genders is how spouses are commemorated. While dozens of married women in this study are referred to as the "wife of" a man, fewer than a dozen men are referred to as a "husband," and in only one of these cases is the wife's name specified. The traditional reason for this inequity is the nineteenth-century belief that a woman's identity is defined by her relationship to men: first to her father and later to her husband. This is illustrated in the American pattern of giving wives the surnames of their husbands. A wife became part of her husband's identity, and this relationship was traditionally unequal regarding ownership of property, wealth, and educational and occupational opportunities. By contrast, enslaved women were not necessarily linked by name to their spouses because enslaved individuals were prevented from legally marrying in Virginia and were frequently sold away from each other.[14] This did not prevent lifelong unions, but it does make it more difficult to locate enslaved spouses and their gravestones.

Another way women are memorialized differently on gravestones is in the choice of motifs. The clearest feminine motifs are roses and lilies. It is rare to find these flowers carved on the graves of men. However, a small percentage of men's graves include motifs from their fraternal associations such as the Elk's Club or Masonic groups. These symbols are rarely found on women's graves, despite parallel associations such as the Order of the Eastern Star for women. Surprisingly, given the inequality between the sexes that dominated most of the period of this study, there are few other gendered motifs. Instead, most mortuary motifs illustrate religious ideas rather than social ones.

A final source of difference between men's and women's graves is the biographical epitaph. For example, the stones for some women describe the deceased as a "kind, tender, and affectionate mother." Men are never described as tender or kind on their gravestones, and only rarely is their identity as a father emphasized. Instead, men's epitaphs focus on their public accomplishments or professions, such as "reverend" or "teacher."

Epitaphs and Inscriptions

In general, gravestone text carvings fall into two main categories: personal information specific to the deceased (referred to here as an "epitaph") and nonspecific information, often taken from biblical quotes or bereavement expressions (referred to here as "inscriptions"). Inscriptions tend to follow changing fashions in attitudes toward death. For example, early twentieth-century markers emphasize a peaceful hereafter, such as "she is at rest" or "he sleeps." The best-known variant in this category is "rest in peace" or "R. I. P." In contrast, early nineteenth-century markers refer to the "death" or "dying" of the decedent.

Inscriptions can be poetic, sometimes quoting from well-known poems. When Florence Jones died at age fifty-nine in 1916, her inscription borrowed loosely from a stanza in Henry Wadsworth Longfellow's 1882 "The Bells of San Blas": "Out of

the shadow of night / the world moves in to daylight / It is daybreak everywhere."
Sometimes it's difficult to determine whether an inscription is locally unique but
more broadly commonplace. For example, Sarah Cobb's 1940 inscription reads:
"Her toils are past, her work is done, she fought the fight, the victory won." None of
the stones in my study contain this inscription, but a quick Google search located
dozens of online examples, found in cemeteries from California to Texas. Presumably there are thousands more that have never been transcribed online.

I use the term *epitaph* to refer to the biographic data carved into a stone. This
includes testaments to the deceased's work, church affiliation, or family life. However, this type of information is uncommon in my study of African American
gravestones, occurring on only 18 percent of the stones. One reason is the cost of
any inscription. Most professional carvers charged by the letter, so the longer the
inscription, the more expensive the marker. Another reason is an emphasis on one's
familial and community relations rather than a focus on the individual. Although
each stone denotes one life, the importance for the community is the individual's
role within the group. Of the 683 epitaphs that I recorded, 31 percent concern the
deceased's military service. This is a misleadingly large number of epitaphs, since
the U.S. government usually provides military gravestones and almost always offers
to add the unit and rank of the veteran. Of the remaining epitaphs, 39 percent deal
with the kinship status of the deceased (83 describe male relationships such as
"father," "husband," "son," or "brother," while 182 reference "mother," "wife," "sister,"
and "daughter"). A smaller number, 9 percent, express "love" or an eternal remembrance in "our hearts" for the deceased. The remaining 21 percent of the epitaphs
convey truly biographic details, such as the deceased's manner of death, education,
membership in social clubs, or a specific emotional appeal (such as "Daddy, we
loved you but god loves you most / we'll miss you. Wife and Children" for a father
who died in 1987). But since these 143 highly personalized stones are a small fraction
of the 6,000 stones in my entire sample, it appears that neither lengthy nor personalized epitaphs are common in the African American cemeteries that I studied. In
these rare cases the epitaph conveys the emotional despair felt by the mourners
and efforts to come to terms with their devastating loss. Such sentiments help us
understand the role of the deceased within the lives of the survivors.

Unusual Epitaphs

Of the gravestones containing epitaphs, 4 percent have unusual epitaphs, such as
the marker for Etta Lee[15] (who died in 1991 at age fifty-three), on which a surviving
family member had inscribed, "You are special in our hearts we will join you soon."
Another example is the grave marker of an eighty-six-year-old woman, a marble
memorial etched with abstract diamonds and squares that reads, "A Grand lady who

wanted to make a difference and did." Even very short epitaphs can raise interesting questions. In the Wakefield Church Cemetery, I found a small marble marker with no design other than the inscription, which reads, "Gertrude Gant / Queen of Victoria / Daughter of B. & P. Gant." At first I assumed the deceased had earned this august nickname over the course of her life, perhaps owing to a profession or a regal bearing. But this stone was for a three-year-old child. Unfortunately, there was no death date, so it is hard to contextualize the stone. Did her survivors mean Queen Victoria of England? Or was it a reference to Victoria, Canada? Or did it refer to an African American social lodge? Of course, the child's age makes it unlikely that she was a member of any organization.

Biographical Epitaphs

Sometimes, biographical epitaphs are rather generic. For example one inscription, "She was an affectionate mother and kind neighbor," occurs on a dozen stones in different cemeteries in this study. A second popular choice is "She was a Loving neighbor and a faithful Christian." Such common, often rhyming epitaphs are probably recommended by the carver or perhaps by a relative or church leader who has seen a similar inscription elsewhere.

In other cases, epitaphs actually teach us about the community. The Wake Forest Church in Blenheim contains more than a hundred stones that illustrate the lives of past congregation members. One such epitaph is for the Reverend Lee Jones, who died in 1923 at the age of eighty-seven. The first half of his stone reads: "Loved by Many, Respected by All, Saved by Grace." This is a rather general statement, but certainly biographical. Below this is a short inscription: "II Cor VIII – 9," a reference to Paul's second letter to the Corinthians 8:9, on the grace and self-denial of Jesus Christ ("For ye know the grace of our Lord Jesus Christ, that, though he was rich, yet for your sakes he became poor."). Below this is a third, biographical epitaph: "For many years, like his father, a preacher of the Gospel, in this his native county." Additional archival research shows that his father was Spotswood Jones. The fascinating part of this inscription is that the Reverend Lee Jones was born around 1843, so his father was probably born around 1820. This is clear evidence that there were African American preachers in America during the antebellum period, despite the laws on the books that prohibited blacks from preaching to groups because of fears of slave revolts.[16] So even though the father's specific burying place and marker were not located (he probably lies under one of the many uninscribed fieldstones in this cemetery), we still learn something about the history of African American religion from his son's elaborate gravestone.

Few prepare their own epitaph before death. There are famous examples of individuals planning their inscriptions, such as Thomas Jefferson,[17] but the average person does not design his or her own stone. So the sentiments expressed by inscriptions are almost always that of the survivors, not the dead. Usually those who selected the stone remain anonymous: it could be a close relative, a distant one, or in the case of an individual outliving other kin, it may be a friend or community member.

The Daughters of Zion Cemetery in Charlottesville contains an interesting series of epitaphs and inscriptions in the Miller/Baker family plot. Three women are buried next to each other: sisters Caroline and Catharine Baker and their mother, Elizabeth Miller, née Baker. A flowery epitaph is carved into Caroline Baker's marble gravestone. Her curved stone reads "sister" across the top and outlines the basic details, "died on March 22, 1890 aged 25 years." Her inscription reads,

> With songs let me follow His flight
> And mourn with his Spirit above.
> Escaped to the mansions of light
> And lodged in the Eden of love.

While researching nineteenth-century inscriptions, I found the rest of the hymn, which begins,

> Rejoice for a brother deceas'd,
> Our loss is his infinite gain;
> A soul out of prison releas'd,
> And freed from its bodily chain.[18]

Further library research located an article in an 1890 issue of the *Richmond Planet* that discusses the circumstances of Caroline's death and funeral: "On Wednesday March 25th the funeral of Miss Carolie [*sic*] Baker took place at Zion Baptist Church. Her home was in Lynchburg, but she died in Baltimore having gone there in order that the doctors might try to cure her disease. She was prepared to exchange homes. A lecture was given by Rev. A. Scott, from Zach, 4th Chapter 10th verse"[19] (a reference to Zechariah 4:10, "For who hath despised the day of small things?").

Clearly it was important to one of Caroline's surviving family members, perhaps sister Catharine, to reunite Caroline with their mother in death because someone had to arrange to have the body returned to Charlottesville from Baltimore. The adjacent stone is for Caroline's sister, Catharine. Her marker reads, "Catharine Baker . . . departed this life July 30th, 1910, aged 48 years." The final stone in this triptych is the sisters' mother, Elizabeth Miller. She is listed as the wife of Ransom Miller, dying in 1887 at the age of sixty-five. Fortunately, she did not live to see her two daughters die young. Her stone appeared to have been erected by "Hund Baker." It struck me as odd that an African American would have a relative with a first name that means "dog" in German. But I proceeded to search for this individual because the name was so unique. This would make him easier to locate in census records, as Baker was in fact a very common name. After fruitless hours of searching and enlisting the aid of a colleague, I finally took a closer look at the stone and realized it read "H and C" Baker, not "Hund." But this led to another puzzle. Were "H and C" Baker the parents of Elizabeth, as her maiden name was Baker? Or was "C" Baker either Catharine or Caroline? And if so, who was "H" Baker?

There are other unexplained issues. Neither Elizabeth's parents nor her husband, Ransom, are buried in this cemetery. So how did these three women, one of whom died in Baltimore, end up buried together in this cemetery? And why did Elizabeth's daughters carry their mother's maiden name, Baker, rather than her married name? Ransom Miller may have been a second husband, or perhaps Elizabeth had her children out of wedlock and chose to give them her maiden name. This case shows how three stones reveal multigenerational family dynamics and kinship ties.

Epitaphs, when present, provide a starting point for recovering the stories of the dead, their contributions to the community as recorded by the community, their personalities (though we must keep in mind that no one is commemorated as being mean or unpleasant), and their relations to others. The grave is the first of many sources for these minibiographies. It is only by supplementing the mortuary remembrance with information from newspapers, city directories, census records, and family stories that we can weave these narratives together to illustrate the history of the African American community, one neighborhood at a time. I discuss this theme further in chapters 6, 7, and 8.

Erected By . . .

Sometimes survivors want to record the fact that they paid for a gravestone. Usually, a surviving relative purchases the grave marker, but in some cases fraternal organizations or charitable groups pay for it. Inscriptions identifying such organizations, often found at the base of a stone, provide a window into African American social and religious clubs. Sometimes these inscriptions are the only remaining historic documentation of smaller organizations. For example, in 1884 the "young men's monumental society" erected a stone in honor of the Reverend M. T. Lewis. Presumably this group devoted its time to fund-raising to pay for grave markers. Almost a century later, in 1977, the Toppers' Club donated a stone for a woman. Many of these clubs seem to be associated with burial societies, a topic I return to in chapter 5.

In other cases, the family member who erected the stone desires credit and inscribes his or her name. For example, in the Daughters of Zion Cemetery Jenetta Dabney, who died in 1891 at age sixty-two, was buried under a marker that read,

"Erected by her daughter, Sallie J. Golden." Sometimes we can deduce who paid for the stone based on the biographical inscription. The stone of a woman named Rosa, who died at age ninety-six in 1990, reads, "Beloved mother, grandmother, and great grandmother." It appears that three generations were involved in the selection of the granite stone.

Who Gets to Commemorate the Dead?

In Charlottesville's Daughters of Zion Cemetery there is an unusual case where two different women paid for two separate markers for one individual, William A. Coles. I learned from his 1917 World War I draft record that he was a "cleaner and presser" in Richmond and, at that time, single. When he died thirty years later, he was commemorated with two stones, erected by two people. The first stone, a simple rectangular marble marker, reads:

Coles

William A. Coles

Son of

Addie Golden Coles

Feb 12, 1891

Oct 5, 1947

Erected by Ella Smith.

The second marker, also carved from marble, lies flush with the ground and reads:

William A. Coles

Died

October 5, 1947

[Erected by] Friend Bea. Gaines.

It is possible that the two women mentioned on the markers split the cost of the two stones and meant one as a headstone (the taller stone) and the flush marker as a footstone. But it appears that each woman wanted to show her respects separately. It is also interesting, and unusual, that while William is described as the son of Addie Golden Coles (1865–1944), no father is listed. Later a descendant contacted me, and I learned his father was William Coles Sr. (1863–ca. 1910s). After much searching, I found William junior listed in the 1930 U.S. Census as living in Richmond; his next-door neighbor was his aunt Lula Golden (then fifty-three years old), who hosted a lodger name Ella Smith (age thirty-five), who worked as a dishwasher in a restaurant.[20] When William junior died at age fifty-six, he was not married, raising questions about the nature of his relationship to the two women who paid for his monuments.

The rest of the Coleses' plot, containing five additional stones, is also interesting because it is dominated by relations among women. On one side of William are his mother, Addie, and his sister, Hattie, who share a stone. On his other side is his aunt Lula Jean. No husbands are listed on these women's stones, although Hattie was once married to a Mr. Montague. Lula was probably single at her death because she retained her maiden name, Golden. Moreover, both of the women who erected monuments to William were seemingly unrelated to Addie, Lula, or Hattie. Finally, the stone between William and Addie and Hattie's shared monument commemorates another woman, Jenetta Dabney (1829–1891), Addie's mother. This example illustrates how gravestone inscriptions and their placement can reveal tangled webs of kinship and friendship.

Are African American Gravestones Distinctive?

When I began this study in 2001, I wondered whether African American graves would have culturally distinctive motifs or markers. In other words, could you distinguish the gravestones of African Americans from other racial and ethnic groups? The answer for central Virginia is no, not clearly. The patterns that distinguish white from black graveyards have more to do with the spreading popularity of a given motif within a neighborhood and the cost of certain styles than with the racial identity of the deceased. The few exceptions are found in the use of obelisk-style markers in slave cemeteries and the cryptic scripts that were occasionally used to inscribe antebellum stones.

To assess the degree of correlation between stone type and race, I selected a subsample from my data set of 1,281 stones from five cemeteries, two black, two white, and one segregated. For each black cemetery I picked a corresponding white cemetery: a black Baptist church (Hickory Baptist Church) and a white Episcopal church (Good Shepherd Church), a public cemetery segregated into white and black sections (Oakwood Cemetery in Charlottesville), and two rural adjacent neighborhood cemeteries that separated white graves from black graves (the Wild Rose Cemetery and Mountain View Baptist Church Cemetery, respectively). Because this initial sample did not include enough black gravestones for a robust sample, I included a sixth cemetery, one founded by a black funeral home in Charlottesville (Lincoln Cemetery).

First I checked to see whether the material of the stone used varied between communities across all of the cemeteries. In these six cemeteries there were four stone types—fieldstone, marble, granite, and metal—and two graves marked by organic memorials. Table 1 illustrates the close correlation between white and black stones. By using a test of statistical significance, I concluded that there was no significant difference by race in the distribution of marker material. This was surprising

TABLE 1 Gravestone material choice in black and white cemeteries

		White (total = 427)	Black (total = 842)
Granite	Count	250	490
	% within race	58.5	58.2
Marble	Count	136	260
	% within race	31.9	30.9
Metal	Count	20	56
	% within race	4.7	6.7
Fieldstone	Count	19	24
	% within race	4.4	2.9
Organic	Count	2	12
	% within race	0.5	1.4

because I had expected African American cemeteries would contain more of the locally available (and therefore less expensive) materials. Note that this subset of data includes postbellum cemeteries, not slave markers (which contained many more fieldstones than contemporary white graveyards).

Next I studied the markers that featured inscriptions. Within this subset of stones, 107 white people's markers had inscriptions, whereas the number of black people's stones with inscriptions was almost double (201). I organized the inscriptions into five categories based on the presence of certain types of words: pessimistic ("died" or "dead"); euphemistic ("at rest," "rest in peace," "asleep," "slumbers," "resting," "weep not," "in memory of," "departed," "victory"); religious ("Jesus," "God," "angel," "heaven," "shepherd," "thy," "faithful," "crown," "blessed," "praise," "gate(s)"; emotional ("loving," "love," "heart(s)," "gone but not forgotten," "sorrow," "children," "baby"); or the rare inscriptions that quote poems. An inscription might fit in two or more categories (e.g., "In Memory of our Beloved Daughter"). Table 2 shows that the pessimistic and poetic inscriptions were rare for both black and white graves. For each row, there is a count for the number of positives and the percentage. For example, 1 white person's marker out of 107 had a pessimistic inscription (0.9 percent), and 8 black people's markers out of 201 had a pessimistic inscription (4.0 percent).

Generally, pessimistic inscriptions were used more often in the seventeenth and early eighteenth centuries but were less popular during the time period of these stones (ca. 1850–2000). Whites' grave markers were more likely to have religious, euphemistic, and emotional inscriptions, probably owing to complex social and

TABLE 2 Inscription types in black and white cemeteries

		White (total = 107)	Black (total = 201)
Pessimistic (%)	Count	1	8
	% within race	0.9	4.0
Euphemistic (%)	Count	72	99
	% within race	67.3	49.3
Religious	Count	39	36
	% within race	36.4	17.9
Poetic	Count	1	5
	% within race	0.9	2.5
Emotional	Count	29	34
	% within race	27.1	16.9

religious factors. Yet this correlation is not strong enough to provide guidance in the field. In other words, religious or emotional terms such as "shepherd" or "slumbers" cannot be used to decide whether a stone belonged to a white person, although it may be suggestive of such an identification.

Finally, I compared the popularity of certain motifs on white and black stones. These results were more conclusive. For this subset of data I only included graves that had at least one motif present and that dated between 1901 and 2000 (there were too few graves before or after to test statistical significance). Some stones featured more than one motif, so the percentages in table 3 add up to more than one hundred. Of the 519 motifs (266 on white stones, 253 on black stones), only one was strongly associated with African Americans: the veteran's cross, found on marble headstones provided free of charge by the federal government to those who served. Three motifs strongly correlated with white graves: ivy (41 percent versus 13 percent on black graves), family name (35.7 percent versus 17.4 percent on black graves), and a fancy architectural design motif (20.7 percent versus 0 on black graves). Ivy is associated with longevity; its popularity paralleled the broader neoclassical/Greek revival fashion of the first half of the nineteenth century. The family name and architectural elements correspond to the family markers that were popular in the twentieth century. The distribution of these motifs points to the availability of economic resources: the cross found on stones provided free to veterans by the federal government appears more than twice as frequently on black graves, whereas the family markers so popular among whites tend to be made of granite, a more expensive stone.

TABLE 3 Motif choice on black and white gravestones

		White (total = 266)	Black (total = 253)
Ivy	Count	109	33
	% within race	41.0	13.0
Rose	Count	19	21
	% within race	7.1	8.3
Floral	Count	151	94
	% within race	56.8	37.2
Lamb / dove	Count	22	13
	% within race	8.3	5.1
Praying hands	Count	32	34
	% within race	12.0	13.4
Light rays	Count	3	1
	% within race	1.1	0.4
Bible / book	Count	31	28
	% within race	11.7	11.1
Cross	Count	22	16
	% within race	8.3	6.3
Veteran's cross	Count	24	63
	% within race	9.0	24.9
Fam. name	Count	95	44
	% within race	35.7	17.4
Architectural	Count	55	0
	% within race	20.7	0

While the presence or absence of several of the motifs did not have a high correlation to race, if we look at the use of these motifs over time, we see that black and white communities selected these designs in different time periods. For example, floral motifs were steadily popular on black graves until the 1940s, when they decreased in popularity for a generation and then increased again after the 1960s. On white graves the pattern is the opposite; the motif increases in popularity during the first half of the twentieth century and then steadily declines in popularity. Similarly, the use of ivy and roses follows different trajectories in each community. Although it is easy to overinterpret what the choice of a rose means on a headstone, a more significant difference is the mortuary style in each community. Even since integration in the 1960s, black and white graves contain different combinations of motifs. And while these differences are not necessarily visible at first glance (these tests do not mean that the presence of a rose on a 1980 gravestone indicates that the deceased is definitely white but that it is twice as likely), they do suggest differences in attitudes toward death. One possible explanation for the different motif selections over time is a delay in the rise of certain mortuary fashions within the black community. African Americans might be copying mortuary styles from white graveyards or waiting for a longer postmortem period to install headstones (which might relate to a lack of economic resources at the time of death). Unfortunately, there is no surviving documentation that explains the choices in gravestone design, and very few descendants could explain the decisions that earlier generations had made in selecting the mortuary motifs.

It would be more satisfying if there were clear African American motifs or inscriptions, but as I argue at the beginning of this chapter, black mortuary practices do not happen in a cultural void but are influenced by surrounding patterns. In central Virginia, African American communities adopted multiple gravestone styles from their white neighbors. This should not be surprising given the nature of nineteenth-century neighborhoods in rural Virginia, where even during segregation most farmers could not afford to live in isolation. For example, in the Jim Crow era, black and white farmers worked together to process harvests in a timely manner, and most of the individuals that I researched in the census were surrounded by neighbors of a different race. This proximity in work and place of residence did not decrease the hardships and inequality experienced by African Americans during this period. But in terms of mortuary patterns, the difference lies in how each community used a similar set of motifs, varying by time and, in some cases, by design.

I hope to create a larger, statewide data set of historic markers in African American cemeteries through future research. In the last decade of the twentieth century, when I was collecting data for this book, very few studies had been conducted on black cemeteries in Virginia. There were a handful of published collections of inscriptions from black cemeteries, but those sources lacked any historic interpretation or context and usually contained only transcriptions, with no indication of the style of the motif or marker.[21] For some regions, such as the Virginian Tidewater, I could not locate any published records of historic African American cemeteries.[22]

Historic African American Motifs

In the eighteenth and nineteenth centuries there were only a handful of motifs found in African American cemeteries in central Virginia that can be labeled as African or African-inspired. This is in contrast to cemeteries south of Virginia that contain African designs and even inscriptions in West African languages. For example, Elsie Clews Parson's study of the Sea Islands off the Georgia coast demonstrated that the tight-knit African American community there retained many African beliefs, some of which were preserved in symbolic grave offerings such as mirrors and shells.[23] Another reason for the paucity of African motifs in my study is that the earliest graveyards date back to the early 1800s and most date to no earlier than 1830. By that time many enslaved individuals in the Piedmont were several generations removed from their African homelands.[24]

Eighteenth-century enslaved communities were established in central Virginia by three primary means: elite Tidewater planters sent their American-born slaves to establish agricultural quarters in areas farther west; less wealthy owners moved with their newly purchased slaves (sometimes first-generation) to the Piedmont; or white farmers purchased newly arrived slaves from traders to meet the labor requirements of the newly established plantations.[25] Philip Morgan estimates that once these communities were established in the Piedmont, the annual natural growth rate within the enslaved community was about 3 percent. In the Piedmont this translated into about thirty-one thousand African American births between 1755 and 1782.[26] These processes resulted in communities that combined generations of African- and American-born slaves.[27] By the end of the colonial period, many Africans had assimilated into the creole culture of enslaved communities, and the retention of African traditions dwindled.[28]

This study focuses on the antebellum period, multiple generations after these forced migrations and after the 1778 law passed in Virginia that prohibited the importation of slaves from Africa or the West Indies.[29] As a result of trade restrictions on British goods (which included Africans), the last legal slave imports to Virginia ended with the onset of the American Revolution.[30] By the early 1800s, Virginia slave owners increasingly relied on local births to increase slave numbers.[31] The result was that the descendants of Africans living in central Virginia in the nineteenth century were several generations removed from their African roots and more likely to syncretize the remnants of their African beliefs with Christian or secular motifs than borrow directly from their ancestral traditions.[32]

Detailed research into the struggles of Methodist, Baptist, and Presbyterian churches to establish a foothold in Virginia during the eighteenth century illustrate the impact of Christianity on the religious lives of enslaved individuals.[33] European Americans were just beginning to establish counties in the Virginia Piedmont when the Great Awakening reverberated through protestant congregations (ca. 1739–1745).[34] Despite conversions and enthusiasm among whites, the first systematic efforts to convert enslaved peoples to Christianity were met with suspicion by slave owners, in part because most eighteenth-century evangelical preachers did not own slaves themselves, and many preached openly against owning slaves.[35] Moreover, slave owners worried that biblical verses would encourage slaves to fight for equality or switch their allegiance to a spiritual master and demand their freedom.[36] These fears were realized when several missionaries concluded that slavery was "contrary to the word of God" and several enslaved individuals drew in part on this philosophy to lead slave revolts (such as the failed Gabriel's Rebellion in the Richmond area in 1800 and Denmark Vesey's Rebellion in South Carolina in 1822).[37]

On the eve of the Second Great Awakening (ca. 1800), few blacks were practicing Christianity, especially outside of urban free black populations. In order to allay white fears about blacks gathering for religious services, many Baptist and Methodist churches switched to biracial services, which ensured that whites could closely supervise the instruction that their slaves were receiving. In parallel with increased access to formal religious instruction, legal doctrine gradually began to recognize the most basic of human rights for African Americans, such as the 1825 act that affirmed that "slaves were rational beings."[38] Even later, in 1841, Methodist missionaries turned their focus to creating plantation missions.[39] Prior to this outreach, only urban areas had plentiful options for black worship; in fact, Richmond and Petersburg, Virginia, were centers for the African American Baptist Church in America.

Most of the enslaved populations that I refer to in this book fall into the former category, living miles away from any church and thus attending services infrequently. In Albemarle County there were only two antebellum black churches, a handful of churches in urban Charlottesville that allowed slaves to attend services in balcony seating, and only one or two recorded instances of rural churches allowing for segregated attendance. Accordingly, it is not surprising that only a handful of the stones I found in antebellum black graveyards contained Christian symbols. Less than a dozen contained crosses (crudely carved and, in some cases, taking advantage of the natural veins in locally obtained stones), and none contained the popular religious motifs found in contemporary white cemeteries, such as Bibles. Chapter 4 discusses the gravestone patterns found in slave cemeteries in more detail.

Black and White Gravestones

If we return to the sample of six central Virginian cemeteries, there are only a few significant differences between black and white cemeteries. These distinctions do not correspond to individual stones but rather to broader patterns. For example, in the adjacent Wild Rose (white) and Mountain View (black) cemeteries, the latter contains three times as many metal funeral-home markers. These markers are usually provided free of charge by the funeral home and are meant to be replaced later with a purchased stone. The higher number in the African American cemetery may point to fewer economic resources. In support of this theory, the Mountain View

Cemetery contains fewer decorated stones (26 percent contain motifs, in contrast to the 89 percent of whites' gravestones that are decorated in Wild Rose Cemetery). Both cemeteries contain stones that date to between 1925 and 2008. Despite this chronological overlap, the Wild Rose Cemetery motifs include a focus on hobbies (e.g., images of deer, football helmets, cabins, guitars, and pets). This popular late twentieth-century American mortuary trend is not evidenced in the Mountain View Cemetery stones. The few decorated stones use more traditional motifs like flowers and ivy.

If we compare the two rural church cemeteries, Good Shepherd (white) and Hickory Hill (black), we see even fewer differences. Both cemeteries contain a diversity of stone types: fieldstones, granite, marble, metal, schist, and soapstone. Both contain a similar quantity of decorated stones (59 percent in Good Shepherd and 53 percent in Hickory Hill) and epitaphs (31 percent in Good Shepherd and 26 percent in Hickory Hill). Some differences are not statistically significant but are suggestive. The white burial ground contains a stone decorated with a Confederate flag. The black cemetery contains several fieldstones that are accompanied by now-illegible metal markers. The most obvious difference between the two sites is the churches themselves. The Good Shepherd Church is built from beautiful stones, whereas Hickory Hill is a cinder-block building with simple ornamentation.

Oakwood, the segregated public cemetery in Charlottesville, contains the fewest differences in gravestones. Again, both white and black grave markers include a variety of stone types and similar quantities of motifs (38 percent of white grave markers and 39 percent of black grave markers) and inscribed stones (26 percent of markers for whites and 18 percent of markers for African Americans). However, there are double the number of personalized epitaphs on white gravestones (42 percent versus 21 percent in the African American section). The content of the epitaphs is not substantially different. Both communities remember the deceased as "mothers," "fathers," and veterans. The difference is quantitative, not qualitative. The most significant difference between the two areas is the segregation of African Americans in a pre–civil rights "colored section." The stones for whites date from 1831 to 2006, while those for blacks range from 1885 to 2006. The disparate early dates illustrate the prohibition on burying enslaved or free African Americans in this public cemetery until after the Civil War, and even then, blacks were relegated to a separate section.

While most individual gravestones do not signify the race of the deceased, their placement within the landscape can be informative, and in some cases, the economic status of the community is revealed through gravestone choices. In the next section I address more distinct differences in African American cemetery landscapes.

Context: American Cemetery Landscapes

Most studies of mortuary material culture focus on the grave marker, but the environmental and geological contexts for memorials are just as important. Our modern conception of a well-groomed grass lawn with orderly rows of stones is not descriptive of traditional American burial grounds. Early European Americans were English, French, Dutch, and Spanish in origin, and their burial practices in this foreign land reflected the syncretism of European beliefs with the harsh adaptations required in the New World. In the English colony at Jamestown, the plan was to bury the dead outside the walls of the fort in accordance with European customs so as not to contaminate the world of the living. But this plan failed after forays outside of the palisaded fort became too dangerous during the early years when the colonists were under attack by native peoples. By 1610 the Jamestown colonists had built a church and were burying their dead within the churchyard.[40] Churchyard burials were common in England. There, important people were buried under the floors of cathedrals, while common folk were buried in churchyards. In America, a more democratic spirit reduced the differentiation between elite and nonelite burial locations.

The first graveyards in Virginia were not manicured and rarely included stone markers because of the scarcity of natural stone in the Tidewater.[41] Some of the earliest stone markers in Virginia were table-style markers that were designed to lie flat, usually mounted on four stone piers. Unfortunately, markers with this design, often carved from soft stone, collect water and are rarely legible today.[42] In Albemarle County, the earliest surviving gravestone in the public cemetery, Maplewood, dates to 1777. It is carved in the table style and marks the burial of Lettitia Shelby, who was visiting from Kentucky at the time of her death.[43] Wealthy individuals occasionally had their gravestones imported from England, but the poor had to do without. Similarly, the wealthy often chose to be buried on plantation cemeteries, while landless colonists were buried in churchyards or paupers' graves.[44] Outbreaks of smallpox, diphtheria, influenza, measles, yellow fever, and dysentery in the eighteenth century, spread in part by the traveling armies during the Revolution, caused city officials to create cemeteries for the many dead.[45] In Virginia, the earliest urban cemeteries date slightly later, to the early nineteenth century; these include Lynchburg's Old City Cemetery (1806) and Norfolk's earliest public burial ground (1825). The use of city cemeteries increased in popularity, while rural landowners continued to use their own lands for family burials. Both types of colonial-era landscapes included dark gray stones, often carved from slate, scattered throughout a burial ground. The movement to bury people in orderly rows came later in the 1800s.

Nineteenth-century cemeteries underwent extensive renovations in Europe and America as the "beautification movement," also seen in cities and parks, resulted in planned mortuary landscapes. In Virginia, one of the first such cemeteries was the Hollywood Cemetery in downtown Richmond, founded in 1847. These "rural style" sites contained meandering walkways, carriage roads, ornamental plantings, and gates that enabled keepers to set hours of operation for visits and burials. Marble came into fashion in gravestones, and cemeteries were landscaped as bright manicured parks, containing row after row of upright, substantial monuments such as obelisks, statues, and family crypts.[46]

Contemporary "memorial parks" resemble checkerboards, with mostly identically shaped markers, often flush to the ground, spaced in a regular pattern across a landscape. The low profile of the gravestones makes it easier to mow and care for the grounds, while simultaneously enforcing an appearance of egalitarianism. Yet within this modern system there are still clear inequalities, particularly the price of each plot, which varies with size and location. Modern cemeteries sell plots in a business model similar to real estate dealings. Plots of land are prorated depending on location, view, and sometimes, proximity to sculptures or parking spaces. In Charlottesville, the plots in the Holly Memorial Gardens all vary in price according to their location. The front half of the cemetery contains different "gardens," each named after the prominent monument that sits in the middle of each respective section, such as the praying hands, the bell tower, the open Bible, and other religiously themed works. These monuments serve multiple purposes, as decorative features and more practically, as orientation so visitors can find their relatives.

To survive as a for-profit modern cemetery, Holly Memorial Gardens has various strategies for organizing its plots. Each memorial is identified with a row number and space. Maps are handed out to mourners. Holly Memorial's marketing approach expands upon the overall "orderly death" attitude characteristic of twentieth-century funeral practices.[47]

The terminology of American burial grounds changed in parallel with the aforementioned landscape modifications. Throughout the eighteenth century, spaces for the dead were commonly referred to as "graveyards," a visceral description of their function. In the nineteenth century, changes in religious ideas and attitudes toward death resulted in a romanticized view of burial locations. At this time the term *cemetery* became popular. It derives from the Greek for "resting place," a euphemism used by Americans to refer to burial grounds. When we turn to the twentieth century, we see a refinement of this trend with the introduction of "memorial parks."

Cultural Specifics: African American Mortuary Landscapes

As in most aspects of life for antebellum African Americans, whether enslaved or not, their cemeteries exhibited patterns and characteristics distinct from European American burial practices. By the time of the first federal census, African Americans made up 40 percent of the population in Virginia.[48] In some western Virginian counties the enslaved population was over 50 percent of the total.[49] As discussed in chapter 2, at this time there were separate slave cemeteries, set aside on agriculturally poor lands within plantations for use by the enslaved community.

In the absence of drawn plans or paintings, it is very difficult to reconstruct antebellum slave cemetery landscapes. There are archival references to evergreen trees and deliberately included plants within these cemeteries. In some cases, white visitors may not have appreciated the intentionality of the landscaping efforts; one such observer referred to a historic black cemetery as a "dilapidated weed-grown graveyard."[50] A more observant visitor realized that "a few flowers or evergreen shrubs had sometimes been planted on the graves; but these were generally broken down and withered, and the ground was overgrown with weeds and briars."[51] It is not surprising that enslaved individuals lacked the time to properly tend to the planted landscape within their cemeteries. But firsthand memories prove that these were sometimes deliberate. For example, one enslaved woman remembered visiting her mother's grave when she was a girl and recalled that the "black stump, at the head of my mother's grave, was all that remained of a tree my father had planted."[52] Other nineteenth-century accounts describe slave cemeteries located in "groves or densely wooded areas" and concluded that these places were selected because they were "traditionally considered to be sacred abodes of spirits."[53] This belief reveals parallels to African beliefs that are discussed in the next chapter.

Today, many of the African American cemetery landscapes that I studied are characterized by profuse plantings including yucca,[54] daffodils, periwinkle, cedar trees, and clusters of perennials. While none of these species is a unique attribute, taken together these plants contribute to an overall impression in many African American cemeteries of a greater focus on the natural landscape rather than the sterile, pruned lawns found in many white cemeteries.

In one slave cemetery, the often invasive species of *Ailanthus altissima* (more commonly known as "tree of heaven") was deliberately planted in a circle around the graveyard. This species was introduced to America from China in 1784 and can easily reproduce itself generation after generation through wind-dispersed seeds and root sprouts.[55] Enslaved populations used what was at hand and did not have the opportunity to purchase the ornamental varieties of plants and trees seen in contemporary white cemeteries, such as willow trees. But some nineteenth-century observers noted the presence of flowers on black graves.[56]

Another characteristic of African American cemeteries is the large number of depressions within the mortuary landscape. Without vigorous maintenance, we would expect depressions to form from natural causes in any pit that is dug down into the earth and then refilled. Among the reasons for soil sinkage are the decay of a wooden coffin and the season of burial (and thus the amount of moisture in the soil as the gravediggers pack the dirt). Most modern cemeteries lack depressions because concrete vaults are inserted above the coffins. This prevents the ground from sinking even if the coffin decays. Because most nineteenth-century coffins were made from wood, first the coffin and later the body decayed. Then the ground above would settle, forming a depression roughly equal in depth to the height of the coffin. In most American public cemeteries, a groundskeeper would refill the holes as they appeared. But in the rural black cemeteries that I have visited, there are rarely any professional caretakers and the ground has settled over the decades, to a degree sometimes alarmingly deep. Throughout this study the term *depression* is used to indicate burials where the sunken earth is the only remaining indication of a planned grave, because the marker eroded away or the grave never had a permanent memorial.

Grave Placement in American Cemeteries

Prior to the more controlled environments associated with late nineteenth-century cemeteries, the most common pattern for grave placement was to allow families to select an area for their dead within church or public burial grounds. This resulted in family clusters until a given area filled up or surviving relatives decided whether a mother should be buried with her in-laws' family or her own relatives. The best way to illustrate this practice is to describe snapshots of an African American cemetery at different time periods. In a map of Charlottesville's Daughter of Zion Cemetery, you can see families distributing themselves across the available area, leaving as much space as they could for subsequent generations. Some families bought multiple plots to give themselves more room. Even after such careful allocation of space, the social status of a deceased person sometimes resulted in special treatment. In one urban cemetery an African American reverend was buried at the entrance rather than within his family plot. He was a very well-known pastor at a nearby Baptist church who died of "consumption" in 1883. His community status, not his family ties, determined his burial location.

Status can apply not just to individuals but to entire families. Cemeteries have wealthy and poor sections, just like cities. Wealthy areas are often characterized by higher elevations, good views, or proximity to roads and paths. In some cemeteries, "undesirables" are buried in a corner or even outside of an enclosed area. Undesirables might include unmarried mothers, suicides, felons, or any other category deemed unfit by the living community.[57]

4

SLAVE CEMETERIES AND MORTUARY RITUALS

Enslavers restricted and denied the human rights of African Americans. However, many masters allowed enslaved people to decide how, and sometimes where, to bury their dead.[1] But African Americans had limited control over the timing of funerals and the graveside commemoration of the dead. This chapter traces the rituals of death and dying within enslaved communities—including funerals, mourning practices, and grieving—and discusses the common features within their cemeteries.

First I review the mortuary rituals celebrated by enslaved individuals, from the death to the wake, burial, and funeral, and from the mourning process to the selection of a memorial at the grave. The experience of an individual man, woman, or child enslaved on a plantation may have included some or all of these experiences. Note that the rituals of contemporaneous communities of free blacks shared similar religious aspects but varied in terms of the church services, location of the cemeteries, and sometimes the gravestone type.

Dying Enslaved

After a brief illness, a mother passes away in the early afternoon, several days short of her fiftieth birthday. Her daughter's grief is barely controllable. While she is surrounded by several of her siblings and her grandparents, her father and other extended kin are absent. She wants to prepare her mother for the hereafter, but first she must return to work for the remainder of her twelve-hour shift. If she can manage to bury her mother that night, it might be weeks before she can arrange a funeral to properly mourn her mother's passing.

This could be the story of any number of enslaved men and women faced with the passing of a loved one. Many enslaved families were separated and worked on different plantations. Most worked six or even seven days a week, from "sun to sun."[2] Funerals and even the washing and preparation of the body often had to wait until the end of the day's work. As one enslaved woman recounted, "We didn alluz hab too much time fuh big fewnul in dem days cuz deah wuz wuk tuh be done an ef yuh ain do yuh wuk, yuh git whipped."[3] To further complicate matters, between the 1750s and the 1830s most states strengthened laws that prohibited the gathering of more than a handful of slaves or required that funerals be conducted during the day or when a white man was present to officiate. These laws were passed primarily out of fear that enslaved people would plot rebellions.[4] Eugene Genovese points out an even more significant aspect of a proper funeral, "the extent to which they allowed the participants to feel themselves a human community unto themselves."[5] Mounted patrols enforced the restrictions on gatherings and sometimes used these laws to disperse mourners at the site of a funeral.

Enslaved mourners did not often control the timing of their funeral services. Moreover, it might take days or even weeks to share the news of a relative's passing with individuals enslaved on different plantations. Therefore, enslaved communities sometimes held a funeral days or even years after the more pressing and practical matter of the burial of the deceased. A white preacher explained the difference, as he understood it, between the burial of the body and the subsequent religious ceremony: "A negro funeral is different from the 'burying,' and is a unique affair. Several weeks after the burial the funeral is preached. . . . [The funeral is] held frequently in the woods, and sometimes as many as three funerals are preached at once."[6]

These "second burials" represent more than simply an adaptation to restricted freedom. They also illustrate a continuation of African mortuary rituals. While African religious rituals varied according to ethnic groups, many societies practiced a "first" and "second" burial. Both relied on the metaphor of death as a journey. The first funeral served as an initial send-off soon after death.[7] The second funeral celebrated the departure of the soul or "spirit" and ensured the deceased "a place in the company of the ancestors." If the ritual was not properly conducted, the living feared that the dead would return to haunt them.[8]

In Africa these secondary rituals could occur days or up to three years after the initial interment.[9] In America, enslaved individuals waited weeks or months before finalizing the funerary rituals. For example, in the Piedmont county of Orange, Virginia, two enslaved women died a month apart from each other and on two separate plantations. Three weeks after the second death, the neighborhood slaves gathered on a Sunday to have their "funeral over Old Judy and Betty."[10] Some scholars argue that the practice of second burials among enslaved African Americans was a catalyst for the development of these rituals within white communities. In 1785, a Canadian visiting Virginia observed that, even among European Americans, "It is the custom in this part of the country to have a funeral service performed two or three weeks after the person is buried."[11]

The mortuary events of both Africans and enslaved African Americans culminated in feasting, singing, and dancing. On American plantations, former slaves remembered the "wailing grief" expressed by mourners, and observers described the event as "an elaborate social function with festive accompaniments."[12] Or, as one white reverend described it, "Several weeks after the burial the funeral is preached and never was there more frolic at an Irish wake than at these funerals."[13] In Charlotte County, Virginia, the Reverend John Holt Rice described his impressions of early nineteenth-century African American funerary ceremonies: "They cry and bawl and howl around the grave and roll in the dirt, and make many expressions of the most frantic grief. . . . Sometimes they can be heard as far as one or two miles."[14] These events exemplified just one of the many rituals African American families created that recognized and strengthened kinship ties, conveyed religious ideas, and extended the social networks of families and individuals who lived on nearby plantations. These rituals provided African descendants with an opportunity to pass on their traditions and beliefs, often mixed with the Christian teachings of the slave owners and itinerant preachers.[15]

Religious Beliefs Concerning Death

It is difficult to track the descendants of specific African ethnic groups in the nineteenth century, especially in Virginian counties that were far from the original port of arrival. The Trans-Atlantic Slave Trade Database demonstrates that most Africans taken to central Virginia would have originally arrived at the York or Upper James River naval district. The largest single group brought to this area came from eastern Nigeria and would have been predominantly Ibo.[16] Other ethnic groups include Kimbundu and Kikongo speakers from West Central Africa.[17] But associating specific individuals listed in Piedmont Virginia wills with their ancestral homelands is complicated.

While research has been done on the diverse religious belief systems connected with these groups in Africa, contemporaneous accounts of seventeenth- and eighteenth-century cultural systems are biased by interactions with European colonists, who introduced European material culture to African cultures, thereby influencing traditional religious rituals, as well as by European authors' interpretations. Anthropologists and historians recognize that current ethnohistoric studies of African groups should not be simplistically equated with the traditions of the seventeenth- and eighteenth-century polities where Africans were captured by slave traders.[18] Moreover, the cultural traditions of past groups in Africa were not homogeneous,[19] and there is sharp disagreement over the survival of these ethnic identities within enslaved communities in America.[20] After the first quarter of the nineteenth century, most North American slaves were born in the Caribbean or North

America and never experienced life in an African village or city. This may help to explain the variety of religious beliefs and mortuary rituals among the enslaved.

Although there is no monolithic African religion in either Africa or the Americas, the following description provides a brief overview of common attributes of African religions. Some of these beliefs are echoed in the mortuary practices of enslaved African Americans.

Across much of Africa there is a focus on ancestor worship. Viewed as the source of "mystical powers and authority," ancestors perform a significant role within the world of the living. The elders within the living community are expected to serve as mediators between the ancestors and the kin group.[21] Ancestors are consulted at gravesites, where supplicants ask for help, forgiveness, approval, and information.[22] The personification of the "ancestors" goes hand in hand with a belief in the survival of the soul after death, a soul that migrates to the spirit world after the appropriate mortuary rituals are conducted. For example, among the Ga people of the Gold Coast, it is believed that the soul of the deceased does not rest until the body has been brought home for burial.[23] Once the body has been properly washed, dressed, and laid out on a ceremonial bed, survivors mourn the deceased, usually through public weeping and singing (we can see remnants of this practice in antebellum "shouts").[24] Most African cultures have strict rituals that govern funerary rituals in order to ensure that the spirits live comfortably in the afterlife; accordingly, many groups place food and drink on the grave to provide sustenance to the spirits.[25]

This chapter demonstrates how slave mortuary rituals represent a syncretism of Christian and African beliefs.[26] It also describes how enslaved African Americans regained a sense of agency over their funerary rituals, despite the limitations imposed by their owners.

Preparing the Body: "Settin' Up"

From firsthand accounts by whites and blacks throughout the South, we learn that the mortuary ritual began with the death watch, often called the "settin' up." This included singing, praying, and "keep[ing] the spirit company."[27] This observance, part practical (to protect the body from animal scavengers) and part spiritual (to watch over the deceased as the spirit left the body) was often held at the dwelling of the deceased. In some cases, the slave owners volunteered space in their own homes.

The first step was to wash the body and wrap it in a cloth. Because of concerns about purity, on larger plantations only certain individuals, often older women, were entrusted with this task.[28] In warm weather, mourners had to contend with the rapid decomposition of the body. Accordingly, the body was buried soon after death. Mourners would then remain with the corpse overnight to ensure that animals did not disturb the remains. This offered enslaved people another opportunity to share songs and prayers. During cold winters, the corpse was sometimes preserved in a root cellar or icehouse until the spring, when the ground would have thawed sufficiently to allow a burial.

Regardless of the season, the washed, wrapped body was laid out on a "cooling board," designed to hold a rigid body while keeping it cool to prevent decay.[29] In the winter, no props were necessary beyond a sturdy plank of wood, but in the summer, ice was packed under the body in a concave storage area.[30]

Next, relatives on other plantations had to be notified. In Georgia, this notification sometimes took the form of drumming that let nearby communities know there had been a death.[31] In Virginia, slaves holding passes to conduct errands or making unauthorized nighttime visits may have carried this information. Funerals were often delayed by several days while the deceased's family was located. Because slavery often caused the separation of spouses, parents, and children, funerals were often poignant celebratory reunions among the living as well as remembrances of the dead.

One of the earliest abolitionist narratives, written by a white man, Richard Hildreth, about a fictionalized slave named Archy Moore,[32] describes an enslaved husband mourning the death of his wife. Archy recalls, "It was a Sunday. The preacher soon left us; and poor Thomas sat the whole day watching his wife's body." After this period of solitary mourning, the plantation community arrives to carry the body to the cemetery: "Towards sun-set, several of our fellow servants came in; and they were presently followed by most of the plantation people. We took up the body and carried it to the place of burial. . . . [The route] seemed to have been long used for its present purpose. Numerous little ridges, some of them new, and others just discernible, indicated the places of the graves."[33] Other slave narratives, penned by enslaved individuals themselves, support Hildreth's tale: "At the funeral, all the slaves from the adjoining plantations obtain passes from their overseers, and come; so this is really a great day for the poor blacks to see each other. If their hearts are sad, they are happy to see their friends, and they all go to some place, and their friends receive such entertainment as it is in their power to give. They stay together till night draws on, and then each leaves for his home."[34]

The Coffin

While some members of the community sat with the corpse, others began making (or in some cases, buying) the coffin. Before the growth of the modern, specialized funeral industry, mourners turned to local carpenters or craftsmen to construct coffins. For enslaved populations, the plantation carpenter may have been called upon to construct a simple pine box. In other cases, the plantation owner may have built the coffin. Elgie Davison described his time on a Richmond plantation: "Massa, he build a wooden box and put the nigger in and carry him to the hole in the ground. Us march round the grave three times and that all."[35]

When boxes were not available, because of their cost or a lack of materials, bodies were wrapped in shrouds. Another well-known abolitionist novel contains a description of a shroud-covered coffin: "On a serene, beautiful morning in the month of May, a small funeral procession might be seen winding its way to the village churchyard; the light coffin was covered with a white pall. The solemn ceremony was performed—'Earth to earth, ashes to ashes, dust to dust.'"[36] The presence of a coffin was not, however, always a sign of respect. After the horrific death of a man named James, Harriet Jacobs observed, "They put him into a rough box, and buried him with less feeling than would have been manifested for an old house dog."[37]

Procession to the Cemetery

After the body was prepared and the coffin built, the mourners wound their way to the graveyard. This solemn processional may have involved hundreds of mourners. In the majority of cases, funerals were the only communal gathering permitted to enslaved individuals. The restrictions imposed on these communities meant that a funeral may have been the only time that extended members of a given family could come together. This rare opportunity, combined with African traditions that suggest that a proper funeral is required to send the deceased off to the afterlife, resulted in large gatherings that expressed both grief and celebration.[38] One anonymous observer writing in the decade before emancipation witnessed a funeral heading to the cemetery: "There were at least 150 negroes, arranged four deep, and following a wagon in which was placed the coffin; down the entire length of the line, at intervals of a few feet on each side were carried torches of the resinous pine, and here called lightwood. About the center was stationed the black preacher, a man of gigantic frame and stentorian lungs, who gave out from memory the words of a hymn suitable for the occasion."[39]

Mourners included relatives, friends, a preacher, and, in some cases, the plantation owner. In *Twenty-Two Years a Slave, and Forty Years a Freeman*, Austin Steward (1793–1860) described the order of the participants in a slave funeral as they proceeded to the graveyard: "First, the old slave minister, then the remains of the dead, followed by their weeping relatives; then came the master and his family; next the slaves belonging to the plantation; and last, friends and strangers, black and white; all moved on solemnly to the final resting-place."[40]

The Midnight Funeral

The funeral was most commonly held at night, often at midnight. Nighttime funerals, held after the long work day, allowed the maximum number of enslaved individuals to attend. The midnight timing can be traced to African mortuary rituals, which were often held at night.[41] A contemporary observer, Mary H. Schoolcraft, described such a funeral:

> As soon as a man or woman dies, their fellow-servants send off couriers to the adjoining plantations, to invite their friends to the funeral. About dark they begin to assemble, and their preacher exhorts, and sings, and prays over the body of the dead man until midnight; when six black fellows take hold of the coffin, and proceed slowly to the negro grave-yard (one of which is on every plantation, and sacredly guarded from outside pressure), accompanied by innumerable torch-bearers.[42]

An illustration from Hamilton Pierson's memoir of life as an itinerant preacher, *In the Brush; or, Old-Time Social, Political, and Religious Life in the Southwest*, depicts a slave funeral, led by torch-bearing mourners, with a boy in the front sweeping the way clean with a branch. The pallbearers follow, carrying a pentagonal coffin to a wooded graveyard (fig. 7).[43] In another account, T. Addison Richards described the songs sung by enslaved individuals: "Perhaps the most remarkable of these exhibitions are those which are wont to occur on occasions of funeral solemnities, celebrated as they generally are, in the deep night-darkness of some dense old wood, made doubly dismal by the ghostly light of the pine torches and the phantom-like figures of the scarcely visible mourners."[44]

During the funeral service a preacher might be asked to give a sermon. Some owners allowed African American ministers to preside over the ceremonies, while others provided a white preacher or, in a small number of cases, the plantation overseer—almost certainly a lay person with no religious training. The last option provided the plantation owner with a way to keep an eye on the gathering. John Antrobus's (1837–1907) famous 1860 painting of a burial on a New Orleans plantation depicts a black preacher standing over a coffin while a white overseer watches (standing to the left, near his horse), and the plantation owners stroll through the woods (almost hidden on the right; presumably they are arriving to pay their respects) (fig. 8).[45]

Because whites were only occasionally present at slave funerals, these solemn occasions afforded the enslaved community the opportunity to select verses, songs (including boisterous "shouts"), and even dances to mourn their dead. A biographer quotes John Jasper, a prominent African American preacher, as observing, "A funeral to them was a pageant. It was a thing to be arranged for a long

FIG. 7 Hamilton Pierson, *Midnight Slave Funeral*, 1881. Original caption "An old-time midnight slave funeral." From Hamilton Pierson, *In the Brush; or, Old-Time Social, Political, and Religious Life in the Southwest* (New York: D. Appleton, 1991), facing 284.

time ahead. It was to be marked by the gathering of the kindred and friends from far and wide."[46]

These services reveal a distinctly African American approach to mourning the dead, one that involved sadness but also singing and dancing. This tradition is in sharp contrast to the Anglo-American traditions of the nineteenth century. One formerly enslaved man, born around 1820, recalled, "A negro funeral without an uproar, without shouts and groans, without fainting women and shouting men, without pictures of triumphant deathbeds and the judgment day, and without the gates of heaven wide open and the subjects of the funeral dressed in white and rejoicing around the throne of the Lamb, was no funeral at all."[47] Several observers noted the singing and drumming that accompanied slave funerals.[48] These services enabled enslaved Africans to retain cultural memories and share them with subsequent generations and also resulted in valuable contributions to American music and culture.

FIG. 8 John Antrobus, *A Plantation Burial*, ca. 1860. (Historic New Orleans Collection, acc. no. 1960.46)

Interrupted Funerals

Not all funerals went smoothly. Because African Americans needed passes for travel at night, many would-be mourners were accosted and often beaten by slave patrols. For example, in Albemarle County the enslaved Harris family tried to hold a funeral one night in 1860. The information about this event comes from a letter written by Thomas Jefferson's grandson Dr. Benjamin F. Randolph (the son of his daughter, Martha Jefferson Randolph). Dr. Randolph lived at the Roundtop Plantation and owned fifty-eight slaves in 1860. That same year he wrote a letter in which he discussed a funeral held by the enslaved population. He relates that their white minister, Mr. Timberlake, was absent from the proceedings, yet Dr. Randolph gave mourners permission to leave work and attend the funeral. "They made my dinner," he wrote, "and placed a cloth over it and then went to the funeral." Unfortunately, a slave patrol arrived, and the mourners had to jump out of windows to avoid being caught.[49]

Graveside Traditions and Ritual Finality

Many African Americans performed graveside rituals as a way to say good-bye to their loved ones. The rituals included not only songs and prayers but material gifts such as offerings of food and water or, in some cases, items used by the deceased.

These final gifts were ostensibly placed in the grave in hope that they could be used in the next life, but they also allowed the survivors an act of closure.

We examine archaeological excavations to learn more about what items were placed in coffins. While many descendant communities prefer that the remains of their ancestors lie undisturbed, there are occasions when exhumations are required to protect the integrity of the burials (such as construction projects that threaten cemeteries). These excavations reveal the use of shrouds; while the cloth does not survive, copper residue remains from corroded shroud pins. A small number of burials contain jewelry, such as rings.[50] In the 1990s, an archaeological firm excavated the cemetery associated with an African American church in Philadelphia, the First African Baptist Church. This antebellum graveyard contained coins on the eyes of several of the corpses.[51] One interpretation of this practice is that the coin could be used to pay for a trip across the river of death or across the ocean to Africa.[52] Sometimes objects of value were buried in the grave to symbolize the social status of the deceased. In other instances, grave goods such as food were intended as a gift to the spirit of the deceased so that he or she might rest in peace.[53]

In the 1830s, Charles Ball, an enslaved man, described a graveside ritual that he observed in western Maryland. He accompanied a grieving couple to the grave of their deceased child and described the goods that were placed in the grave: a lock of the father's hair and "a small bow and several arrows; a little bag of parched meal; a miniature canoe, about a foot long, and a little paddle, (with which he said it would cross the ocean to his own country) a small stick, with an iron nail, sharpened and fastened into one end of it; and a piece of white muslin." The grieving father explained that these items would identify the boy as his son.[54] Several of these items illustrate the belief that the deceased would return to Africa after death, demonstrating that death was perceived as an opportunity to return "home."

Another interpretation is that the objects buried in the grave were the last to be used by the deceased and burying these items discouraged the deceased from returning to retrieve them. A 1925 newspaper reporter commented, "A Gullah negro on the Santee river explained to me that it was their custom to place the last plate, the last glass and spoon used before death on the grave."[55] Florence Postell, a former slave interviewed in the 1930s in Brownsville, Georgia, remembered:

> Dey use tuh put duh tings a pusson use las on duh grabe. Dis wuz suppose tuh satisfy duh spirit an keep it frum followin yuh back tuh duh house, I knowd a uhmun at Burroughs wut use tuh carry food tuh uh daughtuh grabe ebry day. She would take a basket uh cooked food, cake, pies, an wine. Den she would carry dishes too an set out a regluh dinnuh fuh duh daughtuh an uhsef. She say duh daughtuh's spirit meet uh deah an dey dine tuhgedduh.[56]

In addition to the interment of artifacts, other items were left on top of the grave, including shells (especially cowrie), mirrors, glass bottles (including medicine bottles), utensils, water pitchers, ceramic figurines, and dishes.[57] Shells are popular because of their association with water, which we have already seen symbolized a metaphoric crossing over to the other side as well as a more literal reference to the ocean-crossing required to return to Africa. But there is an African correlate as well, in that the shells are believed to hold the spirit of the deceased. Other items included clocks (to tell the time of Judgment Day) and chickens or roosters (which were sometimes sacrificed at the grave of the deceased).[58] In the 1930s, a Works Progress Administration (WPA) interviewer traveled to Eulonia, Georgia, and asked Ben and Sarah Washington, "In some places the people told us that dead people's spirits returned to earth. Is that true here?" In response, Sarah observed that if the dead were provided with graveside offerings, they would not return. "I dohn guess yuh be bodduh much by duh spirits ef yuh gib em a good fewnul an put duh tings wut belong tuh em on top uh duh grave." Her husband added, "Uh puts all duh tings wut dey use las, lak duh dishes an duh medicine bottle. Duh spirits need deze same as duh man. Den duh spirit res an dohn wanduh bout."[59]

Because these items might have been desirable among the living, they were often broken to discourage grave robbing. Jane Lewis, interviewed in the 1930s, warned, "Dem dishes an bottles wut put on duh grabe is fuh duh sperrit an it ain fuh nobody tuh tech um."[60] Breaking the items also symbolized the destruction of the body by death.[61]

After the coffin was lowered into the grave, the assembled mourners would each throw a handful of dirt into the shaft. Harriet Jacobs observed the burial of an enslaved friend when she was a girl in the 1820s and later described the "clods" that "fell on the coffin."[62] The practice of tossing a handful of soil on the grave is documented in many contemporary sources. While this tradition is also practiced among white Christians, there is evidence that it may have had different meanings for enslaved individuals. For example, Kongo rituals include a medicine bag, or "nkisi," which contains dirt from a grave, interpreted as the spirit of the deceased.[63] In the Americas, graveyard dirt was mixed with other items, such as whiskey or shavings from the wooden headstone, and was used by conjurers to bring about certain outcomes or even prepare poisons.[64]

Placement of Slave Cemeteries on the Plantation

Since few antebellum slave narratives or later WPA interviews with former slaves discuss graveyards per se (as opposed to memories of deaths and burials themselves), it is hard to know how to attribute the selection of land and space for burial grounds. Because of the absence of clearly defined expectations in the archival record (e.g., "selected 2 acres for the slave burying ground"), it appears that on many plantations the enslaved community managed many if not all of their burial decisions.

Most of the thirty-six slave cemeteries in my study were located on hilltops, within a mile of the plantation house.[65] The Reverend Silas Jackson, an ex-slave interviewed in 1937, recalled that "at each funeral, the Ashbies [the plantation owners] would attend the service conducted in the cabin where the deceased was, from there taken to the slave graveyard. A lot dedicated for that purpose, situated about 3/4 of a mile from cabins near a hill."[66] To supplement this documentary evidence, we can turn to nineteenth-century drawings and engravings with scenes depicting slave cemeteries in heavily wooded areas.[67] Smaller plants and bushes are not usually drawn, but when we survey the remains of these graveyards today, we find an abundance of periwinkle and often cedar trees and yucca plants. Yucca bears lance-shaped leaves that end in sharp points. One explanation for their popularity in cemeteries is that they were to make certain that the devil does not have a place to sit down.

Gravestones and Markers

Although a slave owner might purchase a stone for the deceased, in most cases the stones were chosen and designed by the African American community without interference from whites. The majority of slave gravestones are small, uninscribed fieldstones. Enslaved mourners usually relied upon locally available rocks, which in combination with the lack of inscriptions, makes it difficult to recognize slave graveyards. But close inspection reveals stones and even paired head- and foot-stones in association with depressions.

The absence of inscriptions is explained by low literacy rates and a lack of time and resources among the enslaved. In the 1830s, several states passed laws that made it illegal to teach slaves to read and write. In Virginia, the General Assembly enacted wide-ranging legislation that prohibited "white persons" from teaching free blacks, "mulattoes," or slaves how to read or write.[68] Some enslaved individuals persevered and taught themselves in secret or relied on the bravery of Quakers or other free people who risked punishment to conduct lessons. But even for literate slaves, it would have been hard to find the time to carve a gravestone. Unlike marble or slate, many of the hard fieldstones would have been difficult to carve.

Thus only a small percentage of slaves' grave markers were inscribed (fig. 9). These fall into two main categories: stones carved by slaves and stones erected by slave owners in honor of a deceased slave. The former included those inscribed by enslaved carpenters, who selected stones and carved inscriptions. One such carpenter was John Hemings, a black carpenter who lived at Thomas Jefferson's Monticello

FIG. 9 *Left,* photograph of inscribed slave gravestone in Brightberry Plantation Slave Cemetery, Albemarle County (photograph by Lynn Rainville, 2008); *right,* gravestone redrawn by Ashleigh Hawkins, 2010.

in Charlottesville, Virginia.[69] When his wife, Priscilla, died, he carved a beautiful stone and inscribed it: "Thesed [*sic*] is placed at the hea[d] of my affectionat[e] wife Priscilla Hemmings Departed this life on friday the M[o]nth of May 1830 age 54." The script is a highly stylized font that includes cursive figures.[70] More commonly, inscriptions are somewhat crudely carved and sometimes include reversed letters, misspelled words, and incomprehensible inscriptions that may have represented an amalgam of English and African words. For example, I uncovered stones that read "Bet8ay" (instead of "Betsy"), "WILLIAM HA / 1816 NO," (unclear meaning), "AMMA" (repeated multiple times on one stone, meaning not known), and the use of the symbol for infinity (which may or may not have been the intended meaning).

Slave owners occasionally erected a stone in memory of an enslaved individual. While this may have been intended as a kindness, these stones contain inscriptions that now often seem paternalistic or racist. Another reason for this charitable act may have been to highlight the wealth of the white owner.[71] Even under the best of circumstances, an owner-erected stone removed the choice of commemoration from the deceased's surviving kin. A plain rectangular stone erected by a white owner on an Albemarle County plantation reads, "Mammy Sarah Jordan—1819–1893— Faithful unto Death." This type of inscription was used throughout the South. For example, a small marble stone in an Alabama graveyard reads, "Uncle John / faithful servant of B. J. Hoole. Died 1883."[72] The use of "mammy" or "uncle" was a way of stating an imaginary familial relationship between owner and slave. The expression "faithful servant" is common on slave gravestones and in literature.[73] A majority of enslaved individuals may well have been "faithful" but hardly by choice. They knew the harsh punishments that awaited them if they dared to display disloyal behavior. Finally, this stone functions as an advertisement for the owner, stating his surname, while leaving out the African American's surname, even though he died after emancipation and therefore almost certainly had a last name. Also omitted is the birth date or age at death for the enslaved "John." The caption that accompanies the photograph of this stone in the Library of Congress American Memory site reads, "In memory of a trusted slave who continued as a servant after he was freed." From the perspective of the emancipated African American, it is more likely that he obtained paid employment in a familiar neighborhood.

Some graves of enslaved individuals were marked with something other than a stone. Documentary sources and archaeological surveys have revealed planted flowers or trees, iron posts, railroad equipment, and links of chains (an ironic choice for enslaved individuals, but the number of chains symbolized whether the deceased had been born free or enslaved and whether they died free). Wooden markers were also used. Harriet Jacobs's autobiography describes the use of a tree stump and inscribed wooden boards in lieu of gravestones.[74]

Cemetery Landscape

Several patterns are found among the landscapes of African American cemeteries. First, bodies were laid in the ground so that the heads faced to the east (i.e., the head lies in the west, the feet in the east). While not unique to these graveyards, in the case of slave cemeteries this practice can be interpreted in two ways. The Christian interpretation is that the deceased will rise on Judgment Day to face his or her maker.[75] A more poignant meaning within enslaved communities was that the deceased rested facing Africa. As noted above, several African American writers refer to "going home" only in death.

Unlike antebellum European American cemeteries, few slave graveyards contain rows of stones. Instead, graves are clustered into groups. Without inscribed headstones, it is difficult to interpret this pattern, but explanations include family groupings, chronological associations, or locations that correspond to the social or economic status of the deceased.

While slave cemeteries rarely included metal fencing or stone walls (both commonly found at contemporary white burial grounds), the enslaved community did make an effort to differentiate the sacred space of the cemetery. In 1867, *Harper's Weekly* published a two-page illustration titled "Scenes on a Cotton Plantation." One of the vignettes included a drawing of the slave cemetery with railroad ties stacked to prevent animals from disturbing the burials. The accompanying text states that the enslaved community went one step further and leaned a "mattock and spade" over the grave for two weeks to "safeguard against the premature resurrection of the corpse."[76] Other accounts suggest that symbolic enclosures were created from planted trees and hedges and possibly even white-washed palings or fences.[77]

The Postbellum Use of Slave Graveyards

Enslaved individuals had few choices about where to bury their dead. Even if the landowners gave them permission to select the location for their graveyards, there would certainly have been limitations on which spot they selected; most owners would have balked at having African Americans buried adjacent to their own houses or gardens, for example. One might assume that after emancipation, African Americans would have established new burial grounds, but this is not always the case, for several reasons. If one member of a couple or family died before 1865, the survivor may have chosen to be buried next to his or her relative, even after emancipation. In addition, not all postbellum African Americans had access to land where they could bury their dead. In rural parts of central Virginia, most independent black churches were founded in the 1870s. This leaves several years between the end of the Civil War and the opportunity to bury one's dead in a churchyard. And while some freed slaves were quickly able to purchase land (and, if they chose to, establish a private family burial ground), others worked as sharecroppers or laborers and thus lacked the resources to own a family cemetery. A final option, burial in a public cemetery, was not always offered to freedmen and freedwomen. Later, segregated sections for African Americans were provided in public cemeteries throughout Virginia, with Jim Crow laws ensuring that the souls of whites and blacks were kept separate for eternity.

In some cases, "slave cemeteries" were used for a decade or two after emancipation. For example, in the slave cemetery at the Redlands Plantation, owned by the Carter family in Albemarle County, there are dozens of uninscribed, undated stones that mark the final resting places of the enslaved community. But there are also a handful of inscribed stones for individuals who were born enslaved but died decades after the end of the Civil War. One such individual was John Sellers, who died in 1885 at the age of ninety-four. In other words, he was born in 1791 and lived most of his life enslaved on the Redlands Plantation. One can imagine why his surviving relatives decided that his final resting place should be alongside the people with whom he lived and worked over the course of his long life, presumably including his wife, Mary, buried under an uninscribed stone at the plantation.

Chapter 8 discusses how these antebellum cemeteries can contribute to the study of enslaved communities and the ways in which they function as an outdoor museum of antebellum African American material culture and beliefs. These death-scapes were, and in some cases continue to be, places of mourning, remembrance, and continuation. In Harriet Jacobs's memoir she recalled visiting the graveyard of her parents over the course of a decade to grieve and to genuflect.

5

THE NETWORK OF DEATH
Funerals, Churches, and Burial Societies

The gravestone is an invaluable source of information, but it is only one of a complex series of mortuary rituals that can reveal much about the culture of the dead. These include rituals of preburial such as wakes and funerals, the participation of funeral homes and churches, and the contributions of burial societies that occasionally helped fund the proceedings. For the past four hundred years, African American families have syncretized belief systems that combine West African, Christian, and evolving American traditions. In funerary rituals, these efforts have created new customs that persist alongside practices found throughout America.

From Home to Hospital

To understand the transition from preemancipation rituals to late nineteenth- and twentieth-century practices, we have to consider broader changes in American attitudes toward death that have impacted African American families. American funerary behavior has been dictated by modern-day sensibilities and expectations, including the participation of funeral homes and other "death care" specialists such as morticians. This professionalism of death has distanced most Americans from mortuary obligations such as cleaning the body and preparing it for viewing in a coffin. This physical and emotional distance is further compounded by the increasing numbers of Americans who die in a hospital rather than at home. Today more than 60 percent of Americans die in a hospital bed, surrounded by doctors and nurses.[1] The hospital may not allow family members to spend the night in the room. In many cases, the sick pass on with no witnesses.

In the nineteenth century, it would have been difficult to die alone. Most Americans died at home unless they succumbed on a battlefield or at sea or suffered a fatal accident at work. When someone fell seriously ill and his or her time was deemed to be near, family, friends, and occasionally a member of the clergy gathered at the bedside.[2] For example, in 1846 in Schenectady, New York, a young mother died of tuberculosis at home, in bed. Her father wrote that "we kept our solemn vigil around her dying bed all night."[3] In 1790 a Virginia preacher recorded his wife's last words: when asked "whether she was happy in her soul she replied 'Yes, O yes!'"[4] This tradition dates to the middle ages, when deathbed gatherings were considered an important opportunity to pass wisdom on to surviving generations. Family members would wait and watch, careful to announce the death only after several simple tests were performed, such as checking for breath with a mirror or listening for a heartbeat. There was a common fear that those who were simply unconscious might be mistaken for dead. This led to the development of a variety of safety devices, designed to alert the living in case someone was accidentally buried alive. One such device was an aboveground bell, connected by a wire to the coffin. If the presumed deceased found him- or herself awake in a subterranean coffin, he or she could pull the wire, thereby ringing the bell and alerting passersby to the mistake. The involvement of American families in these death rituals over centuries contrasts starkly with the twentieth-century tendency toward "death avoidance."[5]

In southern African American communities, a segregated, parallel industry evolved around the care of the dead. In the decades prior to the formation of black funeral homes (ca. 1880s), black churches and secret organizations were already helping to care for the sick and bury the dead.[6] Booker T. Washington bemoaned this focus on dying, complaining, "The trouble with us is that we are always preparing to die."[7] As the popularity of embalming and the professional "death care" industry grew, African American funerals homes were founded, enabling this community to manage their deaths according to more modern sensibilities.

Postemancipation African American Funerary Rituals

After emancipation, black communities in central Virginia had more choices in memorializing their dead. Late nineteenth- and early twentieth-century African American mortuary rituals took several forms, depending on the class and socioeconomic status of the survivors. The first step was always to wash the body and select the burial clothes. The wealthy might purchase a new set of clothes, while poorer families would have fewer choices. Once the body was washed and dressed, it was laid out, usually in the parlor, for the wake. Like preemancipation rituals, postemancipation African American wakes are often referred to as the "settin' up." The wake originated in Europe in the 1400s, when family members watched over the body in case it "awakened" from its mortal slumber (a real fear in the days when some catatonic illnesses could be mistaken for death). For African Americans the wake provided an opportunity for socializing and feasting, often with culturally specific foods.[8]

FIG. 10 Miss Gertrude
White laid out in a coffin
outside her home in Albe-
marle County. (4 January
1919; courtesy Holsinger
Studio Collection, MSS
9862, retrieval identification no. X07251B2, Special
Collections, University of
Virginia Library)

An early twentieth-century photograph taken by Rufus W. Holsinger dramatically illustrates an Albemarle County wake, held at the home of the deceased (fig. 10).[9] Note the contrast between the deceased's status in life and in death. Miss Gertrude White is lying in state outdoors in a very handsome coffin with ornate handles and a beveled wooden rim, covered with beautiful floral wreaths. Several well-dressed friends are in attendance. Floral arrangements were a popular funeral expense. Along with their symbolic message of life budding, blooming, and fading, the flowers' fragrance helped to mask the odor of the slowly decaying body. Miss White's house is visible in the background, in sharp contrast to the elaborate coffin and floral tributes; the porch is haphazardly constructed, the windowpanes broken or missing. There is no explanation for the outdoor wake, but given the dilapidated structure it is possible that there wasn't room for both the corpse and the visitors inside.

It was far more common to lay out the body indoors. A remarkable photograph survives that documents the inside of Benjamin Tonsler's house during his funeral rites (fig. 11).[10] A photograph of Mr. Tonsler sits prominently in an ornate frame. The photo is surrounded by dozens of floral arrangements, several of which hold banners announcing the donor. One reads "Choir 1st Baptist," a reference to the choral group at the First Baptist Church, which Tonsler attended. Many of the flowers are arranged in wreaths, a traditional Greek symbol of honor. Others have been crafted into the shape of anchors (a reference to his Christian faith), stars, and the letter *V*, which might stand for "victory over death."

Mr. Tonsler was the first principal of the segregated, all-black Jefferson Graded School in Charlottesville, where he served for thirty years. His gravestone in the Daughters of Zion Cemetery highlights this accomplishment with an inscription reading, "Erected by the Alumni of Jefferson Graded School and Friends." The

FIG. 11 Mourning flowers in honor of Benjamin E. Tonsler. Note the photograph of the deceased. Photograph taken inside Mr. Tonsler's home 10 March 1917 (he died March 6) by Rufus W. Holsinger. (Courtesy Holsinger Studio Collection, MSS 9862, retrieval identification no. X04907B, Special Collections, University of Virginia Library)

unpolished marble stone is decorated with abstract floral patterns. Benjamin Tonsler's house still stands, located about a mile away from the cemetery, on Sixth Street.

Funeral plans proceeded after the body was prepared. As with collective burial practices, funerals encompassed more than just the individual. The social identity of the deceased was on display, and the ritual surrounding the death was an important event that signaled the status of both the deceased and their surviving relatives. Poor families often spared no expense in burying their dead. In the African American community, the funeral may have provided a chance to confer on the deceased a social dignity that was often lacking in life. Some sociologists have traced the practice back to African traditions that held that the "good dead" continued living in the afterlife, and elaborate funerals and grave goods "helped settle them properly in the worlds beyond."[11] In Charlottesville, the white *Charlottesville Chronicle* newspaper covered the funeral of an African American minister, the Reverend Gibbons, who died 9 July 1886. Alongside the news item is an editorial reflecting on the expense that poor people incur on behalf of their dead. While the Gibbons funeral is not mentioned explicitly, it's clear that lavish expenditure for the minister's funeral prompted the disapproving column.

Historic funeral announcements for the black community often reported on the theme of the funerary oration and the songs that were sung. Black funerals have been described as conveying an "atmosphere of weeping," with an emphasis on emotional responses. One scholar has associated the expressive nature of black funerals with the "call-and-response practices of West African cultures."[12] These dramatic funeral services created a sense of social solidarity that served as a "periodic catharsis for the weight of living black in the United States."[13]

Late nineteenth- and early twentieth-century Virginia society was strictly segregated by race, but whites occasionally attended black funerals. When this occurred, it usually signified that the deceased was held in high esteem by the white community. Often this esteem was based on paternalism. For example, "good negroes" in Charlottesville included African Americans who served the University of Virginia community or well-known business owners. In other cases, individuals classified as "mulatto" were able to partially cross over into white society. For example, when Laurence West died in 1892 at age fifteen, funeral attendees included both whites and blacks. A local African American paper, the *Richmond Planet*, reported, "Mr. Lawrence J., eldest son of Mr. And Mrs. John West, was buried Sunday afternoon at 4 o'clock after a brief illness of four weeks. The funeral took place from the First Bapt. Church, Dr. L. B. Goodall officiating. A large crowd, including a number of white friends, were present. He has passed from labor to reward. The choir sang, 'Asleep in Jesus,' and 'We shall meet beyond the river.'"[14]

The Funeral Business in the African American Community

The American funeral industry became regulated and formalized at the end of the nineteenth century. In the postbellum period, black entrepreneurs recognized the opportunity to serve their community. Despite the beginnings of Jim Crow segregation, white funeral-home owners competed vigorously with this new economic threat. While in life African Americans could not patronize many white businesses, in death they were welcomed by white embalmers and sometimes laid out in the parlors of white funeral homes. More commonly, white businesses competed with black businesses to embalm the body, while black funeral homes hosted the funeral when it wasn't held as a wake at the home of the deceased.

The owner of a black funeral home was often a member of the social, if not economic, elite within his community. His occupation required formal business attire, ornate hearses, and close ties to the community. In Charlottesville, one of the oldest black businesses still in operation is the J. F. Bell Funeral Home. Founded by John Ferris Bell (1890–1959) in 1917, it is one of the oldest family-run funeral homes in Central Virginia. Mr. Bell was born and educated in Petersburg, Virginia, graduated from the Hampton Institute, and later trained as a funeral director and mortician in Chicago. The funeral home is still housed in its original 1925 white clapboard structure, where Mr. Bell and his family lived in the upper floors, reserving the ground floor for business.

In addition to providing embalming and funeral services, the Bell Funeral Home provided temporary metal markers to identify the location of a body until a more permanent memorial could be erected. In 11 percent of the stones in my study, these metal markers were never replaced; I came across hundreds of J. F. Bell markers. One informant told me, "Everybody who is anybody wants Mr. Bell to bury them." Thus, even in death, appearances mattered.

The Role of the African American Church

In central Virginia the postbellum African American community worshipped at churches of several denominations. After decades of segregation and denial of African Americans' right to select their own preachers, the postbellum church served as "an always ready site for cultural redress and spiritual reclamation."[15] The famous civil rights activist and historian W. E. B. Du Bois recognized that in addition to serving as the "social centre of Negro life," the black church was at the center of multiple social groups, including "the church proper, the Sunday-school, two or three insurance societies, women's societies, secret societies, and mass meetings of various kinds."[16] Those who assisted with funerals and burials can be added to this list: black funeral homes and their directors, sextons, cemetery managers, and gravediggers.

Between the early 1800s and the present, the role of the black church in funeral services and cemetery interments changed. While this is not the place for a comprehensive history of the black church in Virginia, Albemarle County can serve to illustrate the intersecting roles of the cemetery with the church and its associated benevolent societies.

Antebellum Worship and Black Churches

Prior to emancipation, the black community could only undertake public worship under the watchful eyes of white men. This regulated observance took the form of white preachers for free black congregations, segregated and often balcony seats for enslaved African Americans within white churches, and supervised black worship. A 1937 Works Progress Administration interview with Reverend Silas Jackson (an African American born in about 1846 in Ashby's Gap, Virginia) recounts: "No one on the place was taught to read or write. On Sunday the slaves who wanted to worship would gather at one of the large cabins with one of the overseers present and have their church. After which the overseer would talk. When communion was given the overseer was paid for staying there with half of the collection taken up, some time he would get 25¢. No one could read the Bible. . . . [The] coachman was the preacher, he would go to the white Baptist church on Sunday with family and would be better informed because he heard the white preacher."[17]

In addition to these supervised formal and indoor worship services, enslaved and free African Americans managed their own religious lives through circumspect gatherings, often held outdoors at night in seldom-visited areas of the plantation landscape, as documented by archival evidence from nocturnal raids in search of runaway slaves. In private, enslaved African Americans created sacred spaces, called "hush harbors" or "brush harbors," where they could worship more freely.[18] By using a series of subtle passwords and signals, enslaved people organized religious ceremonies that blended African rhythms, singing, and Christian beliefs. These secret meetings were led by African American preachers, referred to as "stump preachers." Garland Monroe, a former slave of President James Monroe explained the occupation: "I'm gittin' on to ninety, but I recollec' my daddy an' two older brothers slippin' out nights to go to meetin'. Brothers would tell me all 'bout it nex' day. Dey had what dey called a stump preacher; ole man Tucker Coles it was. Dey call him a stump preacher 'cause he used to git up on a stump an' preach to de slaves."[19]

During this same period, free blacks, who more commonly congregated in northern cities, formed independent black denominations. As early as 1816, the African Methodist Episcopal Church was the first such congregation to organize, quickly followed by the African Methodist Episcopal Zion Church in 1821. But in rural central Virginia, African Americans, free or otherwise, were rarely given the opportunity to publicly form their own congregations until the 1860s. In Albemarle two exceptions were the Pine Grove Meeting House, founded in 1838, and the Mount Eagle Baptist Church, founded in 1854. Unfortunately, no records survive from either church other than their names. Records from the First Baptist Church in Charlottesville indicate that during the Civil War, after the Emancipation Proclamation (1 January 1863), the 812 "colored members" of the church petitioned the white members of the congregation for permission to form an "independent African Church."[20] This became the first black church to be founded in Charlottesville after emancipation.

Postbellum Churches and Twentieth-Century Black Churches

Late nineteenth-century African American churches shared many beliefs with white Christian churches, but scholars have identified unique attributes of black worship. Mark Ellingsen has recognized four traditions within black churches: "(1) concern with personal and group freedom (linking salvation to political liberation), (2) reliance on the image of Africa as the land of origin, (3) emphasis on the Will of God for social justice, and (4) creative style and artistry in worship (worship as existing and to be enjoyed)."[21] The examples cited here come from southern and, more specifically, Virginia churches. The African American religious experience varied in complex ways, according to the worshipper's class and gender and the regional setting of the church, be it rural or urban.

In Albemarle County between 1865 and 1867, several African American churches were founded within newly emancipated communities: Union Baptist Church, African Baptist Church near Carter's Bridge, Union Run Baptist Church, and Mount Zion Baptist Church on Ridge Street in Charlottesville. Between 1868 and 1900 at least twenty-four black churches were founded in Charlottesville, but their attrition rate was high. By 1910 only fifteen black churches were listed in the city business directory. Many of these postbellum churches contained burial grounds.

I recorded about 1,470 stones from black churchyards in my study. Of this sample, 65 percent of the stones were inscribed with a name. A higher percentage of these stones featured epitaphs and inscriptions than those in family, neighborhood, and public cemeteries. Thus there seems to be a greater emphasis on commemorating the dead with an inscribed memorial in church cemeteries. Since survivors select these literary memorials, the widespread occurrence of epitaphs in church cemeteries may point to the increased social bonds present within postbellum black congregations.

I also investigated whether the leaders of these churches were buried under distinctive grave markers, bearing religiously inspired inscriptions or motifs. Without extensive archival research the only means for identifying reverends or pastors was from the stone itself. The appearance of the prefix "Rev." or "Pastor" allowed the identification of ten church leaders, all men. Surprisingly, their graves revealed little of their occupations, other than the use of the title "Rev." Of the ten stones, only four featured religious symbols, and only one of the stones had an unusual motif (a three-dimensional Bible, opened atop an obelisk). Three of the stones contained epitaphs referencing the deceased's occupation. Otherwise, these were nondescript stones of common types, with motifs found on dozens of nearby grave markers. This reinforced one of my earlier conclusions: African American gravestones often focus on community ties rather than individual accomplishments.

Burial Societies

African American churches served many functions for their communities, addressing their members' spiritual, social, and financial needs. Many churches offered membership in "burial societies" for a small monthly fee. These associations served as a form of insurance. For a nominal contribution, members would be assured that their burial needs would be provided for when they died. The cemetery committee was an offshoot of these groups, formed to take care of the landscape and stones within church-owned burial grounds. The noted African American historian and writer Carter G. Woodson explained the context for these associations: "Drawing on the African Negro's penchant for burial pomp, secret societies have been developed mainly around the idea of taking care of the sick and dead."[22]

In Charlottesville, a nineteenth-century charitable group went beyond providing individualized burial assistance, purchasing a two-acre plot of land to serve as a cemetery for its members. The Daughters of Zion Cemetery was founded by a charitable society for African American women in 1873. The first burial was in 1873, and more than two hundred other individuals have since been buried there, most recently in 1995. The majority of burials took place prior to the 1930s, when the charitable group was still active. While there are no extant records from the Daughters of Zion organization, the 1873 deed explains the creation of the cemetery: "for the use of the Charitable association of colored women of Charlottesville, known and styled as 'The daughters on Zion' And used exclusively as a burying ground."[23] The cemetery was used by a wide range of black citizens, from social elites to paupers.

Sometimes a burial association did not provide sufficient resources for a group of poor families. In those cases, indigent individuals turned to their churches and communities for help. One rural black church met the poor's needs by creating a pauper's cemetery on its land. The Chapman Grove Baptist Church was founded in 1900 on land donated in 1898 by Mr. and Mrs. William Chapman. The Chapman Grove Baptist Church Cemetery lies behind the church building. There are about a dozen visible markers past a white picket fence. According to oral history, a former deacon, Mr. Robert Coles (d. 1995), decided to allow burial in the church cemetery of individuals who were not able to afford a plot in one of the larger public cemeteries. Neighbors referred to the cemetery as a "pauper's cemetery."

Only two of the twelve markers in this cemetery contain inscriptions: one for Mrs. Lucy T., who died in 1982, and one for Lucy G., whose dates are not visible. The J. F. Bell Funeral Home database lists more than a dozen additional individuals as being buried in "Chapman Cemetery." The earliest burial in that list is "Miss Lewis," who died in 1963. The most recent burial was in 1994, suggesting that the burials may have ceased after the death of the charitable Mr. Coles.

Reverend Robert Hughes

The gravestone of one of the reverends, Robert Hughes, illustrates the success of a formerly enslaved individual who followed his calling during and after slavery. Hughes died in 1895 at age seventy-one. His birth year, 1821,[24] is the earliest legible on the gravestones within the Union Run Cemetery, located two miles east of Charlottesville. Reverend Hughes's epitaph reads, "Pastor of the Union church for 30 years. And the Zion Hill Baptist Church 20 years." In other words, he was the founding pastor of the Union Run Church, then called the Union Branch Church, when it opened in 1865. His second occupational service was at Zion Hill, located about eight miles north. His stone includes a hand-carved "Holy Bible." Hughes began his services as a reverend during the antebellum period, when he conducted services for his fellow slaves at nearby Edgehill Plantation. A search of the census records turned up his family tree, which led back to Monticello, where he was born enslaved by Thomas Jefferson. His father, Wormley Hughes, was Jefferson's head gardener; Ursula was his mother. When Thomas Jefferson died, Hughes's family was willed to Jefferson's grandson Thomas Jefferson Randolph, who lived at Edgehill. Randolph gave an acre of land to the Union Branch congregation for the construction of its church.[25]

I learned that the reverend's stone had fallen over in the 1970s and had been covered with dirt and grass over the years. In 1997 researchers at Monticello hosted a reunion for the descendants of individuals enslaved by Thomas Jefferson. At the end of the weekend, they gathered in the church cemetery to watch the unearthing of this stone. They rediscovered the grave by combining hands-on fieldwork with oral history. During the gathering, one of the reverend's descendants, Calvin Jefferson, led the group to an area where he had last seen the standing stone. The pastor, Rickey White, used a metal probe and immediately hit the stone. He dug down, brushed away the remaining dirt, and began to read the inscription aloud. The gathered audience erupted in applause.

Surprisingly, while Robert Hughes had ten siblings, none of them are buried here, and neither are his wife and children. This suggests that the reverend was commuting, nineteenth-century style, from another neighborhood or county. Or perhaps his family was buried in a smaller family cemetery, while his congregation requested that he be buried at the church. We can only imagine who decided to bury him at Union Run instead of at the site of his other congregation at Zion Hill. Both had operational cemeteries by the 1890s.

This is only one example of how a burial ground can communicate historical narratives at the local, state, and national levels. Robert Hughes's life story takes us from the antebellum period, when, on some plantations, he would have been whipped, maimed, or even killed for preaching, to the postbellum period, when he successfully founded his own church.[26] A single gravestone's text gives us part of the life story of an individual; its raw material reveals broader technological changes, economic forces, and networks of trade; its motifs and inscriptions point to Christian belief systems; and its geographical setting reveals the community's history. Final resting places serve as containers for the body, but far more significantly, the memorials to these ancestral bodies inform our contemporary identities.[27] This continuity between identity in life and in death is an incentive for honoring all cemeteries as significant sites of cultural memory.

6

LOST COMMUNITIES
OF THE DEAD

Mid-twentieth-century trends toward increased housing development and consequent rising land prices and tax rates forced many African American families to sell their land and attendant gravesites. Difficult economic times also forced families to migrate to northern cities to seek employment. In their absence, many of their historic house sites and cemeteries were destroyed. In other cases, carved fieldstones that once marked graves were removed and stacked under nearby trees to clear the land for cultivation or for animal husbandry. African American family history is lost when the grave sites and homesteads of earlier generations are destroyed.

The following five vignettes of historic African American communities (Milton, Blenheim, Redlands, Free State, and Hardin) illustrate how the landscapes of nineteenth-century lives are lost and why it is important to recover them. These communities were chosen because of the archival, ethnohistoric, and mortuary evidence that survives to document the lives of the African Americans who lived there. I also discuss the importance of preserving oral histories to document the memories associated with these historic places. Using graveyards as a starting point for locating the center of these now vanished communities, I then turn to individual gravestones to recover information about the people in these earlier generations.

Milton

The historic community of Milton, along the Rivanna River, is about a mile from Monticello, Thomas Jefferson's "Little Mountain." Milton was once home to a large tobacco warehouse and a thriving community, but as railroads and highways usurped the commercial roles of canals and rivers, the place and its people withered. Today, there are no businesses in Milton, just a combination of truly historic homes and other old and brand new residences. As in many parts of Albemarle County, the newest residents tend to be wealthy and move into large, custom-built homes, while the longtime residents often struggle to pay rising taxes on small homes that they have lived in for fifty years or more.

In 2004, a University of Virginia librarian living in Milton called me about a rumored cemetery in her backyard. Her house, near a newly constructed road called Lafayette Lane, was built in the 1980s, but the ruins of nineteenth-century homes remained in the nearby woods. After walking around the area for about an hour amid the poison ivy and periwinkle, I failed to see any markers. But I was not ready to give up, so I contacted Billy Hearns.

I had been told about Mr. Hearns's family connections to the area by another longtime resident, Mary Reaves, who was descended from the last African American gatekeeper at nearby Monticello. Mr. Hearns kindly invited me to talk with him about his family history. I learned that his family had lived in Milton for more than 125 years and that he had grown up in his grandmother's house in the 1930s. When he described its location, I realized it was only a couple hundred yards away from the librarian's home. I had located the right person to ask about the cemetery.

Formerly a janitor for a University of Virginia fraternity, Mr. Hearns boasted that he had worked for forty-seven years and only took one day off during that time. He proudly showed me signed yearbooks that the fraternity brothers had given him in recognition of his many decades of service and talked about the large going-away party they threw for him when he finally retired in 2008. Mr. Hearns now repairs old-fashioned lawn mowers and plays piano for a local church. I brought my dulled push mower with me so I could multitask while asking him if he knew of a cemetery near his old family homestead.

Mr. Hearns took me out to his cinder-block garage, which he had turned into a workshop, for our interview. It was the final resting place of grass-cutting devices; pieces were strewn everywhere without a complete lawn mower in sight. He began telling me about his grandmother Mattie while testing the few moving parts on the machine I had brought. He reminisced about the home where he grew up and immediately remembered the spot I was asking about. He insisted on accompanying me there, in his youthful seventh decade of life. Mr. Hearns was excited about seeing the cemetery; his last visit was a distant memory and appears to have occurred in the early 1970s.

We drove out to a periwinkle cluster behind the librarian's house. There was dense ground cover with fallen tree limbs, poison ivy, and rodent holes to avoid. I was worried that Mr. Hearns would trip and spent more time watching him than the ground. We searched for more than an hour, until the sun began to set. Just as I was going to suggest we call it a night, something caught my eye: the setting sun illuminating a fieldstone. A naturally occurring rock had been lightly shaped into a curved headstone. While not inscribed, its mottled surface gave it texture, and a small patch of moss attested to its permanency on the landscape. If we had come thirty minutes later, the absence of sunlight would have allowed the stone to blend into the shades of brown in the carpet of dead leaves. But the burst of late-afternoon sunrays framed the stone perfectly.

With renewed enthusiasm we eventually located four metal markers and six carved fieldstones. Each of these markers was low to the ground or rusted, making them difficult to see against the brown leaf litter. Of the ten, only one marker contained a portion of an inscription, the dates 1925–1927. As I remarked on the dates, Mr. Hearns shared his memory of carrying his infant sister, Marion, to her grave in the late 1920s. "She may lie under this marker," he said. With no inscribed markers, Billy Hearns's memory may well be the only surviving evidence of who was buried there. According to him, his mother, Beatrice Curry, who died in 1948 at age thirty-seven, and infant sister, Marion, who died in 1927, rest there. So do his uncle Joseph (1910–1963) and his great-grandmother Lucy Luck, who was born just after emancipation in 1866 and died in 1935.

The Hearns Cemetery is a classic example of a small family cemetery that began adjacent to a house. If Billy's recollections are correct, one of the earliest burials was of his sister Marion, who was living with her mother in her grandmother's house at the time of her death. It would have been sensible and perhaps consoling to bury an infant nearby instead of paying for a plot in a formal cemetery. By all accounts, the matriarch of the family was the grandmother, Mattie Thomas (1887–1978). Mattie owned forty acres, according to Mr. Hearns, and had built a house on the land. Remains of this structure can be seen along with the debris of everyday life, such as an old hand-cranked washing machine and broken bits of crockery. When Mr. Hearns's mother, Beatrice, died in 1948, the family was still living in the house, but by the 1960s, increased taxes forced grandmother Mattie to sell it.

Here, the story takes an unfortunate and all-too-common turn. Virginia law allows descendants to visit a family cemetery, even when it is located on private property, during daylight hours.[1] However, in the 1960s Mr. Hearns was incorrectly told that he could no longer visit his family cemetery. Even worse, an unscrupulous lawyer told him that she could arrange for him to have access to the cemetery—for a price: the cost of alleged litigious proceedings that she claimed were necessary to enable access. While Mr. Hearns was considering purchasing her services, the lawyer died, and he gave up trying to get access. Thus when the two of us visited the cemetery, he had not been there for forty years.

By the time Mr. Hearns's grandmother Mattie died in 1978 at age eighty-five, the family no longer owned the surrounding land. And as he explained, "Mattie was buried at the other cemetery because it [the family cemetery] wasn't taken care of like it should have been. . . . I guess we just didn't have the proper chance to look after it like we should have." So Mattie was buried many miles away in Charlottes-ville, at the Oakwood Cemetery. Mr. Hearns clearly remembered burying her and specified that in contrast to the unmarked graves in the family cemetery, "I buried grandmamma because I wanted her in a place where I could see her and she could have a headstone. I bought that too." If his grandmother were alive, he admitted, she would have wanted to "have her say" and be buried in the old family cemetery. But its abandoned state was considered unsuitable for their matriarch. Although Mr. Hearns did not contextualize his memories, they occurred within the larger mid-twentieth-century pattern of development and subsequent rising land prices and tax rates that forced many African American families to sell their land.

Blenheim, or Middle Oaks

The immediate postbellum decades—when Mattie Thomas was buying land and establishing a household—saw the founding of many African American churches. Two antebellum churches are listed in Albemarle County historic records: the Pine Grove Meeting House, founded in 1838, and the Mount Eagle Baptist Church, founded in 1854.[2] Two others are labeled "African" and are accompanied by the symbol for a church on an 1867 map.[3] There were probably dozens of other small congregations on plantations with large enslaved populations that were never noted on maps or in other documents.

The presence of antebellum black churches is significant, since a series of early nineteenth-century laws prohibited enslaved individuals from congregating in large numbers and required a white man to be present when African Americans were worshipping.[4] Unfortunately, no physical remains of any of these churches have been located to date, making it difficult to identify the religious centers of these black communities. Hoping to contact descendants of antebellum worshippers and learn about black neighborhood burial traditions, I visited the site where one "African Church" was indicated on a mid-nineteenth century map.

The neighborhood, located at the intersection of five crossroads, is called Blen-heim on the map, though its original name was Middle Oaks. The African Amer-ican Middle Oak Baptist Church was founded here in 1891. The white clapboard building has a simple steeple and an old chimney with an iron grate for shoveling in coal. In the last quarter of the nineteenth century, the church served as the spiritual center of a small but thriving rural community inhabited by a number of African Americans who owned property and ran businesses, including the Blenheim Post Office, a general store, and a blacksmith shop. There was also an African American school at the Blenheim crossroads.

Today, the African American community is much smaller. Large new homes are being built on former fields, and the slowly rising tax base is pushing out African

American families that have lived here for generations. Others among the original families, decades removed from their rural heritage, are moving to cities to find jobs. The only reason a visitor might pause here today is to observe the stop sign at the intersection of the crossroads. But the church still stands and hosts worship every Sunday, and it contains a small cemetery.

Several dozen yards behind the Middle Oak Baptist Church lie a collection of granite and metal markers. Funeral records suggest that more than thirty people are buried here, but only two dozen identifiable markers survive behind the two picnic benches in the churchyard. At first I was puzzled: no burial is earlier than the 1970s, a very strange ninety-year gap for a church founded in 1891.

Charlie Scott

I learned the reason for this gap later, after receiving a call from Ms. Jones, a member of the congregation. She asked me to map and record the original church cemetery, located about a mile away from the church. This cemetery was referred to as the "Charlie Scott Cemetery," in honor of an emancipated slave who gave the land to be used as a burial ground by the Middle Oak Baptist Church. This cemetery is much larger than the church cemetery. It contains more than 110 gravestones, but it is well hidden from the road, and I would never have found it without help from Ms. Jones.

Following her directions, I followed a rural road, parked near a line of telephone poles, walked along a dirt road, and looked for depressions and a fence on the left. When I arrived at the cemetery, I noticed fresh earth on the opposite side of an old fence that surrounded part of the cemetery. A developer had bought the adjacent land and was rapidly clearing land to provide foundations for new homes. It appeared that some of the burials reached into the developer's land—an unfortunate but common occurrence. Because of the ongoing construction next door, it was hard for me to justify an investigation of the depressions, because they might well have been caused by the bulldozers rather than signifying graves.

On the day I surveyed the Charlie Scott Cemetery, no workers were on duty, so the site was very quiet, with only an occasional chirp or scurry breaking the silence. The fence line provided an arbitrary edge for the mapping, but it was less clear how far the burials extended in the other three directions. Only a quarter of the 110 stones contained readable names and dates. The other stones were a combination of illegible metal, eroded marble, uncarved fieldstones, and unmarked depressions.

The earliest legible inscribed stone date is 1871, two decades before the founding of the nearby Middle Oak Baptist Church. All of the burials in this cemetery probably postdate emancipation, because earlier community members were enslaved on nearby plantations and probably would have been buried in slave cemeteries, not neighborhood or church cemeteries. Of the legible stones, seven individuals were born prior to emancipation, between 1823 and 1863. These included members of the Jones, Johnson, Lewis, and Mays families. Some might have been enslaved, though others might have been among the small percentage of free blacks in the region. Four members of the Jones family and two members of the Lewis family are listed as free in the 1790 census for Albemarle County. While these names do not precisely match those of the individuals buried in the cemetery, they may have been relatives.

The black community in Blenheim dates back to the early nineteenth century. Local antebellum histories emphasize the elite white families who lived here: the Carters, descendants of the wealthy and politically powerful Robert "King" Carter (ca. 1664–1732), a burgess and governor of Virginia; the Randolphs, direct descendants of Pocahontas and cousins of Thomas Jefferson; and the Coles, two of whom were private secretaries for Presidents Jefferson and Madison.[5] Surviving plantation homes still cover the landscape in this rural portion of Albemarle County. The physical remains of the African American community are more subtle and more easily forgotten. The African American cemeteries are examples of the material culture that documents the lives of these historically nearly invisible farmers, laborers, blacksmiths, shoemakers, laundresses, and, after emancipation, lawyers, physicians, reverends, and railroad workers.

The family genealogies recorded on the gravestones in the Charlie Scott Cemetery provide a window into this historically hidden African American community. For example, Katherine Lewis's stone reads, "A memorial of Affection and Appreciation To Katherine Lewis / Redlands—1840 / Blenheim—1928 / Faithful unto death" (fig. 12). Redlands, Katherine's birthplace, was originally owned by John Carter (eldest son of "King" Carter) and passed down to his descendants. It was a plantation comprising thousands of acres, located about half a mile from the

FIG. 12 Gravestone for Katherine Lewis, formerly enslaved on the Redlands Plantation. Charlie Scott Cemetery in Blenheim. (Photograph by Lynn Rainville, 2004)

cemetery. An enslaved woman would hardly have chosen the inscription "faithful unto death." This suggests that the Carters paid for her stone.

Other stones reflect the craftsmanship of the mourners, who carved most of the markers by hand. Agnes Lewis (1877–1961) is buried under a unique three-dimensional concrete cross, inlaid with crystals. The styles of the stones change over the decades in parallel with funerary fashions, ranging from unmodified field-stones to marble, granite, and metal. Unfortunately, many of the metal markers are illegible, so the names of the deceased are no longer associated with their final resting place.

Most of the stones display only pithy inscriptions and lack personalized epi-taphs. One exception is the marker of Lena Richardson (1888–1928), who died at age forty. It reads, "She was a kind and affectionate wife. A fond mother and a friend to all." Census records demonstrate that Lena had five children between 1914 and her death in 1928.[6] Her husband, Junius Richardson, was born in 1889 and outlived her by decades, dying in 1975. In contrast to her personalized stone, his is a simple metal marker, indicating only his name and birth and death dates. Spouses often have different gravestone styles when there is an extensive gap between their deaths. This indicates changing funerary fashions as well as the preferences of a younger generation. While Junius probably selected his wife's epitaph and stone, his marker was probably chosen by his children. His children's selection may also have been limited by their financial resources.

Some percentage of family members tend to leave their homes, perhaps for job opportunities or marriages. As a result, few cemeteries serve an entire community. In the case of African American cemeteries, there is another factor that limits our reconstruction of historic communities: the lack of inscribed stones during much of the nineteenth century. The Charlie Scott Cemetery is one of many such ex-amples. As mentioned above, only 30 of the 110 grave memorials contain legible names of the deceased. The other two-thirds of the community lie in anonymity. Unfortunately, there are few publicly available records that document the lives of these individuals. The gravestones are some of the few physical reminders of this hidden history.

Redlands

While the Charlie Scott Cemetery contains the remains of many individuals born enslaved, the stone styles all date to after emancipation. I went in search of the earlier, antebellum slave cemetery in order to discover the types of stones that en-slaved families used to commemorate their dead. From various historic and mortu-ary leads, I knew to concentrate my search on the Redlands Plantation (mentioned on Katherine Lewis's gravestone) and its associated "African Church."

After consulting an 1864 map, I found the approximate location of the antebellum "African Church," about one mile from the Middle Oak Baptist Church. Today
the site is covered in grass and located just off a curving paved road with views of
wide expanses of land, hand-painted fences, cows, and homes at the end of long
drives flanked by brick walls and sculptures. Just before a stone bridge with a re-
modeled span that includes five-foot-high obelisks is an intersection marked by a
large sign that lists a dozen plantations and farms, giving the distance to each—the
sort of assistance you would expect to find in a city center, not a rural area. I chose
the road that passes Nutmeg Farm and Forge Church, founded in 1745. As one of
the earliest white churches in Albemarle County, this church was named after a
nearby iron forge owned by the Carter family. The forge served white residents in
the neighborhood until the 1820s, when it fell into ruin.

What makes this neighborhood unusual is that a white owner, Robert Carter,
gave enslaved African Americans permission to worship here prior to emancipation. A postemancipation document referring to an event that occurred in the 1850s
illustrates the situation. In an Albemarle County Deed Book Robert Carter wrote,
"Whereas 15–20 years ago [ca. 1851–1856] I conveyed to 4 white trustees 1/8 of an
acre which the African Church now stands adjacent to George Rives and W(alter)
Timberlake. A deed was never recorded from no fault of mine. The Colored Baptist
want to replace the church and the congregation not being satisfied with the title.
In consideration of the premises to Charles Sellars as trustee . . . should the church
be abandoned or used for any other purposes it will revert to me."[7]

This pithy document conveys many important details. A white slave owner
deeded the land (via white trustees) for the formation of the church. Decades later,
there appears to have been a dispute over the ownership because of a missing deed.
The congregation was hoping to build a new structure and thus wanted to clarify
the ownership of the land.

At the time, there were several plantations within a one-mile radius: Roundtop,
Redlands, Viewmont, Belair, Estouteville, Enniscorthy, and the eponymous Blen-
heim Farm. Not surprisingly, many of these stately plantation homes are on the
National Register of Historic Places. All of these large antebellum farms required
enslaved labor to ensure their success. Thus there should be burial grounds for
African Americans on most if not all of these historic lands.

Unfortunately, I never found the foundations for the "African Church." But I did
get a lead on a nearby slave cemetery at the Redlands Plantation, which probably
contained the remains of members of the African church congregation. I visited
the slave cemetery at Redlands with University of Virginia professor emeritus of
architecture K. Edward Lay, who had documented the historic 1798 house decades
earlier as part of his long-term project to draw and study domestic structures in

Albemarle County.[8] His expertise provided me with a historic context for the plantation.

Robert Carter, great-grandson of "King" Carter, lived at Redlands in the late eighteenth and early nineteenth centuries. His Georgian-style brick plantation home, also called Redlands, was constructed in the 1790s. When he died in 1810, his son Robert H. Carter inherited the house and grounds and married a granddaughter of the governor of Virginia. The interior of the house is imposing, containing a salon with curving walls, elaborate classical friezes, and Jeffersonian features such as bed alcoves.[9] The exterior displays symmetrical double chimneys, three attic dormers, a columned porch, marble planters, and trees on either side of the entrance. From the perspective of the main house, the slave cabins were intentionally invisible, lying well behind the house at the end of a walkway lined with hedges.

Down the path leading to the slave cabins was an old dairy, a contemporary blue-clapboard child's playhouse, and an outbuilding that stored Delco batteries to provide electricity to the main house during the first quarter of the twentieth century.[10] At the end of this row of structures is a wooden cabin with two entrances and a central chimney designed to open onto each side. Two or more enslaved families lived here in the mid-1800s. On the day of our visit we were met by an elderly white caretaker who lived in one of the cabins. He was not aware of any cemeteries on the property but directed us further down the path toward the stables. We were greeted only by an assortment of hound dogs and curious horses who peered out from their stalls.

When slave cemeteries are located near plantation houses or on hilltops, they are relatively easy to locate. In our search for the Redlands Slave Cemetery, nothing was easy. On this warm spring day, we were following directions from the son of the current owner, who vaguely recalled that the cemetery lay out past the slave dependencies, up a trail that led to a clearing. As we left the canines and equines behind, we immediately faced a fork in the road and veered to the right, following the owner's directions. We hiked for more than forty-five minutes, confronting multiple forks, until we reached a clearing with a small lake the owner hadn't mentioned. As we backtracked, we saw an old stone chimney, the only remnant of a house that may have been occupied by antebellum African American farmhands.

We returned to the stable in search of the granddaughter of the owner, who was reportedly living at the farm. We found her with a friend who remembered stumbling across the cemetery when hiking with her boyfriend. She agreed to accompany us as we returned to the woods, but after walking for a mile, she admitted that she might be disoriented.

The only advantage of these hidden rural cemeteries is that they are less likely to be vandalized or disturbed. This one was certainly hidden from us. We returned to the barn, and our guide pledged to locate it when her boyfriend returned and mark it for us with flagging tape. She would e-mail a revised set of directions and professor Lay and I would return to try again.

As the heat index rose, we made plans for a return trip. In Virginia, the best time to search for hidden or lost cemeteries is within a narrow window of manageable forest conditions, December through March. Before that time hunting season is in progress, and autumn leaves obscure low-lying markers. After March the grasses, bushes, thorns, bamboo, and other dense foliage returns, and by summer it is hot and humid and the woods are filled with ticks, poison ivy, and other hazards that make surveying uncomfortable and occasionally dangerous. We were running out of time to locate the cemetery before the April showers and accompanying plant growth.

Armed with a new set of directions—which led in the opposite direction from our last two forays—we began walking. Our kind friend from the previous visit had laid a trail of hot pink flags. As we sweated, we wondered at the significant distance from the main house and cabins; this was a somewhat unusual layout. After a half hour's walk we came across a huge arrow made from a dozen or more flags pointing into the woods. We would never have seen the grave markers from the trail without this clue. Finally, a further hundred yards distant, we noticed the beginnings of a periwinkle-covered field and several marble markers.

The Redlands Plantation Slave Cemetery contained a surprising number of inscribed and ornately carved stones. However, many of the two dozen stones had fallen over, allowing us to see how the bottoms of the stones were carved and inserted into the ground. While some of the fieldstones were unmodified, many of them had been given curved tops. Some markers contained tantalizing inscriptions, such as letters that look like the initials "B. H." Because of its placement in the upper corner of the stone, this could also be an acronym for "Beloved Husband," just as "I. M." sometimes stands for "In Memory." Another stone, broken in half, read "Home At Last."

Eight of the stones were inscribed with the names of the deceased. One featured a personalized inscription, probably provided by the plantation owner: "In Memory of James Smith a faithful and much loved servant who died Dec. 5, 1850, aged 37 years."

Another inscribed stone commemorated an antebellum death but is hard to decipher (fig. 13). The stone contained eight lines of text. The letters "AMMA" are repeated over and over, suggesting that the inscriber meant to write "ANNO," Latin for "year," referring to the date of death. Or the *M* may be a highly scripted version of an *N*. Or, less likely, more than one person named "Amma" or "Anna" was commemorated on the stone. The number "1848" is repeated at least three times

FIG. 13 *Left,* inscribed marker in Redlands Plantation Slave Cemetery, Albemarle County (photograph by Lynn Rainville, 2008); *right,* marker redrawn by Alice Cannon, 2012.

(the bottom of the stone is hard to read), while "1799" appears at least once. It is therefore possible that the stone records multiple deaths. But if it stands for one person, with the death date mysteriously repeated, he or she probably lived between 1799 and 1848, dying at age forty-nine.

Surprisingly, each of the four markers inscribed with names and dates at Redlands contained a different surname: Sellars, Carey, Wells, and Smith. Two other stones listed only first names, Betsy and Champ, and one stone contained the letters "B.H." This highlights some of the complexity of African American families during the antebellum period. While some African American families retained surnames from antebellum to postbellum times, other related family members selected new last names or, in some cases, lacked recorded surnames altogether.[11] As late as the 1870 census, some African Americans are listed with only a first name. When selected, the surname might be that of a former owner or a famous or admired individual such as "Washington" or "Lincoln." Sometimes siblings took different surnames and wives used maiden names. This makes tracing antebellum African American families very difficult. Such fluidity of surnames often precludes establishing definite family relationships among kin.

The Redlands Slave Cemetery illustrates this difficulty. On one hand, the dates suggest multiple generations, from John, born in 1791, and Edmund, born in 1805, to the individuals born after the Civil War, from 1865 through 1885. Multiple generations should include husbands, wives, children, and grandchildren, some of whom would share surnames. However, of the eight inscribed markers at Redlands, no two bear the same surname. What we do know is that each gravestone commemorates the life of an individual who worked at Redlands and contributed to the longevity of the African American community in this rural village.

The will of Edward Carter, the grandson of "King" Carter and father of Robert Carter, for whom the Redlands house was built, contains interesting information about some of his slaves. The distribution of property at his death in 1792 included several plantations in three counties. After assigning land and slaves to his children, he specified five individuals to be manumitted: "It is my will and desire, that for their long and faithfull service to me. My slaves Stepney who now acts as an overseer, Charles Quashy Wheelwright, Black Smith Phil, W[a]ggoner Lott, and m[y o]ld waiting man Will, be liberated, and perfectly emancipated immediately after my death."[12] Notice that an enslaved individual performed the function of overseer (i.e., managing other slaves). Another interesting fact is that the skilled wheelwright had a surname, Quashy. While Edward Carter freed these individuals, he owned dozens more, and those he allocated to his surviving family members. Since this manumission occurred before the passage of the 1806 manumission/expulsion law that required freed slaves to leave the state, we can probably assume that these freed individuals remained in the community to be near their enslaved families.[13] Perhaps some of their descendants became the founders of the Middle Oaks Baptist Church.

Free State

The cemeteries in the Free State community illustrate the growth of free black communities and their mortuary options. In 1788, an African American woman named Amy Bowles set a precedent for her race and gender by purchasing 224 acres of land in Albemarle County and moving into a predominantly white neighborhood.[14] One of her nearest neighbors was Thomas Carr, a wealthy plantation owner who had ten thousand acres that adjoined her landholdings. Amy had several children with her first husband, including Zachariah Bowles. Zachariah was born around 1770 and married Critta Hemings, also born around 1770. Critta and her famous sister Sally Hemings were both enslaved at Monticello. Critta was one of the few of Thomas Jefferson's slaves to be freed, but not until 1827, when she was in her sixties. Somehow Zachariah and Critta had managed a marriage for decades prior to this, despite the five or six miles between her mountaintop home and his mother's land.[15]

Amy married a second time around 1774, to Thomas Farrow. He died shortly thereafter in 1778, leaving Amy a widow for almost twenty years, until her death in 1797. In her will she divided her land, "plantation tools," and a "stock of hogs" between her two sons, Zachariah Bowles and Thomas Farrow Jr. In the years that followed, Amy's land became home to several free black families. Although the

phrase is not documented until a century later, this neighborhood eventually became known as "Free State."[16]

. Amy's original land purchase was divided generation after generation, but portions of it remained at the center of an African American community until the
last half of the twentieth century. By then the descendants of Amy and her black
neighbors, the Tyrees, Battles, Barnetts, and African American Carrs, had sold all
but a handful of acres.

Today, very little survives of this once thriving African American community.
The documentary record—from wills, deeds, and census records—is of little help.
The only African American descendant of the historic community who still owns
a portion of this land is Phillip Brown. His house is surrounded by a brand-new
development called Belvedere Station, a wistful reference to a former plantation
and an old railroad track line lying five hundred feet to the west. One of the only
topographic reminders of this land's history is a modern road dubbed "Free State
Road," which separates Mr. Brown's land from that of the development. The road
ends in a "T" with one end named "Critta Lane" and the other "Bowles Lane,"
commemorating the antebellum husband and wife. The houses of this African
American community are long gone.

After a year of earthmoving, massive amounts of brush burning, and new construction, the Free State landscape resembles one big manicured lawn. The new
Belvedere Station development, begun by Stonehaus Developers in 2007, was hit
hard by the 2008 mortgage crisis, and only a small fraction of the planned fourteen
hundred units have been built. In 2009, the two dozen finished homes, mostly unoccupied, were surrounded by empty expanses of newly planted grass, planned
streets, and more street signs than residents. The one plot of land that is not empty
is the Bowles Family Cemetery, in the middle of the planned development.

Bowles Family Cemetery

Despite the road names and oral histories that suggest that this area was once home
to a community of free blacks, the physical evidence for this neighborhood was in
ruins or buried underground by the late twentieth century, when Stonehaus began
buying up the land. Two decades earlier Stonehaus had purchased hundreds of
acres at an adjacent location where the company sited its first development, Dunlora, also named after a historic plantation. In the process of building hundreds of
homes at Dunlora, the developers ran across a historic black cemetery, discussed
later in this chapter. By the time they finished acquiring land for Belvedere Station,
they were well aware of the neighborhood's historic significance and the likelihood
of finding more cemeteries and domestic sites that date to the colonial and antebellum era.[17]

Stonehaus hired a local firm, Rivanna Archaeological Services, to try to locate the Bowles Family Cemetery, long rumored to be within this area. The archaeologists eventually found it in 2005, inexplicably buried under several feet of twentieth-century trash. By peeling off the top level of dirt, leaving the more deeply buried human remains undisturbed, archaeologists located more than fifty grave shafts (map 2). There were several stone grave markers, but only one was inscribed. Fortunately, that one stone solidified the connection of the cemetery to the African American residents of Free State. The marker, plain with a pointed top, read, "Mary Bowles, Died Dec. 6, 1882." Mary was married to Edward Bowles, who had purchased land here in the 1830s. Her exact kinship connection to Amy Bowles is not yet clear, but additional research will probably uncover the missing link.[18]

By the end of 2008 Stonehaus had opened the first house within the newly built Belvedere Station development. The development's website invited purchasers to "find your place" within the nascent community. According to the promotional material, "Laced with sidewalks and shared green spaces, Belvedere is designed to be a walkable community, where neighbors greet each other and pause to take in the sweeping Blue Ridge views to the West."[19] Standing in the middle of a hilly roundabout, I had difficulty seeing anything other than high rooflines. It was even harder to find the remains of the historic black community that once lived here. I was particularly concerned about the Bowles Cemetery, excavated four years earlier, which now lay in the middle of the construction project.

To check on the status of the Bowles Cemetery in 2009, I started at Mr. Brown's house, an unchanging anchor on the landscape, walking to the end of his driveway to orient myself. When I had last been here, there were no houses, streets, or signs. At that time the Bowles Cemetery had recently been reclaimed from its burial beneath generations of trash. From the edge of Mr. Brown's property today, it appeared as if the newly shaped topography had swallowed it up again. But then I noticed a cluster of tall trees, very noticeable on the otherwise denuded landscape. These trees enclosed the one area of dirt that hadn't been disturbed during many months of construction. I drove the short distance, realizing that one of the features Stonehaus had added was a parking lot, presumably for future visitors to the site. A year earlier Stonehaus had contacted me, upon the advice of the archaeologists, and invited me to review their plans for a new memorial at the site. I agreed but never heard from them again. The economic downturn may have taken their historically minded gesture off the table.

In its current state, an unsuspecting visitor would be forgiven for thinking that the entire cemetery site was related to drainage. The southern edge of the cemetery is reinforced with cobblestones to prevent erosion, while its southwestern edge contains a large drain. The graves appear inconsequential next to these larger

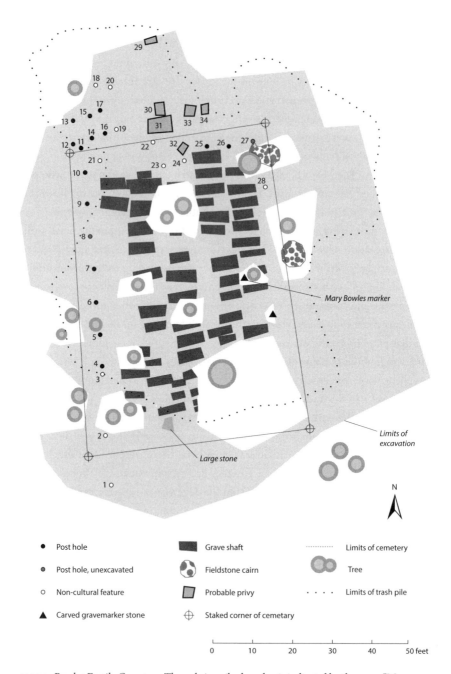

MAP 2 Bowles Family Cemetery. The only inscribed marker is indicated by the name "Mary Bowles" on the map. A total of fifty-three entire or partial grave shafts were located. (Modified from map drawn by Rivanna Archaeological Services, fig. 14 in 2006 report submitted to Stonehaus Development, *Archaeological Identification of Cemetery Boundaries at the Bowles Family Cemetery within Site 44AB374*, by Steven M. Thompson)

and more visible features. The trees were my only guide as I exited my car and walked over a curb onto a surface lightly scattered with remnants (broken pieces of glass, the occasional ceramic sherd, and other small pieces of debris) that remained from the formerly trash-strewn landscape. Since a cemetery lies below, it isn't possible to "clean the dirt" by digging it out. The only way to create a pristine landscape would be to lay down a thin layer of new dirt, being careful not to bury any of the small gravestones. It will be interesting to see how the new residents of Belvedere Station enjoy having a small family cemetery within their midst. This unusual development feature is certainly not highlighted in any of the developers' promotional materials.

The Brown Family Cemetery and the Lewis/Terrell Cemetery

The Bowles Cemetery, dating to the nineteenth century, is the oldest of the three historic African American cemeteries within a half-mile radius. Three other black families, the Browns and the Lewis and Terrell families, created their own cemeteries in the early twentieth century. Mr. Phillip Brown is the only descendant still living in the neighborhood, in a modest house he built for his family in 1966. It lies about half a mile from his parents' house, built in the early twentieth century. His mother's side of the family has owned land here for generations. Employed for forty-one years as a brickmason, Mr. Brown reinforced his home with eighteen-inch-thick walls, faced with beautiful orange stone. Now his land and home are surrounded by Belvedere Station. Despite the developers' best efforts, Mr. Brown refused to sell his land and held on to about ten acres, located in the middle of the planned development. One of those acres contains his family cemetery, just down the hill from his home.

The Brown Family Cemetery lies about two hundred feet south of the Bowles Cemetery and is one of the few in Albemarle County that has remarkably increased its deceased population without the benefit of any additional deaths. To understand how this strange situation occurred, we have to visit the original location of a third cemetery. In 2002 I joined a group of scholars trying to protect an early twentieth-century cemetery that lay within the first Stonehaus development, Dunlora. By the time our group was alerted by a concerned citizen and visited the site, the land around the graves had already been removed to provide foundations for the surrounding homes. The eleven graves were left stranded on top of an artificial twenty-foot hill. The markers included uninscribed fieldstones and metal funeral-home markers.[20] After searching local records, we determined that the decedents were members of the Lewis and Terrell families, former residents in the Free State neighborhood. Stonehaus petitioned the court to exhume the bodies so that they could be moved elsewhere, thereby enabling them to use the land to build more homes. Despite extensive research, our group failed to locate a living descendant to object to the exhumation. Thus the court eventually granted Stonehaus permission to pay an archaeological firm to locate the grave shafts and move the bodies.[21] The only question was where to move them. All of this leads to a strange tale of a land deal for the dead.

Although we didn't know it in 2002, we were only two hundred feet away from the site of Mr. Brown's parents' house and their family cemetery. Eventually the County of Albemarle and the Stonehaus firm approached Mr. Brown to ask if the Lewis and Terrell ancestors could be reinterred in his family cemetery, to which he agreed. When I spoke to him several years after the move, in 2009, Mr. Brown explained his acquiescence. As a boy he had played around the graveyard and had met Mr. Lewis, whose mother was later buried in the cemetery. Mr. Brown's mother had told him that the Browns were related to the Terrells "down the road somewhere" in their family tree. While he wasn't as certain about his kinship ties, if any, to the Lewis family, he figured that he would be saving the corpses from further desecration by giving them a home. But he wanted something out of the deal: a new fence to protect his family cemetery from becoming invisible on the landscape. He also demanded that Stonehaus tend the graves in perpetuity.

So in 2003 a strange parade of hearses and archaeologists drove past the end of the paved road at Dunlora, cut across a narrow channel of dirt, and deposited a recently disinterred group of eleven long-dead individuals back into the ground, within the confines of the Brown Family Cemetery. There the Lewis and Terrell family members joined thirty-three other deceased African Americans in what, this time around, he hoped would be eternal rest. Unfortunately, no one thought to record where the bodies were interred, so they were buried under newly acquired small stones in anonymous graves.

In order to find an unused site for the eleven new arrivals, Stonehaus again hired Rivanna Archaeological Services to scrape the surface of the Brown Family Cemetery and locate the original two dozen documented interments. However, many historic African American cemeteries contain more burials than is at first apparent. One reason for this is the use of impermanent memorials, such as wooden crosses or living plants. A second reason is the difficulty in distinguishing between naturally occurring rocks and deliberately selected fieldstones. By the time the archaeology firm finished its investigation, it had identified a total of thirty-three burials, including the inscribed stones, ten depressions including several that contained fieldstones at the top and base of the hole, one mounded area, and multiple cairns.[22] The last feature was not associated with human burials. Instead, rocks were piled up in four clusters along an old fence line. The drawn plan of the cemetery (map 3) reveals three clusters of burials, dating to differ-

Depression

Mounded

Possible grave
(fieldstones only)

Reinternment

Cut stone grave marker

Metal grave marker

Fieldstone

Mechanically cleared area

Fieldstone claim

Gully

Pit feature/privy

Tree

23–33

Platted boundary of cemetery

Property line

N

0   10   20   30   40   50 feet

MAP 3 Brown/Carr Family Cemetery in the Belvedere subdivision. Graves 23 through 33 are
relocated burials from a nearby cemetery. (Modified from map by Rivanna Archaeological Services, fig. 5 in 2007 report submitted to Stonehaus Development, *Archaeological Delineation of the
Brown/Carr Family Cemetery* [VDHR 002-5052], by Stephen M. Thompson)

ent generations of the dead. But on the ground, the depressions and small, un-modified stones could easily have been misidentified as being part of the natural topography.

The first stones were probably placed here by the Carrs in the 1910s and 1920s when they owned the land. A later set of markers, dating between the 1960s and the 1980s, mark the graves of Brown family members, including Phillip Brown's parents and siblings. He is the youngest and last survivor of thirteen children. Only eight of his siblings are buried in the family cemetery. Three others who died locally are buried in the city's public cemetery, Oakwood. When I asked him why all the children were not buried in the family cemetery, he replied, "Because it was better suitable to be over there . . . where people can up keep the graves." Hundreds of black families in Albemarle County have made a similar decision over the past fifty years, including Billy Hearns and his family. Very few families are conducting new burials in private family plots. The allure of large, tended lawns and landscape adornments, such as statuary and benches, is appealing to many families. Since many of the old family graveyards are located in inaccessible places or near homesteads that have long since been sold out of the family or abandoned, it makes more sense to bury family members in public cemeteries.

For families who wish to bury their dead in private cemeteries today, there are a variety of federal and state laws that govern the practice. In Virginia, twentieth-century laws prevent the placement of cemeteries "within 250 yards of any residence without the consent of the owner."[23] This law does not pertain to preexisting plots on private property, many of which are much closer than 250 yards to historic homes. But if a family wishes to continue burying in a cemetery on land that they no longer own, they have to notify the current landowners before accessing the site and be certain to maintain the cemetery, since abandoned graveyards can be condemned and the bodies removed.[24]

Mr. Brown is part of a continuum of African Americans who have lived in Albemarle County for 250 years. But will Mr. Brown and his descendants—four children and ten grandchildren—still own this land for another one hundred or two hundred years? His eldest son, Phillip junior, now living in Atlanta, hopes to return to Charlottesville and eventually retire on his family's land. On a visit to his father, Phillip junior was out walking when a real estate agent for the Belvedere development spotted him. She asked if he wanted to tour one of their newly built homes. He agreed, and after the house tour she explained to him that within "five to ten years" they would be buying out the "man across the street." Phillip junior pondered this for a moment and replied, "The only man I know over there is my father, and he doesn't have any plans to sell to you, ever." Hopefully the eighteen-inch-thick walls and Phillip Brown Sr.'s determination will withstand the assault from the developers. Either way, Mr. Brown's ancestors deserve to rest in peace, with their newest neighbors, the Lewis and Terrell families, for eternity.

Endangered Species, Gravestones, and a Construction Company: Hardin Tavern Slave Cemetery

Sometimes cemeteries become contentious sites for living communities. In 2003, I was contacted by a neighborhood association and asked to research and map a slave cemetery. The request was standard, but I soon realized that interest in the cemetery was more than historic. The site was once an old-fashioned *ordinary* (a bar with a place to spend the night). Today, a twentieth-century three-story brick home stands at the site, but in the early 1800s a smaller brick building stood here. Known as the Albemarle Hotel, this building was the social and transportation hub of a small community called Morgantown, named after Gideon Morgan, the man who originally owned the land. The tavern owner, Benjamin Hardin, fell into debt and sold the establishment around 1827 to Francis McGee, who operated a tavern at the site. His family is buried adjacent to the house that is located on the property today. The site of the slave cemetery is several hundred feet across Morgantown Road from the original tavern, at the edge of a wooded area. I borrowed the name "Hardin" for the cemetery, since it has never had a formal name. Oral tradition maintains that the cemetery contains slaves who once worked for the Hardin family.

Only eight stones were visible above the ground. Several of those remaining had been disturbed during a storm, which uprooted a tree that held the stones within its root system. None of them was inscribed with a name or dates. There were carved fieldstones of various sizes and a handful of quartz stones. While there is no way to prove that the stones mark slave burials, the site's proximity to the tavern suggests that it was used by the individuals enslaved by one of the former owners, the Hardin or McGee family. As I mapped the cemetery with another archaeologist, three horses from an adjacent field came to investigate. They were uninterested in our labors until one of them realized that my assistant had a sandwich in his coat. Gradually they surrounded him, sticking their noses into his pockets. I had no idea that horses liked peanut butter and jelly. After a small bribe, they left us in peace.

I was happy to map the cemetery, as it contributed to my understanding of antebellum burial grounds. But in this project, the disputes among the living were as interesting as the stories about the dead. When the owners of the tavern initially called me, they admitted that in addition to their historic interest, they were anxious to document the location of the cemetery to determine whether it would be damaged by the proposed expansion of a construction company. The project involved the development of twenty-six acres for use as a garage, office, and maintenance facilities for heavy industrial equipment. The Ivy Community Association (ICA) was formed in part to fight this proposal. The ICA's initial objections stated that the project would damage the environment, threaten the safety of students at an adjacent school, and create a traffic hazard if trucks were allowed to drive on the narrow rural roads. ICA members had previously tried to locate endangered or rare species that inhabited the wooded area and had investigated the possibility that the construction would damage an "intermittent stream" (pursuant to a county ordinance that requires a buffer between a stream and new construction). As the ICA continued to research possible legal objections, several local African American residents came forward and stated that their relatives were buried on or adjacent to the construction company's property. This prompted one of the association members to contact me.

Because the markers were not inscribed, the construction company and even the county planning commission initially denied the existence of the graveyard. So the community organization solicited two affidavits from African American residents: one from a woman who had been told by her mother that her great-grandmother was buried at the site and the other from a woman who remembered her now deceased husband pointing out the location of the graves to her during a horseback ride in the 1950s.[25] The black community that lived along Morgantown Road originated in an 1871 subdivision that had granted land to almost a dozen recently emancipated slaves. Presumably at least some of these individuals were formerly enslaved at nearby plantations.

In the end, the ICA lost its battle. The construction company did modify its construction plans slightly, but eventually the county planning commission gave it permission to build most of what it requested. Ironically, after that victory the company decided to build its construction yard elsewhere. The battle between the construction company and community association raged for almost a year. I should not have been surprised that a historic cemetery was used as a pawn in this sort of dispute. A positive result of the fight was the involvement of one of the residents, Melissa Shore, a documentary filmmaker. She lived near the proposed project and while working on the ICA protest decided to make a film about the stories that she was hearing from the African American community. One resident remembered her father helping with the construction of a wall at Hardindale (the former plantation), while another ancestor helped plaster the Thomas Jefferson–designed rotunda at the nearby University of Virginia. Neither of these stories is found in published histories of the county.

Melissa's project expanded to archival research and oral histories. In her interviews with longtime Morgantown residents, they recalled the days of segregation. The eight-mile bus ride into Charlottesville cost fifty cents for a round trip. One favorite destination was the Paramount movie theater, which was segregated from

1931 until 1964. Mary Dickerson recalled being required to sit in the balcony. The residents' stories also pointed out the changing character of their home. In the 1990s, this quiet rural community became a destination for affluent whites, who valued the rural character of the neighborhood while appreciating its proximity to Charlottesville. One black resident, Bessie Maupin, reminisced, "Ivy used to be a place people drove through to get somewhere. It used to be where people dropped off their maids or their help, but now it's the 'in' place to be." Subsequent rising property values have increased the tax base. Many of the older residents are moving away, and the neighborhood is losing its longtime inhabitants. But the seven people buried in the Hardin Tavern Slave Cemetery will remain at rest, hopefully in perpetuity.

7

GRAVESTONE
GENEALOGIES

A 2006 listing on an Albemarle County online real estate site read, "Don't miss this single family house for sale by agent. This great home is equipped with five bedrooms and five baths. Come and see for yourself."[1] The photograph accompanying the advertisement showed a four-thousand-square-foot redbrick house, complete with a wraparound veranda and white rocking chairs, awaiting occupants holding mint juleps. Nowhere in the listing did it mention another feature of this property: twenty-six permanent residents, lying at rest in the African American cemetery in the backyard. A hundred years ago this was the family homestead of Silas Jackson, a successful African American schoolteacher.

Modern county and health regulations make it difficult if not impossible to create a family cemetery on private property within the city, mostly as a result of health concerns for adjacent living populations. It is only slightly easier to do so on rural land. These regulations state that new cemeteries must be located at least 300 feet from any well and more than 250 feet from any residence unless the owner of the land has given permission and that the property must comprise at least two acres.[2] Prior to these mid-twentieth-century regulations, many American families buried their dead on land held by their ancestors for generations.

There are two basic types of backyard burials: those of the wealthy, who buried their relatives on large estates, and those of poorer families who buried their dead in traditional family plots located near their homes. In Albemarle County, hundreds of African American graveyards fall into the latter category. The following examples illustrate how we can reconstruct family genealogies from surviving gravestones.

Jackson Family Cemetery

Some of the African American cemeteries in Albemarle County have better views than the living households do—prospects worth millions of dollars. The Jackson Family Cemetery, a medium-sized family burial ground, is situated on a ridge in

Free Union with a magnificent vista of the Blue Ridge Mountains to the north, making the land very attractive to developers.

An examination of the real estate sales associated with such properties illustrates the economic incentive for developing lands in Albemarle County, even those with family cemeteries. The Charlottesville area's recent population boom, owing in part to the city's frequent listing as a "top place to retire in," has caused housing values to soar.[3] By 2005, properties on the rural lane in Free Union that was once home to the Jackson family were selling for over $700,000. Real estate listings promoted "idyllic winter mountain views and . . . large, level garden area." A six-thousand-square-foot mansion on Silas Jackson Court sold for $989,000. By 2008, some of the homes on this road were selling for over a million dollars. The road is named after the patriarch of the Jackson family, Silas B., who died in 1936 at age sixty-four.

In 2005, Silas Jackson's descendants began selling off portions of their remaining estate. Despite the land sales, the family retains ownership of the cemetery. But a visitor would never know there was a cemetery behind the opulent new home. The casual observer probably wouldn't even realize that Silas Jackson was an African American, much less that he chose to bury his family in a private backyard burial plot.

The Jacksons have retained the legal right to visit their family cemetery, even if they have to pass through the backyard of a million-dollar home to do so. These descendants helped me locate the burial ground. One of the great-grandchildren of Silas and Bertha Jackson, Ms. Bettie Fitch, offered to give me a tour.

The twenty-six stones located in the Jackson Family Cemetery are encircled by a modern metal fence, probably installed within the last decade as it became clear that real estate development was likely. Over the past seventy-three years, twenty-two individuals have been buried in the cemetery, but there is space for additional family members. The first burial was that of the patriarch of the late nineteenth- and early twentieth-century household, Silas B. Jackson (1872–1936). Born almost a decade after emancipation, Jackson was one of the first African American landowners in Free Union, helping to establish the Amos Church while working as a schoolteacher and postman. He was married to Bertha Collins Jackson (1885–1974), with whom he had twenty children, ten of whom are buried in this cemetery.

All but three of the twenty-six markers are granite, and six of these feature the popular inscription "Rest in Peace." The three nongranite markers are metal, marble, and fieldstone. In 1998 one of the family members was buried under a metal funeral-home marker. Such markers are meant to be temporary, so it is possible that this marker will be replaced with a more permanent marker in the future. The one marble stone is a veteran's stone, in the standard style provided by the federal government for people who served in the military. The lone fieldstone is carved into a triangular shape but lacks any name or date. The style and weathering of the stone suggests that it has lain here for generations.

The Jackson stones are organized into a series of rows. Since most of the commemorated deaths occurred in the second half of the twentieth century, these are flush granite markers, consistent with recent mortuary styles. The stones are grouped into paired head- and footstones. In this mortuary style the headstone provides the chronological data, while the footstones list the kinship relations, "father," "mother," "son," etc. On average, the people buried here died at age fifty-six. This calculation includes two infant children who died before their first birthdays and are buried under stones that read "infant boy" and "infant girl." The burials range in date from the family patriarch, Silas Jackson, in 1936 to a daughter, Helen, in 2004.

Even a small personal cemetery provides insight into American social history. One of the Jackson family gravestones commemorates a veteran from World War II, a first lieutenant in the army who died in 2003 at age ninety-two. An African American woman would have had to overcome the hurdles of both race and gender in order to enter and be promoted to the rank of officer in the mid-twentieth-century U.S. Army.

A second insight derives from the side-by-side granite markers for husbands and wives that symbolize the core of the traditional American family. This graveyard contains several such spousal markers, with men on the left side and women on the right. One unusual stone commemorates a man and woman paired together under one stone, but the man is identified as the "son" of the "mother." Sadly, the son outlived his mother by only six years, dying at age twenty (she died at age fifty-eight). It is not possible to locate the burial site of his father, her husband.

The Jackson Cemetery is not open to the public, since it is located on private land. But a virtual tour of this cemetery online illustrates a typical large twentieth-century family.[4] The cemetery and the named road are all that is left of the physical presence of the Jackson family at their former homestead.

Link Evans Graveyard

Sometimes I have the good fortune to uncover multiple lines of evidence for a past African American community, which in the case of the Evans family led to a burial ground, historic house, and buried artifacts.

In 2007, I received a call from Jennifer Latham, a newcomer to Virginia who had learned that her newly purchased home had been built by a well-known African American blacksmith named Nathaniel Evans. She had seen an article about my work in a local newspaper, the *Daily Progress*.[5] Ms. Latham told me that Mr. Evans was buried across the street in a family graveyard, so I drove out to examine the site.

Evans was known in the area as "Link," and Ms. Latham's house was located on Link Evans Lane. She was in the process of restoring the house's nineteenth-century features, including green shingles that open and close to regulate heat and ventilation, hardwood floors, the original wooden wall beams, and a functioning brick chimney. While showing me her restoration efforts, Ms. Latham told me what she knew about Evans's life as a blacksmith and his successful efforts to buy a house and land in the difficult post–Civil War era.

Today the Link Evans house is one of the only historic buildings left in the neighborhood. Modern homes stand across the street. Ms. Latham's land is much reduced in size from Nathaniel Evans's homestead. Evans originally owned acres of land, housing a blacksmith's shop, a farm, and the family cemetery. Today, the blacksmith's furnace and workshop are buried below the ground. The only evidence of Evans's second profession comes from an enthusiastic next-door neighbor who used a metal detector to locate iron debris at the site of the original farmstead.

For decades the Link Evans Graveyard lay buried by leaves and vegetation. One of Jennifer's other neighbors, an acupuncturist who lives across from the cemetery, contacted me several weeks later, also having seen my request for information on black cemeteries. She described the cemetery to me in an e-mail before a cleanup in about 2002:

> When I bought my house in 2000, the cemetery was just an overgrown patch of black-berry brambles. One day, an elderly black man, his wife, and a young black woman knocked on my door inquiring about the cemetery of their family: Link Evans.
>
> We picked our way through the brambles to identify some of their relatives by the deteriorating headstones. Some graves are as old as the turn of the 19th century.
>
> About 6 months later, a lawn crew came to remove the blackberry brambles and now the cemetery is well maintained by a lawn company. The headstones are visible.
>
> It is tremendously comforting to pull into my parking space at night and see the tombstones. It makes me feel secure and peaceful.

Later, I discovered that a different neighbor owned the land where the cemetery lies, across the street from Ms. Latham. This person did not realize that there was a cemetery on her property when she purchased it. Sometime in 2000, she became aware of its existence, perhaps after the visit of the African American family, and she had the site cleaned. The plot remains in her backyard.

The Evans cemetery is typical of a small African American family cemetery, with fewer than a dozen marked graves as well as several unmarked depressions. Today trees grow throughout the cemetery, but given their small diameters, most are too young to have been planted when the site was in active use. There are a few cedar trees that were either planted by the Evans family or already growing there when the location was selected as a burial ground. According to the inscribed graves, the last burial was in 1932. Sometime after that the house fell out of family hands and the original twenty-five-acre plot was subdivided, leaving the cemetery uncontiguous with the homestead, which lies across a road on the property owned by Ms. Latham.

Today, the immediate area is a predominantly white residential neighborhood. But in the nineteenth century, it was a central location for an aspiring blacksmith, a small rural crossroads with a general store, a tanyard, several mills, and two white churches. Census records document that Nathaniel Evans's father, Perkins, was born in 1808, almost certainly into slavery. In his late thirties or forties, Perkins married Mariah Wood.[6] Nathaniel, their second son, was born in 1850 and married at age twenty-eight in 1878 to Mary Thomas Sammons. They were both twenty-nine when Nathaniel junior was born and forty-three when their last child, Roscoe, was born in 1893.[7] Mary was the daughter of a free black miller, and her mother was Sally Heming's niece.[8]

In the 1880 census, Nathaniel is listed as "Apprenticed to a Blacksmith." In the same census his father, who lived next door, was listed as a blacksmith. Neither man could read or write.[9] Nathaniel was probably apprenticed to his father. When I visited the graveyard site, the current homeowner mentioned that he had found dozens of nails and snippets of metal by using a metal detector in his yard. Apparently, these homes also served as Perkins Evans's place of business.

Mary Thomas Evans predeceased her husband, dying at age seventy-seven in 1927, at a time when Jim Crow laws strictly segregated businesses, schools, and cemeteries. However, private cemeteries allowed families to bury their kin without the indignity of segregation imposed on public cemetery landscapes. Mary's curved, rectangular marble stone is ornately carved with abstract floral leaves and circular motifs. The inscription is simple, reflecting a broader cultural attitude toward women: "Mary Thomas Sammons / Wife of / Nathaniel Evans / 1850–1927." Her husband lies several feet away, parallel to her grave, with a similar marble marker. However, instead of describing him as the husband of Mary, his inscription reads, "Nathaniel Evans / Sept. 20, 1850–Sept. 27, 1932." Note the precision of Nathaniel's stone, in contrast to Mary's, which lacks the specific dates of her birth and death. Unless planned in advance, gravestone carvings are selected by the survivors. It is therefore likely that Nathaniel chose his wife's inscription, while their children selected his, making the effort to specify his exact birth and death dates.

Two of their four children preceded their parents in death and are also buried in the cemetery: Beatrice died at age thirty-four in 1913, and Sarah, the earliest marked burial in the cemetery, died of "a broken heart" at age twenty-two in 1903, when her fiancée backed out on her wedding day.[10] Her early death inspired family members to select a beautiful carved lily for her stone. According to census records, two sons lived longer than these daughters, but there are no stones indicating their graves. Perhaps their graves, if present at all, are among those unmarked. We do know that in the 1930 census (after Mary's death in 1927), Nathaniel was listed as living with his youngest son, Roscoe, a farmer.[11] By the 1930s, blacksmithing had been replaced by machines that produced wire nails, and even metal repairs and forging had become less important with the decreased cost of manufactured goods. Thus the next generations of Evans sons turned to farming instead of learning their father's craft.

Although the Evans cemetery is small, it does contain an interesting array of motifs. The graves of Nathaniel and his wife shared a similar abstract motif. Their two daughters were buried under carved lilies, a flower traditionally associated with mourning. Besides Nathaniel's, another Evans family line is buried in the cemetery; its patriarch is Thornton Evans (1846–1906), Nathaniel's older brother. Thornton is buried with two of his children. His gravestone is plain, with no motif, just a curved marble marker and a simple inscription of his birth and death dates. Two of his daughters have unmarked graves or uninscribed stones. We know that they are in the cemetery because death records list "Family Cemetery" as their final resting place. The second daughter, Mary Ann, married John Grigsby somewhere between 1900, when John was listed in the census as "single" and living at home, and 1905, when their first child was born and died. Today no stone is visible for Mary Ann Grigsby, suggesting that her original marker rotted away or that she lies buried under an uninscribed stone.

Their infant child, Robert, is buried in the cemetery with a common child's motif, a seated lamb. This motif was still popular in the twentieth century as a symbol of innocence, usually reserved for children and occasionally for women. Robert died in 1905; his stone reads, "To the Memory of . . . Robert Leroy Grigsby." The stone lists his birth and death information (he lived for less than nine months) and concludes with the poetic inscription "Budded on Earth, To Bloom in Heaven." Other family gravestones also contain inscriptions. Nathaniel Evans's very typical inscription reads, "Gone But Not Forgotten." In contrast, Nathaniel's daughter Sarah Evans was memorialized with the less euphemistic phrase "Died But Not Forgotten." There is one more Grigsby buried in the Evans plot, probably another one of their daughters who died before her parents, Alfonza E. Grigsby (1900–1919). Her poetic inscription reads, "Death is Eternal, Why Should We Weep?"

There are two uninscribed fieldstones that provide no information. It is possible that they mark the burial of the two missing sons mentioned above. There is also a small metal marker, provided by the J. F. Bell Funeral Home, which contains a slip of paper wedged between two pieces of metal and covered with glass, but the paper cannot be read. Based on the founding year of the funeral home as well as the marker's style, this unidentified family member was buried between 1917 and the 1930s. Near this illegible marker lies a metal floral holder. In the recent past, someone left a wreath to honor another family member. Most of the nine inscribed markers are leaning askew, in danger of falling over and being reburied by leaves. Until that happens, this cemetery serves as both a resting place for the dead and an exhibit that amplifies the historic depth of the house across the street and its original inhabitants.

Response from Descendants

One of the most rewarding things about this work is the opportunity to collect family stories that have never been recorded but that illustrate the important role of African American families in the growth of central Virginia businesses, agricultural productivity, and cultural innovations in cookery, music, dance, religious worship, and many other pursuits. After visiting my cemetery website, one woman wrote, "I have been looking for a few of my family members for some time and you have them listed on your site as being buried at Daughter of Zion. I would like to commend everyone who is working this project for their outstanding work. You have a lovely site with lots of information." Other readers wrote and asked to learn more about the cemeteries: "I would welcome the opportunity to visit Sweet Briar, and to learn more about the research you are conducting. I would like to visit the cemetery. It would be an honor for me to have the opportunity to meet you, and the team investigating the Christian Aid Cemetery." Others offered help: "If I can be of any assistance in your research on African American cemeteries, please let me know." One correspondent wrote, "I spoke with my cousin . . . who lives in Charlottesville. She too is excited about your research and would like to arrange to meet with you when you plan to visit the cemetery. She has a lot of information she can provide about family members buried there."

Sometimes e-mails from site visitors resolve questions about burial sites or link the dead to their living ancestors. Listening to family stories that have been preserved over the generations is a very valuable aspect of the project. Most of these accounts are rarely heard outside of the family, but they illustrate our shared social and economic history one narrative at a time, plotting the successes and failures of individuals as they go about their everyday lives.

One fortuitous contact was with a descendant of the enslaved community at the Mount Fair Plantation, discussed in the next chapter. After conducting research into the plantation's slave cemetery, I published a piece in the local historical society magazine.[12] Three years later, I heard from Sheila Rogers, who had written to the Albemarle Charlottesville Historical Society for any information about her relatives. They sent her my contact information and a copy of my article. She read the article with great interest and in one of the tables saw a list that included her great-grandparents. Her e-mail exclaimed, "THESE ARE MY RELATIVES!"

This is exactly the sort of connection I hope to make between past communities and living descendants. I offered to meet with Ms. Rogers to discuss the records I had uncovered, and I learned that she lived in Oregon but was planning a visit to Brown's Cove in the upcoming year. We eventually met in person and shared our research. I was able to contribute copies of wills listing members of the enslaved community and a time line of the Mount Fair Plantation from its construction to the dispersal of the enslaved community after emancipation. I knew the local story, but Ms. Rogers knew the final ending for many of her descendants. After emancipation several of them moved to West Virginia in search of work in the coal mines. Her relatives were part of a region-wide exodus when many newly freed slaves left their homes in search of work; many pursued jobs in the North or in larger southern cities.[13] The coal mines drew thousands of men and their families, and mining was very dangerous work that shortened men's lives through accidents and various diseases, most notably pneumoconiosis, or black lung. Ms. Rogers contributed other information as she mused about an 1870 census record that listed some of her great-grandparent's children as "black" and some as "mulatto." She noted that most of the photographs she had of her relatives showed light-skinned individuals, some of whom, she commented, could have "passed for white."

The tradition of "passing" goes back to antebellum times and was used by light-skinned African Americans to take on a white identity in certain situations.[14] Later, during the Jim Crow era, very light-skinned African Americans sometimes moved away from darker kin so that they could live as Caucasians. In other cases, the opportunity to pass was a temporary advantage, to gain a seat in an otherwise segregated theater or gain access to a "whites only" business. In Nella Larsen's 1929 novel *Passing*, two light-skinned women discuss the social and economic advantages and disadvantages associated with their ability to pass as white. Even more strikingly, the novel *Caucasia* tells of two biological sisters whose skin color differs enough to enable one to pass as white, while the other moves with her father to Brazil in search of racial equality.[15]

I noticed that the census taker who enumerated Ms. Rogers's relatives classified some of the children from the same parents as "black" and others as "mulatto." This illustrates the arbitrary nature of American conceptions of race. There is no gene for race or ethnic identity, but in America we prioritize skin color as a marker of social and ethnic identity. This masks the complexity of identity, which for most of us is a mixture of dozens or more nationalities. In America there is a long history of interracial relationships,[16] dating back to the arrival of the first Africans in Virginia in 1619. These unions have produced countless descendants of mixed heritage, but because of color consciousness, we divide these descendants into simplistic categories based on one physical attribute, the color of their skin. Assigning related children to different categories demonstrates the absurdity of this system.

Who were Ms. Rogers's descendants, and how did we identify an antebellum couple who lacked surnames as her relatives? I found an answer thanks to the hard work of dozens of individuals in Charlottesville and Albemarle County. One of these researchers, Gayle Schulman, transcribed information pertaining to Albemarle County from a list of enslaved babies and their mothers, which contains information about the children born to enslaved mothers between 1853 and 1864. When I first conducted research into the Mount Fair Slave Cemetery, I searched this record to see if it contained any individuals who lived at Mount Fair. The list is organized by the name of the slave owner. In this case, I was looking for William T. Brown. Under his name, I found that "Charlotte" had given birth to "Cynthia" in 1855. From this I could extrapolate that Charlotte had reached puberty by 1855 and thus established her birth as being in the 1830s. Second, I had the first name of an enslaved individual who lived at Mount Fair. I needed to match a first name to a postbellum surname. My search was made easier for two reasons: Charlotte was a somewhat unusual first name, and as it turned out, she and her husband picked the last name "Brown" after they received their freedom.

I located Ms. Rogers's ancestors by combing the 1880 census of the Whitehall district (which includes Brown's Cove) for an African American woman in her forties or fifties, possibly accompanied by an adult daughter named Cynthia. I didn't find the last piece of the puzzle, which suggested that Cynthia was sold to another owner prior to emancipation, died as a child, or set up her own household. But I did find a Charlotte Brown (aged forty-one, thus born in 1839) listed as "black" and her husband, Thomas (aged forty, born 1840), listed as "mulatto."[17] Now we can guess why the 1880 census taker categorized nine of their children as "mulatto" (although one daughter, Martha, was listed as "black"). Highlighting the arbitrary nature of labeling skin color, the 1870 census taker produced the opposite categorization: each of the Browns' six children at the time, including Martha, was listed as black. In that year, only Thomas was identified as "mulatto."[18] All of the children took their parents' surname, Brown. The oldest living child in the household in 1870 was born around 1860, suggesting that Charlotte and Thomas met sometime in the 1850s, when they were in their teens.

Four of their children were born during the Civil War and six afterward. They may have had more children who did not survive to be counted in the 1870 or 1880 census, including Cynthia. Unfortunately, the 1890 census is not preserved for Virginia, and when we search the 1900 census, the trail goes cold. No one of the right age going by the names of Charlotte, Thomas, Franklin, or John Brown was living in Albemarle County any longer. I searched by the sons' names because sons were more likely to keep their last names as adults than daughters were, as women would probably choose a different surname after marriage. There are many ways to interpret the disappearance of the Brown children from the records. The least likely scenario is that they all died before 1900. While this is possible for Thomas senior and Charlotte (although they would have been only in their sixties), it is less likely that each of their three boys died before 1900. Instead, this may have been the generation that left for West Virginia. Unfortunately, with a common surname like Brown, and without more information on which county they settled in, it is very difficult to trace the Browns in other states to prove that they moved away from Virginia.

The ties between living descendants and their ancestors is documented and enhanced by additional information about their children and a theory about when they met and married during slavery. Though I did not find the graves of Charlotte and Thomas or their children, I learned more about the antebellum community at Mount Fair. On later trips I documented hundreds of individuals who were once enslaved in this rural corner of Albemarle and lived to be buried in church and neighborhood cemeteries located near the former plantations.

A Virginia College and Its History of Slavery

Information collected from African American gravestones provides insight into the notoriously difficult genealogical quandary of how to trace an enslaved family into the postbellum period. Answering this question enables us to build family trees for enslaved individuals and to reconstruct antebellum communities. By pulling together the disparate strands of historic, archaeological, and ethnographic data, we can better understand the social fabric of these involuntary communities and the choices made after emancipation. For example, after the Civil War many former slaves were legally married for the first time after having lived together as husband and wife for decades.[19]

Examination of the enslaved community on the Sweet Briar Plantation provides one example of the need to correlate diverse types of data to better understand a family and its burial patterns. The plantation was owned by a transplanted Vermonter, Elijah Fletcher. One of fifteen children, Fletcher left home in 1810 in search of a job, traveling on horseback from Ludlow, Vermont, to Washington, DC. With the help of friends, he found employment as a Latin tutor in a school in the rural village of New Glasgow, about 130 miles south of Washington in Amherst County, Virginia. Gradually the local planters approached him about tutoring their daughters, since the school was for boys only. He developed an attachment to one of his students, Maria Antoinette Crawford, and in 1813, two years after his arrival in Virginia, he became a southerner through their marriage. Prior to their union,

Elijah sent many letters home in which he expressed his surprise and dismay at the "peculiar institution" of slavery. In 1811, he wrote to his father and called slavery a "curse on any country." This emphatic disgust soon faded after he received two African American children as a wedding gift from his father-in-law, William S. Crawford. Crawford was a large landholder in Amherst who enslaved dozens of African Americans. Little did Elijah know that after Crawford's death in 1815, he would eventually become a large slaveholder himself.[20]

Elijah lived in Lynchburg year-round until the 1830s, when he began to acquire rural lands. In the 1840s he purchased the Locust Grove Plantation, about eighteen miles north of Lynchburg. He renamed the property "Sweetbrier" in honor of his wife's favorite rose. Elijah and Maria had four children: two boys, Sidney and Lucian, and two girls, Indiana and Elizabeth. Three of the children settled permanently in Amherst: Indiana (who later married James Henry Williams) inherited Sweetbrier after her father's death in 1858, changing the spelling of its name to "Sweet Briar"; Elizabeth built a new plantation at Mount San Angelo two miles to the east; and Sidney inherited Tusculum, the former Crawford estate, eight miles to the north. Each of these three children, along with their father, Elijah, owned dozens of slaves. The fourth child, Lucian, fell out of favor with his family and did not inherit a plantation. Indiana was the last sibling to die. She gave most of her land and money to found a college for "white women" in honor of her only daughter, Daisy, who had died at the age of sixteen in 1884. The first Sweet Briar class graduated in 1909, almost a decade after Indiana's death.[21]

Today Sweet Briar College retains more than three thousand acres of farmland. Elijah originally acquired up to eight thousand acres through a series of astute land deals and money-lending schemes and built a small fortune in land and money between 1813, when he married Maria Crawford, and 1847, when he retired from politics and the newspaper business in Lynchburg. During the last decade of his life, Elijah worked at being a "gentleman farmer," planting wheat and barley, experimenting with viticulture, raising livestock, growing orchards, and buying dozens of slaves to provide the labor for these enterprises. Upon his death in 1858, he stipulated that the more than a hundred enslaved individuals who lived at Sweet Briar should be divided among three of his children: Sidney, Indiana, and Elizabeth. Indiana inherited the plantation and forty slaves. Between 1847 and emancipation, sixty members of this community were buried on the plantation in what is today called the "Sweet Briar Plantation Burial Ground."

In 2002 Sweet Briar College held a memorial service to recognize the unnamed individuals who were buried in the slave cemetery. As part of this effort, I mapped the cemetery and discovered a combination of unmarked depressions, hand-carved fieldstones, and ecological and photographic evidence that a deliberate planting of nonnative *Ailanthus altissima* trees originally ringed the cemetery. None of the gravestones was inscribed, so it was impossible to determine who was buried in the cemetery. But the style of the stones, coupled with the location of the burial ground, adheres to the pattern that I found in dozens of other slave cemeteries: within walking distance of slave cabins, located on top of a hill, and containing uninscribed, locally available stones.

This mapping initiated a multiyear project to research the enslaved community of the Fletcher family. Although I would never be able to assign names to individual graves, I wanted to learn more about the African Americans who lived and worked on the plantation and in some cases remained as paid servants in the postbellum period.

The first step was to locate postbellum African American churches that may have served the freed slaves and their descendants after 1865. Based on proximity and on evidence from oral histories, I began by mapping the nearby Coolwell Baptist Church Cemetery. Named after a cold spring, this was one of the first African American churches in Amherst County founded independently of a white congregation, organized by the Reverend P. Ferguson in 1862. The cemetery, in use for more than one hundred years, contains at least 255 individuals. Roughly half of the gravestones have legible dates, but many are carved fieldstones lacking inscriptions or highly eroded metal, marble, or wooden markers. Many of the individuals buried here once worked at Sweet Briar, both during its plantation days and later when it became a college. Oral histories reveal that many of the men and women who worked at Sweet Briar lived in Coolwell and walked several miles on foot to reach work each day. One of these individuals was Signora Hollins, buried with her family in the cemetery. As a child, Miss Hollins played with Indiana's daughter, Daisy.

Fletcher Descendants

When Sweet Briar decided to rededicate its slave cemetery, an effort was made to locate descendants of the original enslaved community. The dean of cocurricular life, Valdrie Walker, an African American woman from an adjacent county, sat down with a phone book; reasoning that some of the formerly enslaved individuals may have selected the surname Fletcher, she began making calls. Amazingly, this strategy worked, and Dean Walker located Jasper Fletcher. It took me several years to tease out Mr. Fletcher's relationship to the enslaved community. His family tradition held that they were descended from Isaiah, an enslaved man who was used as the "local buck." In my naïveté I had no idea what he meant, so he explained that slave owners would select strong and healthy men to sire children with multiple women. Whether this was true at Sweet Briar we may never know.

I did eventually discover that Jasper was only three generations removed from the enslaved community. His father, Patrick Henry Fletcher Jr. (1910–1979) was one of the twelve children of Patrick Henry Fletcher Sr. (1860–ca. 1944) and Jenny Carter (1868–1926). Patrick senior was one of James and Lavinia Fletcher's children. James and Lavinia were both born in 1835 and married, while enslaved, in 1855. Lavinia's connection to the Sweet Briar Plantation can be documented through Elijah Fletcher's probated will, which lists "Lavinia and Nelson," one of her sons. Neither James nor Lavinia used the surname Fletcher until after emancipation.

My efforts to track the Fletcher family history proved how difficult it is to connect antebellum and postbellum communities. On beginning my research in 2001, I had a copy of Elijah's probated will listing the 136 individuals to be inherited and distributed between Indiana and Elizabeth, but I could not recognize the Fletchers, because only a handful of these people used surnames. Moreover, the practice of "hiring out," by which slave owners profited by renting their slaves to others, meant that even families who lived together on one plantation were often separated for part of the year.[22] Thus when the lawyers drew up the division of Elijah's estate in 1860, Lavinia and Nelson were listed but not Lavinia's husband, James. Moreover, Lavinia was not yet using the surname Fletcher, so it was impossible to connect her to the postbellum Fletchers.

Success required working backward from known family members, using the census, marriage records, and chancery suits filed in the local courthouse. These charted family relationships eventually enabled me to build a family tree. By the time a colleague, Bob Vernon, found evidence for the 1855 marriage of James and Lavinia Fletcher, we had the necessary first names to search the antebellum records. Still, we were fortunate that Elijah's estate was so carefully probated. In some cases, the enslaved community is divided into gross groups, such as "15 slaves to be given to each child," with no names provided. But in Elijah's will each individual was listed with an assessment of his or her value so that the human property could be divided equally among his children.

The only Isaiah I found in the historic record was a son of Patrick junior who was born in 1905 and died in 1929, a half century after the end of slavery. But he may have had an antebellum ancestor who worked at Sweet Briar. Without a paper trail, enslaved African Americans can fall through the archival cracks. I learned more about this fascinating family through oral interviews and visits to two of Jasper's postbellum family cemeteries. I was able to trace his family's history into the twentieth century by recording the information from the graves in the Fletcher Family Cemetery on Turkey Mountain Hill and the Broady Family Cemetery near Rose Mill.

Fletcher Family Cemetery

I drove to Jasper Fletcher's home, about ten miles from Sweet Briar, expecting to follow him to the family cemetery in my car. Instead we piled into his ancient truck as we set out on our journey back in time. It was a good thing he chose the truck, because my four-wheel-drive Subaru would not have negotiated the deep ruts and stumps that we encountered on the steep dirt road leading to the Fletcher Family Cemetery. Mr. Fletcher explained that the land had been sold decades earlier and was no longer owned by his family, a situation I encountered again and again with rural cemeteries. Even with Jasper's guidance, it wasn't clear where the cemetery was until we had exited the truck and brushed aside some leaves. Most of the markers in this cemetery were metal or fieldstones difficult to see among the deep leaf litter. Two stones stood out: a marble veteran's grave for Lilbert Fletcher, Jasper's great-uncle, who had been a private in the U.S. Army, and a hand-carved soapstone marker for Jenny Carter, Patrick Henry Sr.'s wife. We never found the marker for Jasper's grandfather Patrick senior, but there were numerous uninscribed stones in the cemetery, and one of them may have marked his final resting place.

Not all of the uninscribed stones were destined to remain anonymous. Jasper Fletcher was able to explain the choice of several rocks within his two family grave-yards, including a striking blue quartz obelisk that marked the grave of his uncle, Lafayette Fletcher (1913–1958) (fig. 14). As Mr. Fletcher related the story, Lafay-ette selected his gravestone when he was a teenager. Years later, upon his death at age forty-five, Jasper Fletcher collected the stone and placed it as his uncle's final marker. This native quartz marker does not show a name, date, or inscription, so

FIG. 14 Hand-selected gravestone for Lafayette Fletcher. Fletcher Family Cemetery, Amherst County. (Photograph by Lynn Rainville, 2006)

this oral history is a unique record of the burial. In another frustrating example, an illegible metal marker lay next to a white stone. At some point, a survivor who knew the identity of the deceased placed the funeral marker next to the rock, but the information was lost when the ink on the piece of paper faded away.

Broady Family Cemetery

After clearing leaves from a number of graves and recording the legible information, we hopped back in the truck for the ten-minute drive to Jasper Fletcher's mother's cemetery. Here again, the land had been sold out of the family, and now the cemetery lies at the edge of a newly built home. Mr. Fletcher had tried to purchase the land, but when the price went higher than he could afford, he informed the new owners about the cemetery and asked them to build far away from it. Instead, the owners chose to build next to it. (Like many cemeteries, it lies on a hilltop with a beautiful view.) Mr. Fletcher later heard that on the first day of construction, a worker uncovered some bones and refused to dig further. While it was never proved that these were human bones, work ceased on the new construction. The owners ended up building their house one hundred yards from the cemetery, on a lower portion of the property. On the day we visited, we found yet another bone, this one lying next to a gravestone. Despite the proximity to a stone and a cemetery, the bone did not appear to be human. We set about photographing and reading the inscriptions, all the while watched by a horse penned behind a fence directly adjacent to the cemetery. The owners must have decided to maximize the utility of the site, even if they couldn't build there. Unfortunately, there was no fence or enclosure for the cemetery, and as we recorded information, we found a lone stone several yards from the others, in danger of being forgotten under a pile of weeds and grasses.

Jasper Fletcher and I located twenty gravestones at the Broady Family Cemetery. Oral tradition maintains that there is a slave graveyard to the south, down the hill, but we only had permission to be in the first cemetery, so a further search had to wait. While the Broady Cemetery included some illegible metal markers and uninscribed stones, there were several granite markers with carved motifs and inscriptions. Jasper Rose (1882–1973), one of Jasper Fletcher's namesakes, was "gone but not forgotten," and Beatrice Lark (1902–1942) was "rest[ing] in peace." A child who died at age nine in 1904 was commemorated as "Our Loved One." Both of Jasper's parents were buried here under a gray granite stone decorated with a carved daisy-like flower and with ivy for his father and a rose for his mother. Some of the earlier stones were hand-carved from concrete. Jasper informed me that he wants to move his parents to the Fletcher Family Cemetery.

Several years later, in 2007, I was contacted by other members of the Fletcher family, Bethany Pace and Annette Anderson. They are great-great-granddaughters of Patrick Henry Fletcher Sr. and Jenny (or Jennie) Carter. After three decades they had decided to hold their biannual family reunion at Sweet Briar. Influenced in part by a website that I had designed to highlight African American heritage at Sweet Briar, they felt that the time had come to learn about their family's residence at Sweet Briar.

After a year of planning, the Fletcher family convened on the Sweet Briar campus for their reunion. Over 170 family members participated in the three-day event in August 2008, meeting with relatives and learning more about the plantation where their ancestors were enslaved. The president of Sweet Briar College welcomed the family members, and several Fletcher descendants spoke movingly about their family's history. I presented genealogical research that tied their family line to an enslaved family that lived at Sweet Briar Plantation. After a series of talks, a visit to the former plantation house (today the president's house), and a visit to the only standing slave cabin, we walked to the slave cemetery, which probably contains the remains of the Fletcher ancestors. When we arrived, the descendants fanned out to walk among the uninscribed gravestones. A hush fell as family elder and Amherst native Jasper Fletcher led the group in prayer. Next, Tracey Carter, visiting from Washington, DC, asked her relatives to pour water over the graves in an impromptu libation ceremony (fig. 15). The memorial ended with family members calling out the names of their ancestors, from the recently departed to antebellum relatives. There may not be inscribed gravestones, but for the Fletcher family the memories of their ancestors are preserved in this small piece of land at Sweet Briar.

FIG. 15 Fletcher family libation ceremony at Sweet Briar Plantation Burial Ground. (Photograph by Lynn Rainville, 2008)

8

CONNECTING COMMUNITIES
THROUGH THEIR
BURIAL GROUNDS

For southern African Americans, the search for their ancestors often leads to an antebellum plantation. But tracing ancestral lines from postbellum families to enslaved, antebellum ones is often circuitous. After emancipation, some African Americans took surnames for the first time. Others, celebrating their newfound freedom, chose new names, which sometimes separates them in the historical record from siblings who did not.[1] Both factors complicate genealogical research. Moreover, many African American communities were dispersed during the depressions of the late nineteenth and early twentieth centuries. Today, very little is left of these historic black neighborhoods. But the plantation cemeteries remain. In this chapter I use a historic slave cemetery to trace an African American community from antebellum times to the present.

The very existence of a cemetery of any size reveals a network of individuals who for various reasons were buried together. The data found in these burial grounds can, with further investigation and a little luck, point us to the living, making it possible to reconstruct antebellum kinship networks. Just as important, the presence of historic burial grounds can connect present-day communities now thriving on the land to their nineteenth-century roots.

Brown's Cove

A modern atlas of Albemarle County identifies a neighborhood called "Brown's Cove."[2] Today, the roads that lead to this mountainous corner of Albemarle County end at the Shenandoah National Park, established from thousands of acres in Virginia in the 1920s and officially dedicated in 1936.[3] During the construction of the park, old nineteenth-century roads that once led over the mountains to markets farther west were closed to the public. In the eighteenth and nineteenth centuries, the Brown family bought the land that led through one of the only passable mountain gaps in the county and charged travelers a toll to use this "three chopped road" (also known as "Three Notch'd Road"), which got its name from the axe markings on trees that signposted the route.

Several of the Brown plantation homes still stand; one, Mount Fair, is even listed on the National Register of Historic Places.[4] The nomination form describes the architectural elements of the "big house" in great detail and lists the surviving outbuildings, dairies, kitchens, springhouses, and agricultural buildings. The Brown Family Cemetery is duly noted, with a list of transcribed headstones. But the presence of a slave cemetery on the same grounds is only briefly acknowledged: "Also contributing is the site of a large slave cemetery located below the house on a small ridge. The graves are indicated by small, upright, unmarked fieldstones."[5]

I began to research Brown's Cove by reading the formally recorded history of the community, which appeared in the form of genealogical entries in a local history book published in 1901. Together with his eldest son, Benjamin junior, Benjamin Brown Sr. assembled a tract of six thousand acres that followed the banks of the Doyles River, then a major tributary of rivers that led to tobacco markets like the one in Richmond. The author delighted in listing the offspring of the family patriarch, Benjamin Brown (1695–1762). Mr. Brown and his wife named most of the children in their large family with names that begin with *B*: Bezaleel, Benjamin, Benajah, Barzillai, Bernard, Bernis, and Brightberry.[6]

Of greatest interest to me about this large rural family was their extensive land holdings and the enslaved labor that was used to work the farms. During the antebellum period, large plantations relied on slave labor to ensure agricultural productivity. The first generation of eighteenth-century Albemarle Browns each owned fewer than a dozen enslaved individuals. By the nineteenth century, several of the descendants each owned dozens of enslaved people. Together, the whites and blacks grew crops and raised livestock including horses, oxen, cattle, sheep, and swine. Since the Piedmont climate and soil were not always favorable to individual crops, they grew a variety, including wheat, Indian corn, oats, hay, hemp, flax, and tobacco.[7] These were supplemented by vegetables, including beans, peas, and sweet potatoes. Antebellum plantations were often self-sufficient in labor, produce, and goods, so to round out the food staples, the plantations produced butter and honey and the inhabitants probably enjoyed milk and cheese from their cows.[8] Crop diversification enabled farmers to take advantage of different markets and optimize their use of enslaved labor throughout the year.

During my five-year investigation of slave cemeteries on the Brown family plantations, I located some of the few Brown descendants still living in Albemarle County, heard various ghost stories, fought a forest with a machete to locate several of the slave cemeteries, and eventually found three antebellum slave cemeteries and four postbellum African American burial grounds in this neighborhood.

Documenting the Slave Cemetery at Mount Fair

Mount Fair was the first Brown plantation slave cemetery I studied. Prior to emancipation, several generations of close to a dozen families lived and worked at Mount Fair. Today, their remains lie in a large cemetery on a hilltop covered in trees and vegetation. A U.S. Geological Survey topographic map depicts fence lines that crisscross the land. Most of the fences are long gone, but the remains of barbed wire and old posts snake through the grave sites. This burial ground apparently began as a scattering of stones placed along a fence that ran up and over the hill. But after decades, the 150 burials associated with several generations of slave families spread across the entire hilltop. Unfortunately, none of the stones was inscribed, leaving us to guess the names of the individuals buried here.

When I first visited the cemetery in the spring of 2002, a young family from the Midwest, whom I'll call the Carsons, owned the house. They had spent a great deal of time and money restoring the 1848 Greek revival home to its former glory, with a copper roof, double-hung sash windows, and an unusual eight-paneled recessed door.[9] The restored structure also included eight-pane casement windows that faced east and west, opening to views of the Blue Ridge Mountains to the west and Pigeon Top Mountain to the east. The second story contained a rare feature for a land-bound house: a widow's walk. Such a feature was more commonly found in seaside homes, where it enabled wives to watch for the return of their seafaring husbands. Despite the historically accurate restorations, the Mount Fair renovations included modern conveniences such as an indoor kitchen (in the nineteenth century, kitchens in large homes were often separate structures because of the risk of fire), bathrooms crafted within former porches, and closets (an expensive and thus uncommon feature in old homes). The separate outdoor kitchen, icehouse, and springhouse remained standing, adjacent to the house; the slave quarters, however, had been in ruins for decades.

As midwestern newcomers, the Carsons were surprised to learn that there was a large slave cemetery on their property. They had, however, noticed the white family cemetery that lay just two dozen yards from their backdoor. This graveyard contained the remains of at least eight Brown family members. As was typical in the nineteenth century, most of the grave markers were carved from marble and a few from granite. Eight of these were legible, but there were also unmarked fieldstones and several illegible markers. The last marked and legible burial in the Brown family graveyard dated to 1925.

When I met with the Carsons and their two young children to ask permission to survey the cemetery, I came prepared with historical research about the Brown family. The Carsons were familiar with the broad strokes of Brown family and Mount

Fair's history, but I inadvertently stumbled across a sensitive subject when I casually commented on the rich history of the house—including the several ethereal haints I had read about at the local historical society. One concerned the "lady in white," a Brown descendant who stood at an upper window at Mount Fair awaiting her husband's return. Other stories featured headless specters, murdered slaves who returned to haunt their masters, and strange noises; one even told of a ghostly dog. I learned some of the Mount Fair ghost stories on a website that hosts the complete text of *From Whitehall to Bacon Hollow,* an unpublished book by folklorist George Foss, who conducted research in Whitehall and Brown's Cove in the 1960s.[10]

A historic home may not seem complete without some ghostly occurrences, but Mrs. Carson hadn't yet heard any of these stories from her neighbors. When I related what I thought was a harmless tale, she became agitated. She then asked me questions about the people buried in the slave cemetery and whether I thought they might come back to haunt the living. I tried to reassure her, but for whatever reason, the Carsons moved out the following year.

The Wisdom of Ghosts

Over the years, the theme of ghosts or spirits returned again and again in my research. Once when I went to search for an old graveyard with a family member, the descendant inquired solicitously whether I would be frightened to enter the graveyard. I assured him that I did this regularly and saw it as an opportunity to recognize the dead, not fear them. He nodded and said that he just wanted to make certain that I was comfortable. But I noticed that when we reached the cemetery he stood at the perimeter of the burials.

Early in my research, I tended to discount the warnings from family members who cautioned me against going into cemeteries alone or walking near graves. Regrettably, I failed to follow up on the reasons for their concern or ask them to share their beliefs about the supernatural. But the more I learned about local folktales (some dating back to antebellum times), the more I came to appreciate the role they served. Many of these twentieth-century versions of alleged hauntings had antecedents in antebellum and postbellum tales that helped African American communities cope with the horrors and vicissitudes of slavery. Moreover, tales of witches, voodoo, and ghosts from enslaved communities paralleled contemporary beliefs among whites (e.g., the Puritans' obsession with witches and spiritualists' efforts to contact the departed).[11] The tradition of "conjuring" empowered enslaved individuals to take control over their circumstances.[12] Moreover, the belief in spirits (or "haints," as they are commonly called in the South) can be traced back to African religious practice. Although not monolithic, many African religions expressed a belief in spirits. These ranged from the belief that the spirit of the deceased eventually becomes an ancestor spirit (to be appeased with grave offerings and appropriate rituals so that it does not come back to cause mischief among the living) to belief in nature spirits (which inhabit inanimate objects) and spirits of misfortune.[13] A former slave interviewed by the Works Progress Administration (WPA) eloquently melded the two concepts in his explanation: "Hants ain't nothing but somebody died outen Christ and his spirit ain't at rest, just in a wandering condition in the world."[14] The belief in spirits is still visible today in Virginia material culture; for example, the West African custom of inviting the spirits to join the living and guard against evil by placing shiny objects in trees survives in the practice of erecting "bottle trees."[15]

The files of the WPA reveal several patterns in tales about ghosts and burials. In stories that take place in Virginia, Thomas Barden noticed four functions of ghosts that can be gleaned from the stories that WPA workers collected during the 1940s: "(1) to reveal hidden treasure, (2) to give advice to or change the behavior of the living, (3) to reveal the circumstances of their death, or to straighten out some problem with their burial or remains."[16]

One of the stories George Foss collected from residents of Brown's Cove was about Jim Royal, "an old slave," which, given the context of the story, probably meant a former slave. Royal was credited with knowing "a lot about black magic" because his "people had learned it in Africa, brought it here with them."[17] His supernatural attributes included ownership of a violin that could put itself back together after being smashed, a magic hoe that worked by itself while Royal fiddled, and the ability to play the violin in the middle of a fire (which worked until the night a drunken man threw whiskey on the fire and burned him up). In another story, a black man who worked at a Brown plantation was chased home by a female specter.[18] Reading dozens of similar stories from the Cove, which describe blacks and whites facing down "haints" or being punished by the supernatural for social transgressions, demonstrates one of the functions of these tales: to identify a shared social network. In other words, the people who knew the story of a headless phantom that traversed the Cove at night were motivated to stay indoors and watch out for each other.

From my encounters with descendants and contemporary owners of historic cemeteries and houses, I learned that ghost stories seem to serve an additional function: they give modern-day communities a role in protecting or passing on knowledge about the dead. For example, Jennifer Latham, the owner of the Nathaniel Evans house discussed in the previous chapter, said that she had been visited by his ghost. The ghost story gave her another level of connection to the past owners, in addition to her efforts to restore the house and help protect the Evans family burial ground.

Thus the spirits of the dead can function in the same way that cemeteries do: as symbols of family and community memory. Stories of hauntings are passed down through generations as cautionary tales and reminders of deceased community members and their family ties, such as those of the once large African American communities that involuntarily clustered at the Brown plantations. More recently, postbellum black cemeteries symbolize kinship connections and historic communities that have otherwise disappeared from the contemporary landscape. Piecing together the clues from these buried family trees helps us reconstruct the histories of these communities. As mentioned at the beginning of this chapter, the formal history of Brown's Cove focuses on a white family—the Browns. It does not include the generations of African Americans who labored in this community and buried their dead on its hilltops.

Field Methods at the Mount Fair Slave Cemetery

My field investigation at Mount Fair began with the realization that I had picked the wrong season for cemetery exploration: the beginning of the hot Virginia summer. I recruited two people to help map the cemetery, one to run a surveyor's total station[19] and the other to help clear the dense growth so that all of the gravestones could be located. In order to decide where to stake the survey machine, it would be necessary to locate the overall distribution of stones. Armed with machetes, each of us headed in a different direction to try to find the edge of the gravestones. The cemetery is shaped roughly like an oval, with a narrow east-west distribution and a long north-south one. To determine the northern edge, we looked for a length of land clear of headstones. It took many hours to reach that northern edge. Just as we thought we had found it, one of us would notice yet another stone, almost hidden under grasses, ivy, and bushes. To our surprise, we came to understand that the cemetery covered several acres, with more than 150 stones and many dozen unmarked depressions (map 4). Unfortunately, not one of these stones was inscribed.

The unmarked slave graveyard is about a thousand feet away from the main house at Mount Fair. This may have resulted from a deliberate attempt to give the slaves privacy during funerals and mourning or an effort on the part of the whites to distance themselves from the enslaved community. Or perhaps it was simply more convenient for the slaves to bury individuals closer to the fields where they worked and, possibly, their cabins. There is very little discussion of slave graveyards in archival records. Whites most often recorded the deaths of slaves in terse fiduciary terms (e.g., "negro boy, died last week, value $100"). As in other southern plantations' records, there is no mention of the decision-making process for laying out the slave cemetery. In this case, the cemetery lies along the edge of a historic

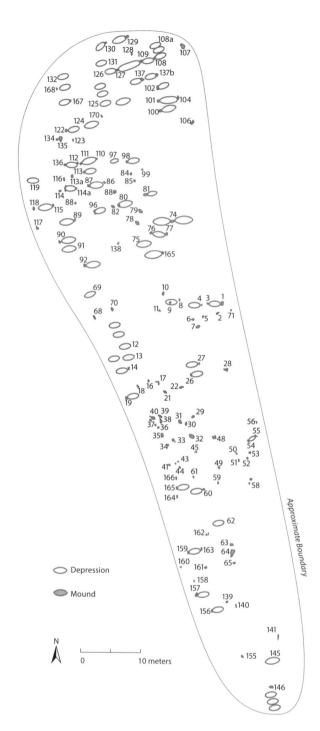

MAP 4 Burial sites at Mount Fair Plantation Slave Cemetery in Brown's Cove. The numbers represent individual stones (some are paired head- and footstones at either end of a depression). (Map by Lynn Rainville)

agricultural field; the burial site may have been provided to the enslaved community because of its location at the top of a steep slope.

I determined that there were 153 possible gravestones at Mount Fair, carved from locally available stones. Because of the clear association between many of the headstones and footstones, it was possible to estimate that more than 120 individuals are buried here. A few of the stones are local quartz. The infrequent use of quartz may have signified a certain type of individual, based on either age, gender, or status within the community or perhaps a certain type of death, such as suicide. More practically, the quartz may have been the first convenient stone that a survivor came across when searching for a marker.

In most cases the 153 stones were either clearly aligned with other stones or set upright; in some cases they marked the head or foot of depressions. In a handful of cases, headstones and footstones were set roughly a body length apart from each other. Some stones were clearly set into the ground to stand vertically, but many lay flush with the ground, possibly toppled by weather and gravity over the course of two hundred years. The gravestones were distributed over one hundred yards roughly north to south and approximately thirty yards roughly east to west.

At first glance, there seemed to be no pattern to the distribution of graves. But a careful study of the cardinal orientation and grouping of stones revealed several noticeable clusters that may correspond to family units. As in many Christian cemeteries, the grave shafts were aligned roughly east to west. Several religions hold that the deceased and any attendant stone should face east, toward the rising sun and, in Christian belief, the direction that Christ is supposed to rise from on Judgment Day. While there is disagreement among scholars as to the extent and nature of Christian beliefs among enslaved African Americans, ethnographic accounts from nineteenth-century communities reveal that enslaved African Americans believed that the head should be buried in the west so that "the dead won't have to turn around when Gabriel blows his trumpet in the east."[20]

There are three clear alignments to the graves in the Mount Fair Slave Cemetery. Those in the northernmost and southernmost part of the cemetery have an approximately four-degree slant to the southwest, while those in the middle sections are angled more dramatically, at about fifteen degrees to the south. This may be intentional, signaling different kinship affiliations within each section, or the cemetery might have been used at three different moments in time. Each new group, when setting out the first graves, might have created a different alignment. The east-west orientation of the graves was probably accomplished by solar or celestial observations rather than a compass, so the orientations would have varied by season. A third possibility is that the demographically distinct communities at Mount Fair (fewer than a dozen individuals in the late eighteenth century, two dozen between

1800 and the 1830s, and up to fifty people between ca. 1840 and the 1860s) buried their dead in three distinct areas within the cemetery.

In addition to the three aligned clusters, there is a clear range of stone size, from as small as 2.5 inches to the largest stone in the cemetery, which measures approximately 30 inches by 23 inches. In nineteenth-century white cemeteries, smaller stones are often chosen to designate child graves. The enslaved community probably used a similar system to denote infant or child deaths. In addition, the quality of the stone (a few are slate as opposed to fieldstone) may have indicated the relative social status of the deceased.

We did not excavate any graves during our study but cleared an area approximately one foot in diameter around each of the 153 surviving stones. This revealed three intriguing artifacts: a horseshoe, a snuff container, and a harmonica (fig. 16). The horseshoe appeared to be associated with a nearby stone; perhaps it was placed there to symbolize good luck or good fortune. While the snuffbox and the harmonica appeared to be haphazardly located, they may originally have been placed on or near wooden markers or unmarked graves. The harmonica may have been played at a grave during a burial; the container may have held tobacco snuff left as an offering.

These artifacts provided dateable objects, useful since none of the stones contained inscriptions or dates of any type. The horseshoe dated to the mid- to late nineteenth century. The harmonica, containing ten holes per side, dated to after 1857, when that style was mass-produced in America. The container was impos-

FIG. 16 Graveside artifacts found at the Mount Fair Plantation Slave Cemetery in 2002, Brown's Cove, Albemarle County. *Left,* nineteenth-century Hohner harmonica; *upper right,* horseshoe with nails; *lower right,* crushed tin, possibly for holding snuff. Artifacts donated to the Albemarle Charlottesville Historical Society by Lynn Rainville. (Scans by Keri Matthews, 2012)

sible to date, but its badly corroded exterior indicated that it had been exposed to the elements for many decades. Although hardly conclusive, this material evidence suggests that the cemetery may have been used as graveyard after the Civil War. It would not be surprising if the freed slaves and later descendants continued to use the cemetery where their ancestors were buried. It does, however, raise an interesting question as to when the last burial took place.

Since we did not conduct any excavations, we were left with some unanswered questions. Did the slaves bury their families together? If so, how was the spacing of burials handled? This second issue would have been particularly difficult for enslaved families to anticipate because of the possibility of forced separation from one's family before death. Third, were impermanent materials such as wood, plants, or artifacts used as markers, and if so, where are the related graves located? A final question is whether oral tradition was relied upon to identify the location of individual burials. This would have been particularly important in the absence of inscribed markers.

Naming the Dead at Mount Fair

By the conclusion of the first day of surveying the cemetery, we had the coordinates required to produce a map. The completed archival research indicated that we were examining a plantation with a moderately sized enslaved population of about two dozen individuals at any given time. Since I wanted to do more than just document the gravestones and tell the history of an antebellum plantation, I endeavored to collect stories from the descendants of the enslaved community to determine, if possible, who was buried under the uninscribed stones. But it was difficult to know where to begin, since the slave records lacked surnames, the markers bore no names, and the last burial was probably conducted about a hundred years ago.

I began the search at the local historical society and then moved on to the University of Virginia archives and the Library of Virginia. These repositories contained Brown family ledgers, census records, last wills and testaments, and probate records. From these records I learned how many enslaved people lived on the farm and, in some cases, their first names. Unfortunately the names of enslaved individuals are usually given only in the wills of their white owners. Only one owner of Mount Fair, Bezaleel Brown Sr., died prior to emancipation, in 1829. His will listed more than forty-eight names for the enslaved African Americans on his property and divided the slaves among his wife and children. Seven "negroes" were given to his wife, who presumably continued to live at Mount Fair until her death in 1847. One man and three children were given to his son William T. Brown, who would inherit Mount Fair and live there until his death in 1876, thirteen years after the enslaved community was emancipated.[21]

Bezaleel's estate appraisal in 1829 provided the names of several additional slaves, although it is difficult to determine whether they stayed on as slaves at Mount Fair or were sold in an effort to settle the deceased's estate. Of one group of enslaved individuals listed in the appraisal, it is noted that "the following negroes are gauged to be worse than nothing." These three individuals are female and may have been young girls: Huldah, Minerva, and Agnes. There are nine additional individuals who appear in the appraisal but were not explicitly willed to any survivor: Ly[d]ia and Lucy (two girls); Mel[il]us, Dicke Wellington, Reuben, Nimrod, and Ada[r]n (five boys); Minor and Reuben (two men); and a woman, Rhoda. The appraisal divided the slaves into four lots for "each claimant." While the first (unlisted) claimant is given ten slaves, the second—also given ten slaves—is Lucy T. Brown, Bezaleel's married second-oldest daughter, who left for Tennessee soon after the reading of the will.[22]

Lucy's departure would have been devastating but unfortunately quite common for the ten people she inherited, many of whom were probably related to the thirty individuals left behind in Brown's Cove. The third lot, also comprising ten slaves, was given to Mary Brown, Bezaleel's wife. Clearly Bezaleel or his executor, his son Bezaleel T., intended to divide up the enslaved community evenly among the owners, according to their ascribed value and not necessarily by African American family ties. A fourth, unlabelled lot consisted of one woman, Me[rn]via, who was given to Sarah Parrott, Bezaleel's third-eldest living child, who lived with her husband at the "Clark Place" on Pasture Mountain, near Mount Fair. Notably, a female slave's name is listed at the beginning of each lot. Two of the headings read "name of or dedud," which I assume is an abbreviation for a deduction from the estate settlement. The names Huldah and Agnes are listed under this category. These two girls appeared on the "worse than nothing list" earlier in the appraisal. Perhaps they were divided up equally because of their perceived low worth, which may have been owing to their young age, a perceived or real disability, or a personality deemed problematic by the executor.

Very little is known about the occupations of the enslaved individuals at Mount Fair, but it is safe to assume that most were engaged in standard agricultural and domestic duties. Two of the men enslaved by Bezaleel, Dick and Wilson, were listed as blacksmiths in the 1829 appraisal of his estate. Several decades later in William T. Brown's 1876 will, there is a reference to a blacksmith shop located on the Mount Fair property, so perhaps these specialists passed down their skills to their children, much like the practice of medieval guilds. Early nineteenth-century documents also refer to several saw and flour mills owned by the Brown family.[23] It is possible that some of the enslaved workers toiled in these mills or built the structures.

More Slave Cemeteries in Brown's Cove

It became clear after completing the research into Mount Fair that it was only one small piece of the social fabric of Brown's Cove. As mentioned above, Benjamin Brown Sr. had many sons. Several of these individuals inherited or built plantations in what became known as "Brown's Cove" in the 1800s. The Brown plantations were numerous: Brightberry (named after one of the sons), Headquarters, Mount Fair, Walnut Level, Buck's Elbow, Rural Retreat, Branch Point, Bachelor's Quarters, Trinidad, and the oddly named Lickin (whose ruins were bulldozed in 1984 to protect grazing cows).[24]

All of the Brown sons utilized slave labor on their plantations. Mount Fair was only one of a dozen possible homes for the families of the enslaved communities. African American families were often separated upon the death of their owner.[25] In the case of the Brown family plantations, the death of one patriarch usually resulted in the dispersion of slaves to a nearby plantation. But these mothers and fathers could not count on leaving together, so families often ended up on adjacent but different plantations. For example, when family patriarch Benjamin senior died in 1762, his will listed the distribution of property and people among his sons: "I give to my son Barzila Brown and his heirs forever all that Tract of land I own on the lower side of the River between the River and the Ragged mountains and one Negro man named Tom: . . . I give to my son Benajah Brown and his Eirs [sic] forever that land and Plantation where on I now live also the Olde Plantation and land belonging to it on the pasture fence and one Negro boy named Cupit and one Negro girl named Franck."[26] These individuals are probably buried in one of the slave cemeteries located on the Brown family plantations, and their descendants may have been as well.

A century and a half later, in 1907, a Brown descendant reminisced about his childhood:

> We stopped at first at the large white house, of a relative, who received us with great hospitality. This farm was adjoining the old ancestral home of Bernis Brown. We stayed overnight and rested with this relative after over ten miles ride, and in the morning crossed the fields and approached the old Brown home from the rear. The path we followed was the one made by the Negroes, long ago, as they passed from one plantation to another on their nightly peregrinations. . . . We crossed the fence several times before we arrived at the foot of the slight eminence upon which the house was built.[27]

His observations demonstrate that the African American community circumvented some of the restrictions of slavery by creating their own social networks. The reference to the trails used by slaves suggests that the black community found a way to be together after their workday ended, despite the many laws that restricted their movements. These connections existed in life and, through communal burial in the slave cemeteries, in death.

Because of the difficulty in moving corpses prior to the invention of motorized hearses, I presumed that each Brown plantation contained a separate cemetery for the enslaved community. However, today each parcel of land has a nonrelated owner, and it took six years to obtain the necessary permissions to search the former Brown plantations. The first time I sought out the slave cemeteries located on other Brown land, I was accompanied by two local residents, Jeanne Morris and Wilson Steppe. Although they didn't live in one of the plantation homes, their neighbors did. Jeanne invited me to their Brown's Cove house so that we could set out together in their four-by-four vehicle. I was having difficulty imagining why we would need four-wheel drive in the relatively low-lying foothills of the Shenandoah valley; little did I know we would be driving over ditches and through fields with five-foot-high grass.

Headquarters

Our first stop was Headquarters, the home of Thomas H. Brown, built in 1769, with an 1818 addition. This house contained an innovative feature for the nineteenth century: running water, pumped to the house from a higher elevation. This half-brick, half-frame building contained fancy moldings and original plaster, made from lime, sand, and horsehair. The outside walls featured molded brick cornices from Wales and, originally, beaded weatherboards with cut nails.[28] In the mid-nineteenth century, local Methodist preachers used the home, then owned by Thomas's son, Horace, as a retreat during the hot summer months "on account of the bracing air, quiet seclusion, and generous fare."[29] Continuing in this generous spirit, Thomas Brown opened up his home to convalescing veterans after the Civil War.

The slave cemetery lay upward—nearly straight upward—from the house. We drove, tilted at an angle, toward an area where Wilson remembered seeing stones. A short while later we found a short row of fieldstones buried by foliage. None was inscribed. I snapped some photos, and we returned to the car for our next stop, Brightberry. This home lies in a valley, surrounded by pastures. Built around 1818, the two-story hall-parlor frame dwelling stands at the entrance to a gap that leads up and over the mountains. Instead of driving up to the house, we drove past a pond on an old road, right to the fenced-in cemetery. Protected from errant plows, the stones were all still standing, but, again, covered in very high, tick-infested grasses. I took some photos, but didn't linger in the overgrown site.

Brightberry Slave Cemetery

Several years later, in 2007, I received an e-mail from the owner of Brightberry, who had heard of my work. She invited me to come out to map the cemetery on her land. The enslaved community at Brightberry was given prime real estate for its burial ground. The cemetery lies on a hill overlooking the big house and the rolling green hills of the Shenandoah valley to the west.

Unfortunately, there were only two inscribed stones, and they were separated in date by more than one hundred years. The 1987 stone was carved from marble and read "Franklin D———," who died in his fifties.[30] It was not clear whether he worked here or was a descendant of the nineteenth-century community. The older stone was a carved fieldstone and very hard to read. It contained four straight lines that appeared to have been carved first, to provide a guide for the inscription. The legible part read "Mrs ——— Jul 1, 1863," the latter presumably the death date (see fig. 9, p. 63). A nearby marker contained a similar set of four lines, but these were crooked and lacked any visible inscription. The remaining sixty stones were carved into various shapes, such as obelisks and curved markers, and also lacked inscriptions. The large number of stones, coupled with the stone dating to 1863, strongly suggests that members of the enslaved community are buried here.

The Walnut Level Slave Cemetery

In the twenty-first century, Brown's Cove has retained its rural character. The roads are narrow and curvy, and fields extend for thousands of acres, even though there is little active farming among the many multimillion dollar homes. The twenty-first-century Brown's Cove farmers are more likely to raise prizewinning horses or to hunt and fish on their weekend retreats than to engage in the daily tasks of planting and harvesting. Another phenomenon in this once predominantly agricultural community is a repurposing of old plantations. The story of one Brown plantation, Walnut Level, illustrates the reuse of historic buildings and the impact this has on the local mortuary landscape.

Built around 1810, Walnut Level is a brick "I-house" (so named not for its shape but because the two-story structures were first identified in Illinois, Indiana, and Iowa).[31] For much of the nineteenth century, Walnut Level was owned by Captain Bezaleel Brown Jr. (1793–1878). Bezaleel lived here with his wife, Elizabeth, and their six children and fourteen slaves. The Browns grew wheat, tobacco, apples, and other marketable items. Today only a handful of apple trees remain, and the livestock consists of chickens and cows. A nineteenth-century painting depicts the original outbuildings that once stood around the plantation house. Although none of the buildings are identified, historic records and the existing old foundations suggest that they included a dairy, an icehouse, and a slave cabin. The residents of the latter structure were most likely the house servants, required to live close to the big house. The painting also depicts two trees in the location of the cemetery for whites, which may have been deliberate symbolic plantings.

Since 1971, Walnut Level has been home to several dozen developmentally disabled adults (referred to as "coworkers") who live and work on the modern organic farm along with two dozen volunteers and a small paid staff. The farm was initially organized by parents who wanted a better future for their disabled children and chose the name "Innisfree" for the community. Together, its members grow food, weave, bake bread, and enjoy each other's company in this bucolic setting.[32]

Today the Innisfree maintenance man, Tom, lives in Walnut Level's historic big house with his wife and three children. Several years ago, he tore up old floorboards in the house in an effort to level the floor and discovered a cache of collected artifacts buried near an old chimney. They included nineteenth-century toys (a ceramic doll's head, a metal silhouette of a pistol, wagon wheels), ceramics (broken pieces of old blue and white patterns), and more modern trash, including a pink child's fork with a man's body for a handle, a bargain-basement plate that inexplicably depicted the Wright brothers' airplane flying behind a Native American man on horseback, and the only complete artifact, a small tea dish. When I turned the last find over, I found a "Made in China" sticker. Perhaps during the last renovation a child collected these treasures and hid them.

The next step was to determine whether any of the antebellum landscape was left intact. I had inquired beforehand to see if anyone knew whether there was a slave cemetery on the grounds of Innisfree, and I arranged to meet with the gardener, Tricia, who had worked on the farm for many years. When in answer to my query she noted the presence of a slave burial ground behind the greenhouse, I breathed a sigh of relief; this would be an easy quest. But when I asked about inscribed stones, it became clear that she was describing the burial ground of the Browns, the original white owners of Walnut Level.

I decided to visit anyway to find out if there might be another burial ground with less visible stones that may have been missed over the years. When I arrived, a coworker was pushing Tricia's new baby in a stroller, while other residents worked in a nearby greenhouse. Three portable chicken coops were visible in the distance, and twentieth-century houses and barns were clustered nearby. Tricia led me behind the greenhouse, pointing to the graves only a few feet distant. The cemetery was surrounded by a three-course-wide stone fence (fig. 17), its low height more closely resembling a garden wall. I wondered out loud about its origins, and Tricia informed me that the Innisfree residents had constructed the wall within the last two decades to protect the gravestones. The reasons for this

FIG. 17 Walnut Level Plantation Cemetery for members of the white Brown family, Brown's Cove, Albemarle County. Today, Walnut Level is the site of Innisfree Village. (Photograph by Lynn Rainville, 2009)

concern were evident when I mapped the stones and noticed that one footstone had been cleft in half, and the matching headstone was nicked. The last direct Brown descendant moved from Walnut Level in 1863, and before the wall was constructed, the cemetery had fallen into disuse. Members of Innisfree had cleared the site of brambles, righted stones, and planted a dogwood tree in the center of the small graveyard. A cedar tree—perhaps one of the trees depicted in the old watercolor—grows nearby.

Tricia remembered that empty grave shafts were observed when the foundation was dug for the nearby greenhouse. Some of the funerary remains may have been exhumed and reburied elsewhere. Another scenario is that the remains decayed so thoroughly that the only clue was a subtle change in soil color, which may have caught the eye of the workers in the 1980s. We'll never know who was buried in the graves, but one possibility is that they contained the remains of favored house servants. Since most slave gravestones are uninscribed, it is more likely that their grave memorials were accidentally removed or displaced over the decades.

The visible three-person white cemetery at Walnut Level reveals important patterns in small family cemeteries that should be considered in the study of historic black cemeteries. If this had been a small African American cemetery with uninscribed stones, I would have guessed that the three stones were the remains of a married couple and their child and would have missed the longevity of the cemetery (which turned out to span more than three generations) and the complicated burial practices. Unfortunately, there is no easy method for correcting such misjudgments when the grave markers are not inscribed. One partial solution is to collect oral histories and record graveyards while there are still descendants living nearby and to gather any documented information, such as burial locations recorded in a family Bible.

In this instance, with the aid of the inscriptions and historic research, I learned that the cemetery contained one individual from each of three generations of the white Brown family. An unknown number of graves are missing, probably hidden underneath twentieth-century construction. The earliest burial in the white cemetery commemorates the owner of Walnut Level, Bezaleel G. Brown (1787–1825). Neither his wife, Elizabeth Early Michie, nor any of their children are buried here. Only his daughter Frances E. Brown is buried alongside her father. Frances died in 1834 at age twenty-three, most likely unmarried. The third preserved burial is that of John J. M. Parrot, who died in 1853 at the age of two. He represents the third generation, Bezaleel's grandson, born to one of his daughters, Martha, who married Charles H. Parrott. Then there are the uninscribed or destroyed graves that lie under the recently constructed greenhouse. A report on file in the director's office at Innisfree states that "the markers of older graves have disappeared." Unfortunately, if any names were associated with these markers, they were not recorded in the report. Perhaps the stones were not inscribed or their carvings, if any, were lost over time.

Toward the end of researching Brown's Cove I reread a 1984 report and noticed the preface, which began, "I am indebted to Miss Eugenia Bibb, a descendant of Benjamin Brown, Sr."[33] Benjamin was the patriarch who first moved to Brown's Cove; Miss Eugenia Bibb is my next-door neighbor in Charlottesville, twenty miles away from the Cove. My family and I live in a house that Miss Bibb's father built in 1952, a house built by a relative of the individuals buried at the Walnut Level Cemetery. After only eight years of living in Charlottesville, I am already part of a series of interconnections that lay the groundwork for the future recording and explanation of Albemarle County history.

Although I located the white Brown Cemetery, I was not able to find the burials of the enslaved community at Walnut Level. We know that the antebellum owner, Bezaleel G. Brown (1787–1825), owned slaves, because they are mentioned in legal documents pertaining to Bezaleel's estate when it was appraised after his death. In the appraisal the enslaved community was listed just before a "mahogany side board." The community included eighteen people: four adult men, six adult women, four boys, and four girls. Unfortunately, there is no indication of the family relationships.[34]

The appraisal does not indicate how the enslaved community was distributed among the living Browns, and Bezaleel died without a will, so we do not know where these individuals ended up—although it is possible that Bezaleel's wife, Elizabeth, inherited them. She continued to live at Walnut Level for another three

decades, until her death in 1858. In 1830, the year of the first census after her husband's death, she is listed as the owner of twenty-four enslaved individuals, which
may have included some or all of the original eighteen persons from her husband's
estate. After Elizabeth died, her property passed to a relative, Horace Brown, who
sold the house to someone outside of the family five years later in 1863, Charles W.
Antrim.[35] Within two years of this sale, all of the Brown's Cove slaves were emancipated. In the 1870 census almost every white surname is mirrored in a black family
name, such as Woods, Brown, and Davis.[36] Many of the postbellum Brown plantations were surrounded by African American neighbors with shared surnames. This
strongly suggests that some of the formerly enslaved individuals remained in the
neighborhood after the Civil War, as was the case in much of the war-devastated
former Confederacy.

A tantalizing memorial to the descendants of the enslaved community was a
photograph on the wall of the Innisfree director's office, showing a 1935 apple-
packing shed with the work crew standing in front. A local historian and photogra-
pher, Phil James, created this reproduction from an old photograph, thoughtfully
including the names of the individuals on the back. Three of the two dozen people
in the photograph are African American, standing off to the left of the group. They
are identified as Will Jackson, Martha Conaway Jackson, and "Herbert." Given their
apparent ages in the photograph, I would estimate that they were born in the 1860s
or 1870s and thus represented the first postemancipation generation. Some of their
descendants continue to live in Brown's Cove to this day, as I discovered on later
visits to African American family cemeteries in the Cove.

Burials at Walnut Level continue into the present. Many of the "coworkers" remain in the Innisfree community until their deaths, and the organization works
with a local hospice to give individuals end-of-life care. In the three decades of
Innisfree's operation, several deceased residents have chosen to be buried on the
five-hundred-acre grounds. Each of these has been a scatter burial, in which the
ashes of the deceased are strewn beneath trees. Thus a new generation of burials
and community ties has begun.

9

COMMEMORATING AND
PRESERVING HISTORIC
BLACK CEMETERIES

Sometimes the presence of an African American cemetery is obvious—when an area is enclosed with barbed wire or contains visible markers or is adjacent to a church, for example. But often, what remains is so subtle that it is likely to be missed by the casual observer. Left unmarked, these cemeteries are more often subject to inadvertent or intentional destruction. There is no single correct way to commemorate a cemetery, but any efforts to do so should focus on respecting the individuals buried at the site.

Solomon Family Cemetery

Sometimes even narrowing down the possible location of a cemetery is not enough to help locate it. For many years I dropped in on the local African American genealogy group meetings to report on new findings and ask if anyone had additional leads, but eventually I stopped making those announcements because they made me feel like the angel of death, focusing on the dead and buried. But one of the leads that arose during a meeting seemed relatively easy to pursue. A member of the group was searching for a family cemetery within the city limits of Charlottesville. Her family name was Solomon. Unfortunately, the cemetery had been disturbed during the construction of a new apartment complex. And yet the developer was using the family name, calling the complex "Solomon Court Apartments." An advertisement beckoned, "Enjoy the serenity and quiet of country-like living in beautiful Charlottesville—without sacrificing the easy access to shopping, business, and entertainment offered at Solomon Court."[1] Decades earlier this site had been situated in the country, whereas today it lies along a very busy thoroughfare squarely within the city of Charlottesville. The only remaining evidence of the "country" is a rustic-looking wooden fence and some landscaped flowers. Otherwise there is very little unpaved surface area.

I visited the complex hoping to locate the cemetery, bringing my dog as a cover for my explorations. It was possible that the cemetery lay in an undeveloped area of the site, perhaps adjacent to the trash compactor that sat in a lightly wooded area or in one of the small patches of grass left for resident canines. The welcoming sign for Solomon Court included a warning against soliciting or trespassing, making it difficult to conduct an extensive search (such as probing the ground for buried markers), and eventually I gave up. Now, years later, I drive by the site once a week en route to deliver lunches for Meals on Wheels. With each pass I scan the perimeter of the property, hoping to notice a misplaced tree or rock that might suggest a place of burial, but without success so far. Even though my colleague had shared her memories of a twentieth-century family cemetery and its approximate location, I was unable to find it. This story highlights the need to locate and map these sites before they are covered over or destroyed.

Commemorating African American Graveyards

In some cases, descendant communities may prefer the anonymity of an unmarked burial ground, which decreases visits from nonrelatives. But there are also many examples nationwide of memorials designed by descendants[2] and of successful, culturally sensitive memorials for African American burial grounds that attempt to incorporate African and Christian belief systems. There is no "right" way to memorialize a cemetery, but it is possible to suggest what should be avoided.

For instance, it would not be appropriate to enclose an antebellum slave cemetery with a wrought-iron late-Victorian-style gate. Not only are the material and style anachronistic, but the late nineteenth-century emphases on enclosure and on demarcating the division between "sacred" and "secular" space was less relevant to enslaved communities. By necessity, many slave cemeteries took advantage of opportune locations along fence lines, in rocky, inarable soil, or in wooded areas. Most of the slave cemeteries in my study appeared to grow randomly, extending beyond the original clusters of graves and often past original fence lines. If a historic slave cemetery must be enclosed, either to protect it or to identify its location, I recommend building a low stone wall or selecting symbolically appropriate perimeter markers, which might include hedges, yucca plants, fieldstones, or artwork. The goal is to create a symbolic barrier between sacred and profane ground, while avoiding anachronistic enclosures such as a twentieth-century chain-link fence. A relatively impermeable boundary, such as a high stone wall, may not be appropriate given the original open nature of most black cemeteries. The inclination to enclose property is more often seen in public cemeteries and some white churchyards.

A more important step in memorializing a site is to erect some type of sign commemorating the family names, if known, or at least the name of the plantation formerly associated with the burial ground. A sign will protect the identity of the site so that it is not forgotten or overlooked by future generations. The placement of a sign is particularly important at burial grounds that lack inscribed stones, since future generations would find it difficult to connect the names of historic families to these burial grounds without a marker of some kind.

The design of such a sign can be complicated. Sites from all American states are eligible to be nominated for the Historical Highway Marker program. Those that meet the program's standards are entitled to a standardized gray metal marker that stands about six feet high and includes space for a one-hundred-word inscription indicating the historic importance of the site. The advantage of these markers is that they are both durable and recognizable as part of a national effort to signify historic importance. A possible disadvantage is that the style of these markers may seem anachronistic, depending on the date and location of the individual cemetery. Fortunately, these signs can be amended if community members want a different design in the future. Initial efforts should include contacting any descendants and discussing plans for the sign with any community members living in the neighborhood of the cemetery today. Ideally, such discussions will result in a more site-specific design.

Another issue for historic black cemeteries is efforts to clean up the sites. Some of the best-intentioned communities ask volunteers to help neaten the cemetery by removing trash and pruning weeds, but aboveground artifacts may be part of an earlier graveside mourning tradition, and floral remains may be part of a deliberate effort to use plants to mark gravesites. This does not mean that actual trash should not be cleaned up, but experienced professionals should be contacted to document the association between depressions and plants and between graves and artifacts.

A Highway Marker: Rose Hill Church Cemetery

To commemorate the graves in a hard-to-find churchyard, I requested grant money to design a permanent marker for the rural Rose Hill Church Cemetery. I was concerned that the historic association between the church and the graveyard would be lost over time; the majority of current congregation members had never visited the cemetery because it lay distant from the church.

In my attempt to find the cemetery, I spent hours talking to local residents and scouring aerial photographs, but I searched in the wrong place for weeks because of conflicting directions from my informants. Someone finally pointed me in the right direction—a mile away from the church, down an unmarked dirt road. The cemetery lay within an overgrown forest down a narrow, weed-covered lane, pitted with ruts and too narrow for a car to traverse safely, past ruins of old houses, recent trash, and hunting stands.

With the help of Derek Wheeler, a professional archaeologist from Monticello, I spent several days mapping a total of 215 burials. The perimeters of the cemetery were poorly defined, although the road to the north created a border on that end. The remaining three sides appear to have expanded beyond the original estimates, and a dozen or more burials lay outside of the asymmetrical polygon that figuratively enclosed the burials—figuratively because there was no standing fence, just property markers buried at the four corners.

A marker for the Rose Hill Church Cemetery could be modeled after those used in Virginia's Historical Highway Markers program. The church liked the association, so I searched for a sign maker and met with the congregation after their Bible study to ask what information they would want on the marker. Initially, they felt it should include their church icon (a rose) and the names of all of the people buried in the cemetery. With over two hundred interred individuals and only twenty inscribed markers, this presented a monumental research task, as well as a logistical challenge in fitting the names on one piece of metal. After more discussions, the congregation eventually settled on a final text identifying the cemetery as the "Rose Hill Baptist Church Cemetery" and explaining, "The Rose Hill community came into existence around 1880. In May 1882, residents purchased land to build a church. Later a school was constructed next to the church. The earliest known burial dates to 1917." They added a Bible verse: "Blessed are the dead which die in the Lord . . . that they may rest from their labors. Rev. 14:13." The completed marker was erected at the site in 2004. In addition, I prepared a cemetery brochure with a map of the burials, transcriptions of the readable markers, and a history of the church. These efforts to map and identify burials encouraged the church to clear the road in 2005 to make the cemetery more accessible.

Unfortunately, the Rose Hill Church Cemetery did not qualify for the state or national registers of historic places; only a handful of African American cemeteries have. The goal of the National Register of Historic Places, created in 1966 and maintained by the National Park Service, is to recognize the "districts, sites, buildings, structures, and objects that are significant in American history, architecture, archeology, engineering, and culture" at the local, state, and national levels.[3] Each of the nationally recognized properties can be searched in the National Park Service's online database,[4] making these resources available for planning, management, research, education, and interpretation efforts. Yet despite the National Register's seemingly inclusive goals, it is perplexing to learn that of the eighty-five thousand sites in the register, fewer than 2 percent concern African American history.[5] This is unacceptable, for as the archaeologist Barbara Little has noted, "Listing in the National Register serves to authenticate the worth of a historic place. It is this authentication that gives the National Register power in public perception."[6] The inclusion of more African American sites would broaden the definition of heritage within many communities and help the general public to understand the historic importance of African American cemeteries and other sites.

A Stone Wall: The University of Virginia's Slave Cemetery

Individual communities can and do commemorate historic African American cemeteries without National Register recognition. Sometimes these local memorials work well to highlight the sanctity and significance of these sites. But sometimes, good intentions fail to adequately memorialize them. And even if a site has been commemorated, these sacred spaces can still be very difficult to locate on the modern landscape, as the following tale demonstrates.

One of the more inventive but unfortunately unnoticed cemetery markers that I have found is at the University of Virginia. Unknown to most students and faculty, there is a slave cemetery in the front yard of several university residence halls, the Gooch/Dillard Residence Area. Today this site is blocks away from the plantation house it was originally linked to and covered with twentieth-century buildings. When I first heard about the cemetery, I was told the name of the dormitory and thought it would be easy to locate. Instead I spent an hour searching the area, asking students and staff at work in the surrounding buildings if they knew about the cemetery. None did. After climbing the outdoor stairs and hills crisscrossing the area, I sat down on a stone wall to look at a map and saw that the wall was inscribed with the words "Graveyard Site: This area contains unmarked graves believed to be those of slaves owned by the Maury family, owners of Piedmont in the nineteenth century" (fig. 18). I had found the site but was disappointed that there were no traces of the gravestones.

I later learned from an old newspaper clipping that the site had originally contained seventy-five graves, but by 1983, when the cemetery was rediscovered, there were no surviving aboveground markers. When the university needed to expand student housing, it selected this site for the construction of three dorms, planned in an interlocking pattern to surround the site of the cemetery. The available building space was thus maximized, leaving the cemetery itself as a buffer and open space between the dorms. The burial ground is surrounded today with a road and remains wooded, with only a handful of walking trails passing through the site.

As the memorial inscription indicates, the African Americans buried here had been enslaved by the Maury family, who lived at nearby Piedmont Plantation. The plantation house still stands, but it too is out of context, surrounded by faculty housing. Given the size of the cemetery, it is probable that it holds the remains of more than one family.

FIG. 18 Stone memorial at the site of the University of Virginia Slave Cemetery, Charlottesville. (Photograph by Lynn Rainville, 2012)

Kitty Foster Cemetery

More recent local memorials combine artistic sensitivity with the practical need for identification. One successful example is again at the University of Virginia, on the site of a free black cemetery referred to as the Kitty Foster site. In 1993, a university parking lot expansion uncovered the remains of a dozen grave shafts. This site now lies across the street from some of the university's largest academic buildings (such as Cabell Hall), but in the nineteenth century it was a free black neighborhood called Canada. University records demonstrate that several of the residents in this community worked as carpenters and laundresses for faculty and students. The graves were found on land owned by a free black named Catherine "Kitty" Foster, who lived from around 1795 to 1863. She purchased the land in 1833, and it remained in her family until 1906, when the land values in the neighborhood began to increase, and most of the African American residents moved away. An 1832 receipt shows Professor Turpin requesting the proctor of the university to pay Kitty Foster four dollars for "washing before commencement."[7] Foster had at least two daughters and two sons. The former probably assisted her with the washing, while her sons were indentured to local craftsmen.

In 1993 the tops of a dozen grave shafts associated with Kitty Foster's family were uncovered, and then, after a discussion with local residents, they were reburied. In 2003, a new construction project was begun, and in the process two more graves were discovered in a previously unexplored part of the site. Once the grave shafts were outlined (several feet above the bodies), the remains were not disturbed further. Eventually a total of thirty-two graves were found distributed across the property.[8] The large number of burials suggests that this site was used by commu-

FIG. 19 Kitty Foster Memorial at the University of Virginia, Charlottesville. (Photograph by Lynn Rainville, 2011)

nity members, not just by one household. This complex of free black graves was incorporated into the design plans for the South Lawn Project that was built around this site years later, in 2010. The burial ground is preserved as part of a one-acre park that includes a footprint of Kitty Foster's now razed house, whose foundations were uncovered during the archaeological work (fig. 19).

Commemoration, Interrupted: The Monticello Parking Lot

Thomas Jefferson's Monticello is also home to a displaced slave cemetery. A burial ground of at least some of the plantation's enslaved people was found a century and half after their original burial, in a wooded "island" deliberately left undisturbed as the visitor's parking lot was built around it. In 1990, after reviewing historic and ethnographic evidence that pointed to the presence of a burial ground, archaeologists conducted remote sensing and uncovered the tops of two dozen grave shafts. A decade later, a more sophisticated geophysical test was undertaken, and the magnetic anomalies were tested with limited excavations in 2001. During this noninvasive fieldwork a total of twenty burials were located but not uncovered. These burial sites were marked by depressions in thirteen cases and by a total of ten stones (paired together as head and footstones). The sunken ground and aboveground fieldstones did not always correspond to the belowground features. Using statistical modeling, the archaeologists estimated that the cemetery originally contained 40 to 110 graves.[9]

After the archaeologists documented the location of the coffins and shroud burials, the Thomas Jefferson Foundation erected a split-rail fence around the area and put up a sign. Subsequently, the foundation held a competition to design a memorial for the site; entries were submitted, but now, over a decade later, no effort has been made to implement the winning design. Monticello opened a new multimillion dollar visitors center in April 2009. The slave cemetery lies only a stone's throw away from the handsome new building complex, yet it did not reap much of a reward from the capital campaign that funded the new construction effort. The two improvements made since 2001 are a new sign and a gravel pathway that leads to the cemetery from the new visitors center. The waist-high interpretive marker lists the "enslaved people who died at Monticello" and contains a list of individuals who might be buried in the cemetery, illustrated by archaeological maps that indicate the location of the graves.

The Search for the Avoca Gravestones

Unmarked cemeteries, as we have seen, are subject to vandalism, destruction, and sometimes, as in the example that follows, displacement. On behalf of the Avoca Museum, I traveled one hundred miles south of Charlottesville to Campbell County to document a slave cemetery connected with a plantation that had been owned by a wealthy and successful Virginia family, the Lynches. The plantation was originally called Green Level, but the family inexplicably changed its name to Avoca in 1868. Today the museum retains the name Avoca and is located in the Lynch family home, built in 1901.[10] The then director of the Avoca Museum, Frank Murray, arranged for me and two of my Sweet Briar students to spend a day locating and mapping Avoca's slave graveyard.

In this instance there was a rich oral history to work with. Gladys Fauntleroy Winston had owned Avoca before turning it over to the museum. In 1993, her son Pete, born in 1923, shared his memories of the house and cemeteries with museum personnel. He began by drawing a sketch of the plantation, commenting on historic features, many of which are no longer extant, and the homes of former residents. He recalled natural features such as a "big spring" that supplied the plantation with water through a gravity-fed tank and a "duck pond" in the backyard of the house. He remembered dozens of outbuildings, a cornhouse, stable, springhouse, slave quarters, tobacco barn, mill, icehouse, and several homes. He indicated the Lynch Family Graveyard by a roughly square dotted line with a cross in the middle. Local tradition held that favored servants were buried under some of the uninscribed stones.

Across a road and over an early twentieth-century railroad track, an X marked the spot of a "slave graveyard." Pete Lynch explained that the graveyard "was in this area, distinguishable a few years ago as a grove of high trees." The drawing was roughly to scale, and Lynch had thoughtfully included a north arrow (often absent from informal maps). Our two clues were the rough distance from the house to the graveyard and the visible environmental context of the trees. Unfortunately,

Pete Lynch had passed away by the time my students and I arrived to locate the cemetery, so the map would have to be our primary guide. But we did have a third source of evidence: the descendant of a woman who worked as a servant in the Avoca kitchen remembered that her aunt described a graveyard that was located "across the train tracks."

When my students and I arrived in late April, Mr. Murray gave us a brief tour of the imposing Victorian mansion constructed in 1901, the third house on that property. Two previous family homes built on that site had burned in 1879 and in 1900, respectively. The mansion's interior included Queen Anne–style arched doorways, elaborate banisters, pine paneling, batten wainscoting, and historic furniture. Because the house was unoccupied between the mid-1970s and the mid-1980s, it required repair before opening as a museum. Today's meticulous interior restoration was achieved by a collaboration between the Lane Company (a furniture and drapery business) and *Country Living* magazine. The end result is a stylized glimpse into the lifestyle of the last century. Regrettably, the planners failed to reconstruct the antebellum slave cabin with a similar degree of accuracy.

In contrast to the display of Victorian wealth within the house, the museum also exhibits the Juliette Fauntleroy Native American Artifact Collection, which includes arrowheads, ceramic sherds, axes, celts, and other prehistoric artifacts. Throughout Virginia, people make a hobby of collecting objects from everyday life lived thousands of years ago. I later learned that oral tradition held that the first burial in the "slave graveyard" was a Native American who drowned in the nearby Staunton River.[11]

As my students and I stood in the Lynch Family Graveyard and looked out across the railroad tracks, the trees in the foreground and background blended into an impenetrable forest. Consulting the decade-old map sketched by Pete Wilson, we piled into my car and drove across the tracks, keeping in mind that in the antebellum period they would not have presented the raised barrier that they are today. The copse of trees became more prominent as we drew closer. More significant to a cemetery location was the elevation of the site, preferred to ensure that the burials remain above the water table. This was particularly relevant at Avoca because the site lay in the floodplain of the Staunton River.

We parked alongside an unplowed circular area and trudged in through knee-deep grasses. Two large trees, both over one hundred years old, flanked a possible opening, which they might have marked in the absence of a metal gate. We spread out and walked up and down an area enclosed by dozens of smaller, younger trees. Hay bales lay just outside the overgrown circle, reminding us that if it weren't for the more recent undergrowth and fast-growing trees, the land beneath our feet would have been significantly disturbed by plowing.

FIG. 20 Displaced gravestones at Avoca Slave Cemetery in Altavista, Campbell County. (Photograph by Lynn Rainville, 2004)

Instead of rows of gravestones or even unmarked depressions, we discovered a curious pattern of two clusters of stones lying amid copious poison ivy. The stones had been stacked, some against trees, some next to each other (fig. 20). Although the stones were locally available river cobbles, they were modified into several shapes: columnar or obelisk styles (a pattern also found in the Lynch Family Graveyard), squat markers, a headboard style, isosceles triangles, and less modified circular stones. There were only four other stones visible within the circle of trees, partially buried rocks that did not appear to be shaped.

Here were stones that appeared to be modified by people, presumably for grave markers, but no graves. The clusters of stones could not possibly be in situ, because there was not enough space between the stones for the burial of a body. We photographed each stone and wondered what could have produced such an unusual pattern. Later, we reexamined the various oral histories of the site and discovered that a cattle farmer had grown tired of his cows tripping over the rows of stones and had placed them against the trees. It's hard to imagine a community accepting this action at a formal public or church cemetery. Otherwise, many maintenance personnel would choose a similar solution in modern cemeteries, where irregularly spaced grave markers wreak havoc on mechanical lawn-mowing methods.

When we finished mapping the displaced gravestones, we retraced our steps, combing the circle to try to locate the original depressions, which would have given us a better idea of the stones' original placement. But decades of farming and livestock grazing had obliterated any clues.

In the end, we could only guess at the number of individuals originally buried here. An accurate count depended on whether headstones were paired with footstones (in which case there were about twenty burials) and whether impermanent markers were used alongside the stones (in which case the circular copse could have held dozens of burials).

The Lynch family owned a large amount of property, so it is likely that this cemetery is one of several slave cemeteries associated with Green Level. The site we located was far from the big house; this may indicate that it was used to bury field slaves. Conversely, the uninscribed markers within the Lynch Family Graveyard adjacent to the mansion may have been for the house slaves.

As part of the grant that funded our investigation, the museum pledged to clean up the site regularly, trimming the grasses and trees so that the gravestones were more visible, albeit displaced. Several years later the museum finished clearing the site and erected an informational sign at the cemetery. Almost a decade later, in 2012, the museum unveiled the restored cemetery. Volunteers, including members of the Boy Scouts, Sons of Confederate Veterans, and Sons of Union Veterans, helped build a new road, erect a split-rail fence, and construct new signs. This project included resetting the stones in rows, despite the absence of depressions or other information as to the original location of the burials. While efforts have been made to conduct additional oral history interviews with descendants of the enslaved community, relatives have yet to be located.[12] All too often, these untold stories lie buried with the dead.

The Church and the Parking Lot

The last three examples in this chapter highlight endangered slave cemeteries, but twentieth-century and even twenty-first-century cemeteries are also at risk. I first noticed the historic Mount Calvary Baptist Church on my way to visit the Hardin Tavern site. The church is most notable for a large hand pointing to heaven, mounted on the highest part of the steeple. This dramatic symbol of faith caught my eye, and when I drove by an old cemetery seconds later, I assumed the two were related. Subsequent research revealed that the church was one of the earliest postbellum African American houses of worship in Albemarle County, founded in 1869, and its original cemetery, dating to around the same time period, was located several hundred yards west of the church.

From a preservation perspective, it is always unfortunate when communities and their burial grounds are separated by geographical distance. Noncontiguous features are in danger of losing their historic context. The historic Mount Calvary Cemetery did not have a sign, nor was it completely enclosed. Its four sides were surrounded by sites that could infringe on the graves: a school to the west, railroad tracks to the south, a house to the east, and Morgantown Road to the north. Months later I received permission to map the cemetery, and as we recorded the 150 burials, several members of the community stopped by to see what we were doing. The first was Henry Waller. Several of his relatives were buried in the cemetery: two distant ancestors, John G. Waller (1879–1952) and George Waller (1874–1964), and two veterans born in the twentieth century, Kyles Waller (1923–1967), who served as a technician in World War II, and John Gilmore Waller (1913–1981), who also served in the army during World War II. Henry Waller visited their graves regularly and was happy to see that someone was documenting the individuals buried in the cemetery.

None of the visitors could tell me why the cemetery wasn't located closer to the church, but two years later I had an answer, when a preservationist who worked for the county asked if I could map "an old cemetery" that lay behind the Mount Calvary Church. At first I thought the researcher was confused and explained to her that the historic church cemetery lay to the west, not directly behind the church. She explained that there was an even older family cemetery behind the church. No one knew who was buried there, but the church had recently requested permission from the county planning commission to expand its parking lot into that area.

The planning commission told the church that it needed to identify the boundaries of the old cemetery first. The church didn't have money to pay a professional surveyor, but several county employees knew of my interest in black cemeteries. I agreed to visit the site, draw a map of the stones, and make recommendations for the placement of a parking lot adjacent to the cemetery that would avoid disturbing any human remains.

The Mount Calvary Church represents the center of a once-thriving African American community that extended along Morgantown Road. Today this community is threatened by rising taxes and property values. Property deeds in this area illustrate numerous small divisions of land that run perpendicular to an east-west railroad track lying to the south of the church. These lots housed dozens of African American families who purchased land here after the Civil War. Prior to the founding of the church, this community worshipped at the nearby white Saint Paul's Episcopal Church.

At the Mount Calvary Church I was greeted by Deacon Burnett. Despite the proximity of the graveyard to the church and oral histories suggesting that the people buried in this cemetery were black, no one in the current congregation remembered who was buried there. Further, although there were over fifty markers and many more unmarked depressions, only one inscribed metal marker remained. The cemetery has a fragmentary barbed-wire and wooden fence around its northern edge and drops off precipitously to the south where a railroad track cuts through the cemetery.

Most of the burials were marked with locally available fieldstones, some carved and some unaltered. There was also one pink quartz stone and one metal marker. The metal marker had a fragmentary piece of paper in it, highly eroded and ripped. The legible letters read "A[ ][ ]" and "[initial] Co[ ]per." Although it is hard to prove, the paper may be associated with the burial of Alice Cooper, who died in 1937 at age one hundred. A local funeral database listed her burial site as "Ivy Depot," a historic name for the larger community surrounding the site. I named the graveyard the Cooper Family Cemetery in Alice Cooper's honor because I was unable to locate descendants of any of the other burials.

Unfortunately, no other marker in the cemetery contained a legible inscription. As the other markers were naturally occurring fieldstones, they were probably never inscribed. There was some diversity among the fieldstones: some were flush with the ground, others were carved into a two-dimensional headstone reminiscent of nineteenth-century gravestone styles, and still others were upright blocks. Considering the presence of roughly fifty gravestones and many more unmarked depressions and the total area that was originally enclosed by the fence, I estimate there may be as many as 250 burials in this cemetery, suggesting that this was probably a community burial ground that predated the contemporary Mount Calvary Baptist Church. This illustrates again the difficulty of researching the history of a burial ground lacking marked graves.

Within the past decade the church ran out of space at its historic cemetery and established a new burial ground directly behind the church, in front of the Cooper Family Cemetery. The two dozen modern gravestones include temporary metal funeral-home markers, marble veteran's stones, and granite stones, the most prevalent type. This new cemetery is distinct from the historic one in several ways, such as the number of granite memorials, the fancier motifs found on the stones, and the elaborate aboveground grave offerings. When I visited, most graves were adorned with plastic flowers, often placed in metallic urns that accompanied the stones. Several featured heart-shaped wreaths, flower stands, and statues of lions and angels. The praying hands motif was very popular in stone decoration, as were carved flowers. The markers were deliberately spaced apart within the cemetery, giving families contiguous individual plots within which to bury their dead, which is desirable to family members. The difficulty is in remembering which plots are full. In the past, gravediggers would dig test pits to see if a plot still had room. As far as I knew, the church was not keeping a map, but presumably it encourages everyone to use some kind of marker to keep track of the available spaces. In Albemarle County, some churches have devised a different strategy, laying out straight rows of stones to keep track of exactly who is buried where.

This particular cemetery-mapping project highlighted the tension between a congregation and the county planning commission. My final report indicated that the Cooper Family Cemetery was much larger than initially thought, and thus a larger buffer zone would have to be allotted. To the contrary, the church was trying to put in as many parking spaces as possible to meet the growing congregation's needs. A year after I mapped the cemetery, the church asked my advice on putting up a fence around the Cooper Family Cemetery, a requirement that the planning commission had set as part of the building permit. I assumed that the church had gone through with its plans to erect a protective fence.

In the end, the church took a much more dramatic step. The late nineteenth-century church was torn down to build a new six-thousand-square-foot building. The church saved the replica wooden hand, which, in turn, had replaced a century-old carving that pointed to heaven, atop the steeple. Decades earlier church leaders had removed hand-carved wooden silhouettes of tearful African faces that once decorated the side of the church.[13] They hope to display these historic artifacts in the new building. The rest of the historic church was demolished, much to the dismay of a handful of longtime parishioners, neighbors, and preservationists.

The access roads to the new parking lot were laid down directly through the church's own more recent cemetery (the one located directly behind the original church and in front of the Cooper Family Cemetery). When I visited in 2009, years after my initial research, this newer cemetery had been cut into two halves to accommodate the roads, and the church had not followed the instructions of the planning commission; the Cooper Family Cemetery still lacked a protective fence. On the day I visited, boulder-sized chunks of dirt from the drainage construction had landed in some of the burial depressions, and the newly landscaped fill was within inches of the cemetery boundary. I informed the Albemarle County Planning Commission of the disturbances, and the church again agreed to put up a fence to more clearly delineate the boundary between the parking lot and the historic black cemetery.

Preservation Activities

Even when a cemetery is properly marked, the stories it might have told are very often lost. Many markers are never inscribed or are now illegible. Of those that remain readable, restoring them professionally takes skill and expensive supplies. Nonetheless, there are simple steps that anyone can take to help preserve these sites for future generations.

The most effective way to preserve and protect African American cemeteries, or any abandoned American burial site, is to share the stories of the dead with the living. The more community residents who locate, visit, and learn from these cemeteries, the less likely it is that these sites will be unintentionally destroyed. These visits don't have to involve morbid or depressing discussions of death. Instead, use the opportunity to record new stories about the cemetery residents. Or take photos of the stones in various seasons with different light conditions to improve the readability of eroding inscriptions. Bring a mirror to direct raking light at a shallow angle across hard-to-read stones.

Another simple step is to register any family or unmarked cemeteries with local authorities. You can begin with your local planning commission, which maintains accurate tax maps for properties. Cemeteries are not always indicated on deeds, but if you make officials aware of their existence, they might note their locations on a topographic map or land deed.

A more involved method is to record the information from all of the stones within the cemetery. The ideal way to do this is to sketch a map of the stones and number each grave (regardless of whether you can read the stone). Photograph each stone, and as you do so, record any legible information such as the name of the deceased, death date, age, inscription, epitaph, motifs, etc. If you are taking digital photos, burn a CD with the *original* image files from your camera, before you label or manipulate the images. This will preserve a clean copy of each photo. Once you start editing the photos (cropping them, rotating them, or saving them into different formats), you lose some of the original clarity in the photo. You should have backups of this information, ideally in separate locations. It is also helpful to give a copy of the transcribed stones and photos to a local historical society, often the first stop for genealogical researchers. Churches are another potential repository for this information.

Recruit volunteers (perhaps a local scout troop or elementary school would enjoy the outdoor project), and begin with a cleanup of the grounds. A cemetery that looks abandoned or contains trash will only encourage more littering. When cutting the grass, be careful to hand-trim around markers so that the blades of mowers and weed eaters do not damage the stones. One strategy is to plant a ground cover, such as periwinkle or ivy, to decrease the need for regular mowing. Consider removing any young trees that are growing close to stones, since over time, tree roots and the trunk itself can destroy them.

A crucial preservation action is to assess the condition of the stones and determine which, if any, should be cleaned. It is a mistake to think that because most markers are made of stone, they are impervious to damage. Harsh chemicals, the bristles on brushes, even the simple act of removing lichen can damage a friable stone. With the exception of granite, most stones are fragile; even the act of grave rubbing can damage some inscriptions. Identify any brittle stone faces with flaking lettering or delicate surfaces. These should be cleaned only by a professional. Stable stones can be wetted with water and then brushed lightly with a soft-bristled brush.[14] Work from the bottom to avoid streaking, and rinse thoroughly once you have scrubbed the entire stone. Do not use cleaning solutions (not even dishwashing soap) without consulting an expert, since the effective cleaning agent varies with each stone type. In my study, many markers were soapstone, which should only be cleaned with water. If you are not certain about the stone material, consult with a geologist or professional cemetery conservator.

If funds are available for the upkeep of a cemetery, consider hiring a professional cemetery conservator to assess any damaged stones and offer advice. Gravestone conservation is a specialized field that involves stabilizing stones if physical decomposition or eroding inscriptions are present and repairing any fallen or broken stones. Before hiring a professional, consult with interested parties to decide on the priorities for the graveyard. Some burial grounds will have dozens of fallen or broken markers. It will probably not be economically feasible to fix all of the stones, so prioritize your goals.

If financially feasible, archaeologists or surveyors can be hired to produce a professional map of the graves. This is most valuable in large cemeteries (over fifty graves) or in cemeteries that are still accepting new burials. In the process of drawing the map, a surveyor or archaeologist can ascertain where existing graves are located, including those that lack aboveground features. This will allow the community or church to better plan where to dig new graves.

Before beginning any conservation project, make certain that you have permission to work in the graveyard. This includes knowing who owns the land, since the owner may be distinct from the families of the people buried there. Finally, be sure to check any state or local ordinances that govern the alteration of funerary monuments.[15]

Virtual Cemeteries

Another way to preserve and share information on cemeteries is to create a website. With financial support you can hire a professional website and database designer and create a searchable site that includes photos of each gravestone, a numbered map, information about the history of the site, and even walking tours or interactive educational sections. The website African-American Cemeteries in Albemarle and Amherst Virginia (http://www2.vcdh.virginia.edu/cem/) is the result of my research and was created with the help of several generous grants. A small sample of other cemetery websites with searchable databases is listed at the end of the bibliography.

A searchable online database that has been a tremendous resource for my own research is the J. F. Bell Funeral Home Records database (http://www.virginia .edu/woodson/projects/bell/). In the 1990s, the founders of the Charlottesville African American Genealogy Group (CAAGG) embarked on an ambitious project to record the names of individuals who were buried by J. F. Bell, a historic black funeral home. Working with the funeral home, which had saved a large number of records, the group began compiling data. After working through the funeral-home records, they decided to check these records by comparing them to the official death certificates on file in Richmond at the state archives. The CAAGG project expanded beyond one funeral home to encompass thousands of African American deaths in Albemarle County. They collected information for deaths between 1917 (the year that the J. F. Bell Funeral Home was founded) and 2001, when they compiled the information. Although sometimes incomplete, death certificates contain a wealth of information, including the deceased's parents and mother's maiden name, spouse if any, cause of death, address at the time of death, occupation, birthplace, place of death, and burial location.

Unfortunately the last category, the place of burial, is sometimes vague, such as "Family Cemetery," or abbreviated in such a way as to conflate multiple places: "Zion Ch. Cem," "Zion Cem," "Mt. Zion Cem"—which may represent three separate cemeteries or just one. Several years into my own research, I helped the group migrate their impressive database, with more than eight thousand names, to a searchable online database.[16] This became my first source of information upon returning from a newly recorded cemetery.

Don't be daunted by these examples of websites with searchable databases; if you don't have the financial resources to mount a fully developed site, consider hosting a blog or a wiki. Templates for both types of sites can be downloaded free of charge from various sources, such as wordpress.com or pbwiki.com. With minimal effort anyone can design a simple website that provides information and graveyard locations. An online presence will help researchers locate family members buried in the cemetery and will promote awareness of the family and community. A website can also be used to ask for remembrances, photographs, or letters that enhance the historical record even further.

10

CEMETERIES AS CLASSROOMS
Teaching Social History with Gravestones

When I began my research into historic African American cemeteries, I envisioned local residents lingering over old tombstones, reading epitaphs and poignant inscriptions aloud. While some of this vision has come to pass, it became clear that some segments of the interested audience would not be visiting the cemeteries in person. These included older members of the community who were not able to travel easily, busy families, nonlocal descendants, and former community members who were interested in learning about these historic sites from a distance. With contemporary technologies, such as online databases and digital photographs, I was able to post photographs of individual stones online so that anyone could view them. But I wanted to find a way to interest someone who wasn't related to the deceased and also to demonstrate how gravestones can reveal the histories of past communities.

To achieve this goal I designed walking tours of publicly accessible cemeteries. Most of the cemeteries that I studied were privately owned family cemeteries or were located on private land. While state laws allow descendants to access their family burial grounds even if they lie on private land, members of the public would not be granted access. So I began with a public yet forgotten site called the Daughters of Zion Cemetery, named after an African American women's sororal organization.

Daughters of Zion Cemetery

As related in chapter 5, the Daughters of Zion purchased a cemetery for the burial of members and their families in 1873. It lies one half mile from Charlottesville's popular downtown mall, a bricked pedestrian area for shopping and dining. A fitness center was built across the street from the historic cemetery, and its large picture windows provide a bird's-eye view of the memorials. From a distance, the markers appear pristine, and their patterning in organized rows is visible. Unfortunately, a visit to the site reveals years of neglect and vandalism, with overturned markers, strewn bottles, and broken stones. How did such an unusual effort, a mutual aid society's Reconstruction-era purchase of land for an all-black cemetery, come to this end? Was there anything I could do to reclaim the site's history and encourage local residents to respect the dead?

My first challenge was to highlight the significance of the African American cemetery. Most visitors to this area come to Oakwood, the larger, segregated cemetery across the street. Few notice the unfenced two-acre plot of land, geographically removed from Oakwood by a narrow street, that comprises the Daughters of Zion Cemetery. When mentioned in historic documents, it is often conflated with Oakwood, once a predominantly white cemetery with a segregated section for "negroes." Beginning in 1936, the Charlottesville city directories listed the Daughters of Zion Cemetery as the "Oakwood Cemetery (For Colored)," a serious error that continued until 1953, when both cemeteries were incorrectly lumped together as the "Oakwood Cemetery." Even as late as 1975, a local newspaper erroneously reported, "The heritage of Southern segregation is marked for generations to see in what is now called Zion Cemetery, adjoining Oakwood Cemetery off Cherry Avenue. Called then the 'old Oakwood section,' Zion was the place the black people of the city were segregated in death."[1] This implies that the "Zion Cemetery" is a part of Oakwood Cemetery and that African Americans were buried there against their wishes. To the contrary, a segregated section within Oakwood contains African Americans who did not have a choice as to their final resting place, while the Daughters of Zion Cemetery contains the remains of the organization's members and their loved ones, buried in purchased plots of their own choosing.

Some of the invisibility of the Daughters of Zion Cemetery is due to the nature of the landscape. The cemetery lacks a fence or border of any kind. It includes a level portion with dozens of trees and a second low-lying area at the bottom of a steep slope. While it contains almost two hundred markers, many have fallen over or are low to the ground. Its proximity to the much larger and better-kept Oakwood Cemetery camouflages its location within a sea of gravestones. The Daughters of Zion Cemetery sits in an isolated urban corner between dead-end streets, one of which separates it from the larger cemetery. The lack of traffic results in frequent visits by underage drinkers and homeless campers; both groups leave behind copious amounts of trash.

This cemetery is unusual in being established by a sectarian burial association founded by women. The nature of this "secret society" coupled with the lack of surviving records gives us few documentary leads. The all-female organization appears to have been one of a dozen or so all-black fraternal societies in Charlottesville, many of which had affiliations to national lodges.[2] The Daughters of Zion may have been motivated to found a burial ground by African Americans' lack of control over black burials within Charlottesville's public cemeteries, which at that time set aside segregated areas for African American burials. With a $600 purchase of land, the Daughters of Zion could bury their dead where and how they wished. The 1873 land deed stated their goal for the cemetery: it was to be "for the use of the Charitable association of colered [sic] women of Charlottesville, known and styled, 'The daughters on Zion' And used exclusively as a burying ground."[3] In postemancipation Charlottesville, the opportunity to purchase a cemetery plot would have been an important step toward claiming full citizenship. For some families, such a plot may have been the first piece of land they owned. Over the next several decades, the increasingly successful urban African American population buried its dead here. In contemporary newspapers the cemetery was also referred to as the "Society" cemetery, reflecting the social status of many of its residents.

The cemetery grew between the 1870s and the 1930s, until the demise of its charitable association in 1933. A court case that year noted that "all the members of the said organization known as the Daughters of Zion are now dead, and . . . [the] organization has disbanded and become extinct."[4] During the same year, the organization lost the title to its meeting hall, which it had purchased in the 1880s.[5] Burials continued after this point, but it is unclear who supervised these new interments.

As the years passed, the cemetery fell into disrepair. Without regular maintenance, grass covered the footstones, ivy and other vines grew through cracks, and fallen or displaced stones were eventually buried by decaying leaves and soil, resulting in an aura of neglect and even abandonment. The cemetery deteriorated for decades until the City of Charlottesville stepped in and claimed ownership of the site, noting that it was "heavily overgrown and appear[ed] not to have been maintained for 20 to 30 years."[6] After a deed search failed to turn up any living owners of the property, the city acquired control and is now responsible for the maintenance of the property under the jurisdiction of the Parks and Recreation department.

Today, some 140 years after the Daughters of Zion purchased the land, the cemetery is used only occasionally for burials by families that have interred the dead there for generations. Older monuments and family plots owned by residents who have moved away are falling into a state of disrepair, but we can still learn much from the 136 surviving gravestones.

It is possible to imagine the postbellum landscape, when the cemetery was first laid out. We don't know how the members of the organization selected this site, but presumably they wanted a convenient, urban location, which would make transporting the dead from one of the nearby black communities easier and would enable a larger number of mourners to attend funerals. In the nineteenth century, funerals were often much larger than they are today and served a social function, as relatives and friends gathered to grieve and memorialize the deceased. Another advantage to this site was its proximity to an existing burial ground that probably gave the area a more sacred character. But in contrast to Oakwood's hilltop location, the Daughters of Zion site straddles both high and low topography. The northeastern portion of the site is at the bottom of a steep slope. Because of its proximity to the underlying water table, this acre was almost unusable for burials. The higher ground, where a grassy expanse is dotted with mature trees, resembles a park. There is no evidence that a wall or fence ever enclosed the site, but there are faint traces of a road that once divided the cemetery into two halves and would have allowed horse-drawn hearses to pull into the cemetery.

Late nineteenth-century mortuary practices are still evident in this historic landscape. Participants in the tours I conduct there must enter the site via the old road. If you stand in the middle of this narrow alley and look carefully, you can discern slight depressions in the ground on either side. Only a handful of stones remain standing along the road, but once you train your eye to notice the depressions, you begin to see the original layout of the plots and the regularity that is visible from the second story of the fitness center across the street (map 5). A surviving plot purchase receipt indicates that burial plots were available in at least two sizes: "twenty feet square" and nine feet by eighteen feet.[7] In 1877, the trustees of the cemetery, the husbands of the female members, sold a larger plot to Cornelia Gilmore and her heirs for twenty dollars. The deed specifies the plot's location: "One whole Section No. Two . . . in the first row of sections . . . on the left hand side of the Alley, leading from the Gate of Entry, into said Cemetery."[8] The "alley" is the road that remains today. Unfortunately, the exact location is unknown because no markers survive for Cornelia or her family.

Twenty-two years later two male trustees sold Tamar Wright "a certain half section, on the south side of Charles Goodloes Section."[9] Because her plot was roughly half the size of the Gilmore plot, she paid ten dollars for the space. Again, no markers survive for Tamar Wright or her family, but the Goodloe plot is very visible (indicated by gravestone numbers 69 to 84 in map 5). Their twenty-by-twenty-foot plot is the only one that retains a fancy black iron fence, a symbol of their economic success.

After an African American woman or her family purchased a plot, how did survivors choose to commemorate the dead? Most of the 136 surviving grave markers are carved from marble or granite, and almost all of them have carvings containing the name of the deceased and her or his death dates, at a minimum. But this homogeneity encompasses a wide variety of stone sizes, motifs, epitaphs, and inscriptions. One-quarter of the stones contain a personalized message, either a quote from the Bible, a piece of biographic information, or a sorrowful message. The three most popular inscriptions ("Asleep in Jesus," "Gone but not Forgotten," and "At Rest")

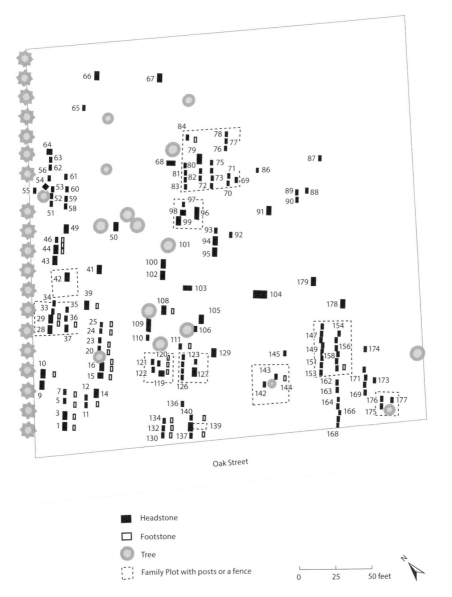

MAP 5 Daughters of Zion Cemetery, Charlottesville. (Map by Lynn Rainville)

are commonly found in late nineteenth- and early twentieth-century gravestones of both black and white individuals. Other inscriptions occur singularly but display broader patterns in commemorating the dead. For example, several indicate trust in God: "God will take care of me," "In God we Trust," and "We loved thee well but Jesus loved thee Best." Others are fatalistic: "She hath done what she could" and "Death is certain, the Hour unseen." Still others are poetic: "With songs let me follow his flight and mount with his spirit above. Escaped to the mansions with light and lodged in the Eden of Love" and "Yet again we hope to meet thee / when the day of life is fled / When in heaven with joy to greet thee / where no farewell tear is shed." Some families chose to highlight the deceased's membership in a fraternal or sororal organization. Two stones reference the male and female variants of the Elks Club: the Williams Lodge No. 11 of the Improved Benevolent and Protective Order of Elks of the World and the Queen Esther Temple No. 7, both local chapters of national benevolent organizations.

Very few of these inscriptions are biographical or truly personal in nature. Aside from gendered pronouns, these inscriptions are interchangeable among any number of individuals. Who would not want to "trust in God," "escape to the mansions with light," and be "in heaven with joy?" The half dozen personalized stones are usually "In Memory of" a "beloved" husband, wife, or mother. And two recognize the kindness of the deceased: "As a Father devoted / As a son affectionate / As a friend kind and fair" and "Tender mother and faithful friend." And yet even these inscriptions are found on hundreds of gravestones in other American cemeteries. One might guess that survivors would use these inscriptions as an opportunity to say something deeply personal or specific about the deceased, but in the nineteenth century the opposite is true; gravestone inscriptions rise and fall in popularity in parallel with attitudes toward death, but very few are original compositions. In the twenty-first century, there is a greater focus on individualism, illustrated by photographs of the deceased or an unusual design that commemorates the deceased's hobby or identity.

Only four individuals in the Daughters of Zion Cemetery are biographically memorialized on their gravestones. All four are men engaged in elite occupations, including a school principal, a doctor, and two reverends. One of these, Jesse Herndon, who died in 1889 at age thirty-nine, was buried under a marble marker that features a disembodied hand holding a Bible. The inscription references his leadership in the Zion Union Church. The other reverend, M. T. Lewis, also died young, at age forty, in 1883, and was buried under the most elaborate memorial in the cemetery, a tall rectangular marker topped by a stone cushion. The face of the memorial, embellished with architectural flourishes, bears personal information on one side and a Masonic symbol on the other (fig. 21). A four-sided iron fence stands in front of the

FIG. 21 Grave of Rev. M. T. Lewis (1843–1883) in Daughters of Zion Cemetery, Charlottesville. (Photograph by Lynn Rainville, 2012)

marker, enclosing the location of the body. Each of its four posts is topped by a vase evoking a container for an "eternal flame" and bears four-pointed flowers and extra crossbars to prevent easy access to the consecrated ground within. The third individual noted here is Benjamin Tonsler, a much-beloved principal of a local African American school. His marker is a plain rectangle with only a few carved flowers and an epitaph in the form of a tribute. The bottom of his stone is inscribed, "Erected by the Alumni of Jefferson Graded School and Friends." The fourth individual was a doctor whose stone bore a lengthy inscription, which unfortunately is no longer legible.

With the exception of inscriptions that mention black schools or social organizations, nothing about these motifs or inscriptions would identify these graves as African American. This is due in part to the urban population who purchased these gravestones instead of carving the memorials by hand or making them from locally available materials. There is far greater stone variability in the rural and small family graveyards that I recorded. But this cemetery served an urban elite who ordered gravestones from the same catalogs that whites did. Even at the height of the Jim Crow era and later state-sanctioned segregation, mail orders could be placed by anyone. Sears and Roebuck catalogs, among others, offered standardized gravestones for sale. Unfortunately, receipts that would indicate where the Daughters of Zion members purchased their stones are unavailable.

Can we use information gleaned from gravestones to reconstruct the social history of a living community? At the Daughters of Zion Cemetery we could gather only a limited amount of biographic data from the gravestones themselves. But by collecting birth and death dates from the 136 legible stones, we can trace broader patterns in the demographics of this African American community. First, the median age at death for the cemetery population was the then relatively old age of sixty. This statistic may be misleading, because infants and young children were sometimes buried under smaller or more impermanent memorials, such as tiny fieldstones, wooden markers, or even bushes or flowers. Their burial data may thus be missing from the surviving graves. A second interpretation for the higher-than-average lifespan is that the social group itself, the Daughters of Zion, may have appealed (or even been limited) to elders within the community. Unfortunately, there are no surviving membership records, so it is impossible learn more about the group's composition or even to determine what percentage of individuals within the cemetery were associated with the sororal group. The two stones mentioned above clearly commemorate individuals from two additional local lodges.

Third, an earlier researcher observed that there is "a striking generational gap" between those born before 1920 and their children, born after 1920.[10] Of the 124 legible birth dates, all but four date to before 1920. In other words, subsequent generations chose to be buried elsewhere. This demographic shift signals changing domiciles, as the younger generations migrated north or to larger southern cities to find employment or education. Charlottesville did not provide African Americans with education beyond grade school until 1927, when Jefferson High School opened.[11] The absence of more recent burials may also signal changing burial options for African Americans after the end of segregation in the 1960s. By that time, burials in the adjacent Oakwood Cemetery were no longer segregated, and in the 1980s new "memorial parks" were opened within the city limits. Younger generations may have found those options more appealing, or they may have lost the social memory and association with the long-defunct Daughters of Zion organization.

One of the most common types of African American cemeteries is the church cemetery, organized by a religious institution and usually located adjacent to the church. The Daughters of Zion Cemetery is an interesting example of a secular organization purchasing land for burials. I initially assumed that most of the families had belonged to the Mount Zion Baptist Church, a nearby historic black church that bore a similar name and was located only four blocks away. Further research revealed that there was no strong correlation between the cemetery and any one church. It was possible to identify church membership for 20 percent of the burials; of this number, "41% of those buried in Zion Cemetery attended First Baptist Church, 24% attended Mt. Zion Baptist Church, 7% attended Ebenezer Baptist Church, and the remaining 28% attended various local churches, including Zion Union Baptist, Bethel Church, and the Church of Christ."[12] The multiple places of worship associated with the deceased reflects the fact that this cemetery emerged out of a social network and not a religious one. It points to the unity and strength of the black community during times of social and racial upheaval, from about

1870 until the 1950s, when the number of burials dropped off precipitously. In this cemetery, community in death served as a comfort to the living.

Individuals

The grave markers in the Daughters of Zion Cemetery are a testament to the dedication of a women's organization determined to provide its members, their families, and their friends with a dignified burial in a place of their choosing. The graves also reveal the demographics behind the social organization, preserving the bodies and memories of this pre–World War I generation of African Americans. Can we search further and learn about the lives of these individuals, beyond the four social elites discussed earlier?

The grave markers are the first clue to individual lives. A dozen pairs of men and women share stones. In all but one case, these pairs are husbands and wives; the exception is a mother and son. In other cases, couples are buried next to each other with matching motifs or stones. In many instances families share a plot, with children lying under miniature versions of their parents' stones. Several of these stones reveal rich stories. I sorted the birth dates from the cemetery and learned that the earliest birth date was 1795, that of Delia Johnston, who was buried side by side with her husband, Phillip, under matching curved soapstone slabs. Phillip was born in 1813 and lived until age sixty-five in 1878, while Delia was born in 1795 and died in 1895, a remarkable century-long lifespan. Moreover, she married a man eighteen years younger than herself, and it appears that they were married for over fifty years, spanning the antebellum and postbellum periods. Unfortunately I have not been able to find them in the census, city directories, or marriage records. Their rapidly eroding gravestones are perhaps the last physical memorials of their lives.

Nearby stands a single stone with a poignant inscription. This plain stone contains the names of two children, born to "A. T. & Louise E. Buckner." Their first daughter, Annie, died in 1873 at age six. Her stone is one of the earliest remaining gravestones in the cemetery. Annie's sister Hattie died eight years later in 1881 at age two. Despite the gap in their deaths, the dual inscriptions are evenly spaced across the height of the stone. This strongly suggests that an earlier, perhaps impermanent memorial marked Annie's grave and was later replaced by a stone commemorating both children. It is possible that this was Annie's original stone and that enough space remained on it to add her sister Hattie's name and birth and death dates—although leaving just enough space for a second child's name below the first is either a coincidence or demonstrates a morbid anticipation. It is more likely that the family decided to purchase a joint marker for their daughters after Hattie's death. Two adjacent graves contain memorials for their brother, John T. Buckner, who died in 1888 at age three, and their sister Susie, who lived the longest, dying at age twenty-eight in 1910.

When I first noticed the children's gravestones, I didn't realize they were buried next to both of their parents. I located their mother, Louise or Louisa, but the stone for their father, Anthony E. Buckner, had fallen over, and I wasn't able to identify it until I enlisted help to lift the stone. Anthony was the last family member buried in this cluster, dying in 1923 at age seventy-eight. The stones told the story of his family tragedies. Four of his children died young, at ages two, four, six, and twenty-eight. While his family was suffering these losses, he lived next door to his father, Robert Buckner (1803–1901). From the census records it appears that Robert and his wife, Susan, had a very large family with eight or more children, the last one born in 1871, just two years before Anthony's own first daughter, Annie, was born. It is not clear from the census records whether Anthony had any other children with his wife Louisa, but it appears that none of their children survived long into adulthood. He lost Louisa, who died at age fifty-eight, in 1909, and married Mary Churchman sometime later. Curiously, his stone, located next to Louisa's, reads, "In Memory of Anthony T. Buckner . . . Erected by his wife and son." Since he died in 1923, fourteen years after his first wife's death, the stone was clearly commissioned by his second wife. And yet she is buried twenty-five miles away in the Piedmont Baptist Church Cemetery, while his son is unaccounted for. Was he a child of Anthony's first marriage, absent from the census records, or a son from his second marriage? In any case, it is somewhat surprising that the stone did not identify Mary, given the preexisting Buckner family plot.

An obituary appearing in the white newspaper upon the death of Anthony and Louisa's last daughter, Susie, provides a final insight into their lives. "Susie J. Buckner, the only daughter of Anthony Buckner, one of the city's most worthy colored residents, died at 2 o'clock yesterday morning. The funeral will take place at 3 o'clock tomorrow afternoon from the First Colored Baptist Church, the service to be conducted by the pastor, Rev. R. C. Quarles. The many friends of Anthony Buckner, both whites and colored are with Him in his bereavement."[13]

Ironically the obituary provides almost no information about Susie, instead using the announcement of her death to praise her father, Anthony. The anonymous obituary appeared in a newspaper written by and for whites. It was unusual for a white newspaper to report on black deaths unless the white community considered the deceased to be socially significant in some way. The 1880 census lists Anthony as a waiter in Charlottesville, and in the 1920 census he is listed as the proprietor of a grocery on Main Street. He must have been successful in addition to being well liked, because by 1920 he owned his own house on Main Street, surrounded by white neighbors, and was able to read and write. His second wife, Mary, however, was illiterate.[14]

The custom of white residents memorializing some African Americans deemed "worthy" is a paternalistic carryover from the antebellum period, when favored slaves were given condescending and misleading kinship titles such as "Aunt" or "Uncle." Far from conveying respect, these titles overlooked surnames (some but not all enslaved people had last names) and presumed a naturalized relationship between whites and blacks. For example, Margaret Lewis is buried in the Daughters of Zion Cemetery under a very plain, small, rectangular marker, carved from marble. There is no motif or personalized epitaph, just a short inscription: "Margaret Lewis, Died Feb. 27, 1915." Her obituary explained that she was an "old-time colored nurse," caring for Mr. John Shepherd at the time of her death. The text continues, "'Aunt Margaret' as she was familiarly called, was held in high esteem by all who knew her. She was kind, gentle and faithful in her duties. She was born a slave more than 70 years ago, having belonged to the Meade family. She was the mother of 13 children all of who, together with her husband, have been dead a number of years."[15] Her stone stands alone; it is not clear where the rest of her family is buried.

In the postbellum period, in the face of widespread prejudice and inequality, some members of the white community made a point of identifying "good" or "worthy" African Americans, who presumably pleased them in some way or whom they considered well behaved. Many of the social elites within the African American community had learned to coexist with the white community and were considered "worthy" because of their profession or social success. Several of the obituaries referenced this status among the Daughters of Zion deceased. For example, when Jesse Cary died in 1897, the white newspaper wrote, "Jesse Cary, a well-known carpenter and one of Charlottesville's most worthy colored citizens, died suddenly Saturday afternoon about six o'clock at his home on South Fourth Street. His funeral took place from Ebenezer Church at 1:30 this afternoon and was largely attended."[16]

When Susan Fleming died in 1931, she was memorialized as a "well known colored nurse" who "ministered to many white people of this community, by whom she was held in high esteem."[17] Other African American doctors and nurses who were buried at Daughters of Zion were not mentioned in the white newspaper, so presumably what made Mrs. Fleming of interest to whites was her ministrations to their community. An even more telling obituary described a local barber, J. P. Fleming, as "industrious and obliging."[18] In segregated Charlottesville, African Americans were often publicly valued in the memory of whites if they accepted a powerless status. This public passivity was rewarded in the obituaries penned by whites. After desegregation in the 1960s, obituaries for deceased African Americans who are buried in the Daughters of Zion Cemetery cease to contain such demeaning language. Instead, black deaths are reported on their own merits, without reference to whites or the white community.

Walking Tours

There are dozens of other families buried in the Daughters of Zion Cemetery. An attentive visitor would notice many more stories of loss, longevity, and family connections. I've shared these stories and more with students from the nearby University of Virginia and members of the public who have joined me on Black History Month walks. However, it shouldn't require a formal tour to encourage more residents to stroll through this public cemetery. With increased visitation, the vandalism problems and neglect at this site would likely be lessened.

When I take students from Professor Patrice Grimes's University of Virginia's education classes on tours of this historic cemetery, their comments encourage me that guided tours are one way to effectively share the significance of the cemetery's history. One student wrote, "Although I was skeptical of the idea at first, I soon realized that cemeteries were not boring, but rather very historic and interesting places to explore. I had no idea how much interesting historical, sociological, and psychological implications that could be derived from just a cemetery. In addition, as a teacher, I am constantly looking for new and original experiences to share with children, and after taking this tour of the Daughters of Zion Cemetery, I am certain that taking students to a cemetery could be a very unique teaching opportunity." Another student envisioned a lesson plan that asked students to imagine the lives of those buried in the cemetery, such as "the suffering they endured from racism, their desire for a special cemetery all their own, the difficulty they may have had in acquiring property due to their race, and similar social issues relevant to the lives of those interred in this special place." This future teacher hypothesized that "students would likely feel a connection to these families who lived where they live, and would be made to see how different their own lives are. This type of examination of civic history would be a far cry from reading texts about the lives of African Americans in the U.S. in the nineteenth century. It is this personal connection which is so essential to history education; students must be made to feel they are living *in* history, not simply reading *about* history." This perceived connection between material culture and past lives is exactly what I strive for; at the end of one tour Professor Grimes concluded, "Every time I take a walking tour with you, I learn so much about the neighborhood 'right under my nose.' Thanks for helping me to appreciate it and for sharing your talent with our students."

More recently I worked with an architectural historian, Gardiner Hallock, to document the cemetery's history in order to nominate it for the National Register of Historic Places. Using categories recognized by the register, we concluded that its regional significance pertains to two primary features: it "remains the only site that relates to Charlottesville's Daughters of Zion Mutual Aid Society," and it is "one of the few sites in the City that retains a connection to the vital role played by reconstruction-era African American mutual aid societies in the development of post-emancipation African American communities." In March 2010 we learned that the cemetery had been placed on the state and national registers. I am working with neighbors and members of the university community to raise funds to purchase and erect the $1,500 highway marker that the site now qualifies for. This prominent sign would enable visitors and passersby to understand the significance of the cemetery and learn more about its unique history.

The story of the Daughters of Zion Cemetery and those of the other cemeteries in this book revisit the question I undertook to answer for my friend Leah—or for anyone interested in history and culture—at the outset of this project: Why are historic cemeteries important, and why should we care about them? What is left in a now-dilapidated burial ground such as the Daughters of Zion Cemetery, or any historic cemetery, to hold the interest of contemporary viewers? One scholar observed, "To control a museum means precisely to control the representation of a community and its highest values and truths."[19] If we substitute the term *cemetery* for "museum," we see why historic cemeteries need to be cared for and preserved. Gravestones can teach us lessons in American civics as told through portraits of individuals and their communities, depicted in the details found on their headstones. The storylines in these mortuary museums illustrate national values: the worth of the individual, the primacy of the family, the depth of religious beliefs, the importance of patriotism. Through their monuments, cemeteries show us American concerns regarding social mobility and reveal changes in attitudes about death and the afterlife over time. They can also demonstrate some of the darker aspects of our shared past, the legacies of slavery and segregation. Cemeteries are instructional spaces that, if read correctly, have much to teach us about our social and moral values and about our shared history.

Appendix:
Gravestone Recording Forms

GRAVE MARKER RECORDING FORM

Name of cemetery: _____ *Stone number:* _____

TYPE OF MARKER

____ Headstone

____ Footstone

____ Tomb, table, or barrel vault

____ Family monument

____ Unmarked depression

____ Uncarved fieldstone

Oriented in which direction? (E, W, N, S)

MARKER MATERIAL

____ Slate

____ Soapstone/schist

____ Marble

____ Granite

____ Metal

Other:

Color of stone:

SIZE OF MARKER

Above ground height _____

Width _____

Thickness _____

SHAPE OF MARKER

____ Rectangular

____ Curved

____ Three-dimensional

CONDITION OF STONE

Inscription: Legible / illegible

Fallen or broken: Yes / no

Overall condition: Excellent / good / fair / poor

PHOTOGRAPHS TAKEN

Number of photos _____

Orientation of photos _____

Negative/photo number _____

MORTUARY SYMBOL

__ Skull, faces, or bones   __ Wreath

__ Vegetation (e.g., ivy)   __ Masonic symbol

__ Cross, Bible, or angel   __ 3D statuary

__ Dove, lamb, or animal   __ Geometric symbol

__ Urn and/or willow tree

__ Lettering only (plain)   Other: _____

Above ground artifact: _____

SKETCH

INFORMATION INSCRIBED ON THE MARKER

Name of deceased _____

Date of birth _____

Date of death _____

Age _____

Inscription _____

Other data (veteran?) _____

Carver (if known) _____

Date form completed: _____ *Form completed by:* _____

INDIVIDUAL BIOGRAPHICAL FORM

NAME AS LISTED IN OFFICIAL RECORDS

Last name _____

First name _____ Middle name _____

Maiden name _____ Nickname _____

Buried in Cemetery: _____ Stone Number: _____

Individual Number: _____

INFORMATION INSCRIBED ON THE MARKER

Name (as it appears on marker) _____

Date of birth _____ Date of death _____

Age _____ Sex _____

Mortuary symbol _____ Type of marker _____

Marker material _____

Inscription or epitaph _____

Other data (pronoun, veteran status, etc.) _____

ADDITIONAL INFORMATION ABOUT THE DECEASED (does not replace a family tree)

Mother _____

Father _____

Spouse _____

Siblings _____

Other kinship affiliation _____

Address at time of death _____

Place of birth _____ Place of death _____

Cause of death _____

Occupation _____

Church _____ Funeral home _____

Published obituary _____ Death certificate located _____

Notes: _____

_____

_____

_____

_____

Date form completed: _____ Form completed by: _____

Notes

1. Finding Zion

1. Historical Census Browser, University of Virginia Library, Geospatial and Statistical Data Center, Slave Population search, http://mapserver.lib.virginia.edu/php/newlong.php?subject=9.

2. To test this approach I counted the number of "blacks" and "mulattos" listed during one year, in the 1860 mortality list. There were 298 deaths in Albemarle County from January to December 1860; this is at the end of the period cited here when the overall population figures were higher. Thus the eighty-six deaths per year is a conservative estimate.

3. The punishment for free blacks congregating to learn how to read or write was up to twenty lashes, while any white person instructing them could "be fined not over $50.00, also be imprisoned not exceeding two months." If a white person assembled slaves to teach them to read or write he or she would be fined ten to one hundred dollars for each pupil. Guild, *Black Laws of Virginia*, 175–76.

4. In later years I located a handful of archaeological reports on slave cemeteries, but as they were in the gray area of literature produced by contractors, few libraries carry these titles. Two other single-cemetery studies were published: in 2003 a book was released describing a community study of a slave cemetery (Rawlings, *Gone but Not Forgotten*), and in 2008 a journalist wrote about her efforts to record a slave cemetery (Galland, *Love Cemetery*).

5. Library of Congress, Prints and Photographs Division, *Historic American Buildings Survey,* reproduction no. HABS VA, 2-NOGAR.V, 1, survey no. HABS VA-995.

6. Ibid., 4.

7. Free black population of Albemarle County compared to its enslaved population, 1820–1860, Historical Census Browser, University of Virginia, Geospatial and Statistical Data Center, accessed 28 December 2008, http://mapserver.lib.virginia.edu/.

8. For example, Samuel Miller, Albemarle, Virginia. U.S. Census 1930, roll 2434, p. 10B, enumeration district 10.

9. *Richmond Planet,* 12 April 1890.

2. Locating and Recording the Dead

1. Historical Census Browser, University of Virginia, Geospatial and Statistical Data Center, "Free Colored Males" and "Free Colored Females" results, http://mapserver.lib.virginia.edu/index.html.

2. As a colony of Great Britain, Canada freed its slaves in 1843, much earlier than did the United States.

3. "Old City Cemetery," *Lynchburg Insider,* accessed 29 February 2012, http://www.the-lynchburg-va-insider.com/old-city-cemetery.html.

4. The U.S. Census Bureau compiled only two slave schedules, one in 1850 and one in 1860.

5. Rainville, "Home at Last," 59–64.

6. Hildreth, *The Slave,* 82–83.

7. Named after Brightberry Brown (1762–1846).

8. Lay, *The Architecture of Jefferson Country,* 55.

9. U.S. Census 1810, Fredericksville, Albemarle, Virginia, roll 66, p. 187, image: 0181426; U.S. Census 1830, Albemarle, Virginia, p. 232, NARA series M19, roll 197, family history film 0029676.

10. Even though Brightberry is a private home (not a business) it can be found as a "place" on VA Home Town Locator, accessed 15 March 2012, http://virginia.hometownlocator.com/maps/feature-map,ftc,2,fid,1675010,n,brightberry.cfm.

11. Brightberry's wife, Susan Suca Thompson Brown (1776–1832), one of his daughters, Millie Brown (1788–1852), and one of his sons, Horace L. Brown (1807–1882), are buried here. There are several illegible and unmarked stones, one of which may mark the grave of Brightberry himself.

12. For more information on additional slave cemeteries in Albemarle County see Rainville, "Home at Last"; Rainville, "Saving the Remains of the Day"; Rainville, "Social Memory and Plantation Burial Grounds"; and Rainville, "An Investigation of an Enslaved Community."

13. Undated blueprint for the Oakwood Cemetery, in Dr. Scot French's possession, and oral remembrances recorded by him in the early 2000s regarding the possible presence of a fence.

14. See J. F. Bell Funeral Home Records, http://www2.vcdh.virginia.edu/jfbell/.

15. Later I learned from a descendant that the family calls this the "Douglas Cemetery." Unaware of this, I had used the designation "Thompson Family Cemetery," found in J. F. Bell Funeral Home Records, http://www2.vcdh.virginia.edu/jfbell.

16. U.S. Census 1880, Whitehall, Albemarle, Virginia, roll T9_1352, p. 69.3000, enumeration district 3, dwelling 30, family 30.

17. I retained the name "Thompson Family Cemetery" for the site that I found first, where Robert Thompson was buried. This experience highlights the difficulty in determining how to best identify historic cemeteries, based on community knowledge, family tradition, or funeral-home or death-record data.

18. Library of Congress Veterans History Project, http://www.loc.gov/vets/vets-home.html.

19. The URL is http://www.facebook.com/AfricanAmericanCemeteries.

3. *The Accidental Museum*

1. African symbols appeared on stones in slave cemeteries located farther south in the Carolinas, Georgia, and Florida. See, for example, Parsons, *Folk-Lore of the Sea Islands;* and Stokes, "Gone but Not Forgotten," 184, 189.

2. Olmsted, *A Journey in the Seaboard Slave States,* 405.

3. Ibid., 449.

4. Bromberg and Shepherd, "The Quaker Burying Ground in Alexandria, Virginia," 57, 59–60.

5. Vlach, *By the Work of Their Hands,* 43–45.

6. Wilkinson, *The Complete Temples of Ancient Egypt,* 57–59.

7. Hollis, "Otiose Deities and the Ancient Egyptian Pantheon," 67.

8. Dozens of pages of transcribed archival documents and Carr family history are available on the Ivy Creek Foundation website, http://ivycreekfoundation.org/history/familyhistory.html. The foundation owns the historic Hugh Carr farm.

9. Dethlefsen and Deetz, "Death's Head," 502–10.

10. Stannard, "Death and Dying in Puritan New England," 1305–30; Jackson, "American Attitudes to Death," 298.

11. Delaney and Rhodes, *Free Blacks of Lynchburg, Virginia*, 67–69.

12. Sears and Roebuck catalog (1902), 809.

13. Coincidentally, in March 2012, I spoke with a man who grew up in Amherst County and attended the church where this stone was located. The deceased was his uncle, who died at age forty-six. He remembered that his uncle was "a very religious man" who "took a knife to his heart and killed himself."

14. A comprehensive study of pension requests from African American soldiers and their dependents reveals that "married" slaves did occasionally share surnames. Although postbellum in date, these petitions reveal antebellum naming patterns because the applicants had to prove their dependency on the soldier prior to the end of the Civil War. Regosin, *Freedom's Promise*, 73–75. In this book there are many examples of surnames shared between husbands and wives such as Harriet and Joseph Berry (23–36) and Huldah and Robert Gordon (62–64) (she took his surname upon his death in 1862, to enforce family continuity), and Rena and Miles Easson (70–72).

15. To protect the privacy of the more recently deceased, I do not include surnames of individuals who died after 1959, in keeping with architectural definitions of "historic" (older than fifty years).

16. For example, an 1804 Virginia statute prohibited "nighttime religious meetings of slaves," and by 1819 this was broadened to include any evening assembly of free black or enslaved persons. May, " Religious Assembly Laws in Antebellum South Carolina and Virginia," 247–48. Yet enslaved preachers, like the Virginian John Jasper (1812–1901), managed to circumvent these laws.

17. Thomas Jefferson's epitaph reads: "Here was buried Thomas Jefferson, Author of the Declaration of American Independence, of the Statute of Virginia for Religious Freedom, and Father of the University of Virginia." Transcription by the author on a visit to Monticello.

18. Charles Wesley, "Rejoice for a Brother Deceased," in Hare, *Epitaphs for Country Churchyards*.

19. *Richmond Planet*, 5 April 1890, 3.

20. U.S. Census 1930, Richmond, Richmond (Independent City), Virginia, roll 2478, p. 23B, enumeration district 63.

21. See, for example, Boxley, *Gravestone Inscriptions in Amherst County, Virginia*.

22. While traditionally published records are scarce, Nadia Orton began a Facebook page titled "African American Cemeteries of Tidewater Virginia" in 2000. The page contains hundreds of photographs (some of which mark the graves of whites) but no comprehensive or searchable list of black interments or cemeteries in the region.

23. Parsons, *Folk-Lore of the Sea Islands*, 213–15.

24. The transatlantic slave trade was permanently abolished by Congress in 1808; thereafter the American slave trade was supplied through biological increases. Morgan and Nicholls, "Slaves in Piedmont Virginia, 1720–1790," 215, 217; Walsh, "The Transatlantic Slave Trade and Colonial Chesapeake Slavery," 15; Deyle, "The Irony of Liberty," 39–40, 43, 50.

25. Walsh, "The Chesapeake Slave Trade," 146, 149, 155–56. The African-born individuals in southern Virginia primarily came from Bight of Biafra and West Central Africa, while individuals from Upper Guinea and the Gold Coast disembarked in the northern Chesapeake.

26. Morgan, "Slave Life in Piedmont Virginia," 435–38 and table 2.

27. The American Revolution further disrupted the then British-dominated transatlantic slave trade, and vague promises of freedom from British forces convinced thousands of Virginian slaves to leave their owners, resulting in a severe labor shortage. Frey, *Water from the Rock*, 210–11, 219.

28. Morgan, "Slave Life in Piedmont Virginia," 441–44.

29. Guild, *Black Laws of Virginia*, 60.

30. Minchinton, King, and Waite, *Virginia Slave-Trade Statistics,* xvi.

31. Deyle, "The Irony of Liberty," 50–51.

32. This in contrast to other regions where African beliefs are clearly illustrated through grave goods, such as shells and broken vessels placed on graves in Columbia, South Carolina (Ingersoll, "Decoration of Negro Graves," 69); the use of "African drums" to announce a funeral in the Sea Islands (Roediger, "And Die in Dixie," 168); and a cache of West African *minkisi* of quartz crystals, pierced discs and coins, beads, pins, a rounded black pebble, and a painted sherd found underneath the floor of an antebellum big house in Maryland (Leone and Fry, "Conjuring in the Big House Kitchen," 372, 379).

33. Frey, *Water from the Rock;* Frey and Wood, *Come Shouting to Zion;* Boles, *Master & Slaves.* For a discussion of the growth of Baptist and Methodists churches and the presence of black preachers in the Piedmont, see Morgan, "Slave Life in Virginia," 472–79.

34. Frey, *Water from the Rock,* 18.

35. For example, the Society for the Propagation of the Gospel, a missionary arm of the Anglican Church, attempted to convert and school African Americans. Ibid., 19–21.

36. Ibid., 247–50.

37. Ibid., 247.

38. Ibid., 278.

39. Ibid., 287.

40. Kelso, *Jamestown,* 163–68, 159.

41. Two of the rare exceptions are a surviving gravestone from 1673 in Saint Paul's Church in Norfolk (Mason, "The Colonial Churches of Norfolk," 152) and a gravestone erected in 1744 in the Denbigh Churchyard in Warwick County (Mason, "The Colonial Churches of Warwick and Elizabeth City Counties," 379). The stones were recorded in 1941.

42. A husband and wife pair documented several inscriptions from these old gravestones (dating from 1760 to 1784) in the Tidewater region in the 1930s while they were still legible. Gray and Gray, "Out-of-the-Way Tombstones," 38–42.

43. Woods, *Albemarle County in Virginia,* 49.

44. Following in the European tradition of poor relief (dating to legislation passed in 1536), the American colonies began caring for their sick poor as early as the 1640s, when some municipalities paid doctors to administer their services. These payments included funds to bury deceased paupers such as "Arther Mcclain" in a Virginia parish in 1732 and a "Poore wounded seaman" in South Carolina in 1698. Almshouses or poorhouses were founded slightly later in the 1730s (e.g., in Philadelphia [1732], Charleston [1736], and New York [1736]). Deutsch, "The Sick Poor in Colonial Times," 569–70, 574.

45. Ranlet, "The British, Slaves, and Smallpox in Revolutionary America," 217. For example, the earliest burial in the Blandford Cemetery in Petersburg dates to 1781, that of a British major general who died from a fever related to either malaria or typhus.

46. Bender, "The 'Rural' Cemetery Movement," 204–5; Ames, "Ideologies in Stone," 642, 651–53.

47. See http://www.hollymemorial.com.

48. In 1790 the total number of enslaved individuals in Virginia was 292,627, while the total population of the state was 747,550. Historical Census Browser, University of Virginia, Geospatial and Statistical Data Center, accessed 28 December 2008, http://mapserve.lib.virginia.edu/.

49. For example, in the 1790 U.S. Census enslaved individuals constituted 51 and 54 percent of the population in Goochland and Louisa counties, respectively. Both counties are located in the western half of the state.

50. Ingersoll, "Decoration of Negro Graves," 68.

51. Olmstead, *A Journey in the Seaboard Slave States,* 405–6.

52. Brent, *Incidents in the Life of a Slave Girl*, 92.

53. Frey, *Water from the Rock*, 303.

54. Yucca plants, or *Yucca filamentosa*, are native to the southeast and may have first been selected for deliberate planting by Native Americans, who grew the plant near their settlements for fiber and soap. Benny Jensen, "Yucca filamentosa," 2005, accessed 14 March 2012, http://www.bennyskaktus.dk/Y_fila.htm.

55. Gomez-Aparicio and Canham, "Neighborhood Models," 70 (citing S. Y. Hu, "Ailanthus," *Arnoldia* 39, no. 2 [1979]).

56. Olmsted, *A Journey in the Seaboard Slave States*, 405–8; Puckett, *Folk Beliefs of the Southern Negro*, 571.

57. Interestingly, the Ibo in Nigeria also segregate suicides by "put[ting them] in the bad bush; there is no lamentation for them and no sacrifice." Thomas, "Some Ibo Burial Customs," 166.

4. Slave Cemeteries and Mortuary Rituals

1. Genovese, *Roll, Jordan, Roll*, 195. Peter Randolph (an emancipated slave) remembered that "most of the owners will grant their slaves [the] privilege" of having a funeral. Randolph, *Sketches of Slave Life*, 13.

2. Elizabeth Sparks, quoted in a 1937 interview in Hurmence, *We Lived in a Little Cabin in the Yard*, 29.

3. Jane Lewis, in Georgia Writers' Project, *Drums and Shadows*, 147. Most WPA interviewers and early twentieth-century ethnographers were white. The efforts of these individuals to capture the pronunciation of words by southern African Americans often reveals the prejudices of the interviewer. Though potentially offensive today, the dialect that results, is retained in these direct quotes from historic documents and is a product of its time.

4. Genovese, *Roll, Jordan, Roll*, 194. The first law that prohibited enslaved blacks from gathering for funerals was passed in Virginia, the Act of 1680 on Negro Insurrection. May, "Holy Rebellion," 237. Subsequent legislation, such as the 1804 statute that prohibited "nighttime religious meetings of slaves," fine-tuned this law. Ibid., 247.

5. Genovese, *Roll, Jordan, Roll*, 195.

6. Long, *Pictures of Slavery in Church and State*, 20.

7. Frey and Wood, *Come Shouting to Zion*, 23; Sobel, *The World They Made Together*, 218.

8. Sobel, *The World They Made Together*, 218.

9. Ibid., 24–25.

10. Harry Toulmin, *The Western Country in 1793*, 29, quoted in Morgan, *Slave Counterpoint*, 644.

11. Hunter, *Quebec to Carolina in 1785–1786*, 214, quoted in Sobel, *The World They Made Together*, 218–19.

12. Schoolcraft, *The Black Gauntlet*, 54; Hatcher, *John Jasper*, 36.

13. Long, *Pictures of Slavery in Church and State*, 20.

14. From "Report to the General Assembly's Committee on Missions, 1809," cited in Morgan, "Slave Life in Piedmont Virginia," 479n81.

15. Genovese, *Roll, Jordan, Roll*, 197–99.

16. Walsh, "The Transatlantic Slave Trade," 11–14.

17. Walsh, "The Chesapeake Slave Trade," 139–70.

18. Jamieson, "Material Culture and Social Death," 41–42.

19. Seeman, *Death in the New World*, 17.

20. At one end of the spectrum is the suggestion that many African traditions were preserved after the forced journey from Africa (e.g., Chambers, *Murder at Montpelier*), while other scholars argue that Africans were quickly forced to assimilate into European culture (e.g., Morgan, *Slave*

Counterpoint). Walsh (*From Calabar to Carter's Grove*) charts a middle ground, concluding that the "inconclusive evidence . . . suggests a mixture of forced adoption of European culture, tenacious retention and later adaptation of some African ways, differing self-preservations tailored to different audiences, and other ambiguous mergings of custom, belief, and outward appearance" (169–70).

21. Kopytoff, "Ancestors as Elders in Africa," 129.

22. Ibid., 132–34.

23. Adjei, "Mortuary Uses of the Ga People," 87–88.

24. Ibid., 89.

25. O'Donnell, "Religion and Mortality among the Ibo of Southern Nigeria," 56.

26. There was also a small percentage of Muslim Africans who arrived in the Americas during the colonial and antebellum periods (Austin, *African Muslims in Antebellum America*), but I found no evidence of these beliefs in the gravestones that I studied.

27. Georgia Writers' Project, *Drums and Shadows*, 11, 125.

28. Roediger, "And Die in Dixie," 169.

29. Rundblad, "Exhuming Women's Premarket Duties," 178. A Mississippi folktale also related how an African American man, presumed dead, sat "up on the cooling board and said 'What am I doing here.'" Dorson, "Negro Tales of Mary Richardson," 19.

30. This practice would have been restricted to wealthier individuals who owned an icehouse or enslaved individuals who were given ice. The practice was more common prior to the Civil War, before embalming techniques were developed. Robert Wells documents the use of ice to preserve an infant in 1846 in New York state in *Facing the "King of Terrors,"* 48.

31. Georgia Writers' Project, *Drums and Shadows*, 140.

32. Hildreth, *The Slave*.

33. Ibid., 82–83.

34. Randolph, *Sketches of Slave Life*, 15.

35. Elgie Davison, in Hurmence, *We Lived in a Little Cabin in the Yard*, 35.

36. *Cassy, or Early Trials*, 32.

37. Brent, *Incidents in the Life of a Slave Girl*, 49.

38. For example, in New Kent County, Virginia, a reverend preached a funeral sermon "over a poor old slave who died in the Lord" to two hundred slaves, as well as an unstated number of whites. Morgan, *Slave Counterpoint*, 643.

39. Viator, "The Night Funeral of a Slave."

40. Steward, *Twenty-Two Years a Slave*, 39.

41. Genovese, *Roll, Jordan, Roll*, 197.

42. Schoolcraft, *The Black Gauntlet*, 162.

43. A similar ritual was recorded in the early twentieth century by an anthropologist studying the Ibo of Nigeria. An informant told him about a coffin being carried during a funeral "after dark with torches. The procession was led by a slave wearing a rain hat with a fly whisk on his shoulder." Thomas, "Some Ibo Burial Customs," 186.

44. Richards, "The Rice Lands of the South," 731.

45. Burns, "Images of Slavery," 49–50.

46. Hatcher, *John Jasper*, 37.

47. Ibid., 38.

48. Olmstead, *A Journey in the Seaboard Slave States*, 25–27; "Letters on the Productions, Industry, and Resources of the Slave States"; Randolph, *Sketches of Slave Life*, 14–15; Georgia Writers' Project, *Drums and Shadows*, 106–7.

49. Randolph, farm diary, 28 August 1860. Sam Towler, an Albemarle County researcher, uncovered this reference while researching the African American community that lived in the Carter's Bridge neighborhood.

50. Rathbun, "Health and Disease at a South Carolina Plantation," 241.

51. McCarthy, " African-Influenced Burial Practices and Sociocultural Identity in Antebellum Philadelphia," 5.

52. Parrinder, *African Traditional Religion*, 107.

53. Genovese, *Roll, Jordan, Roll*, 198. Unappeased or angry spirits could cause death. Sobel, *The World They Made Together*, 217.

54. Ball, *Slavery in the United States*, 265.

55. Brannon, "Central Alabama Negro Superstitions."

56. Georgia Writers' Project, *Drums and Shadows*, 58.

57. Bolton, "Decoration of Graves of Negroes in South Carolina," 215; Ingersoll, "Decoration of Negro Graves," 68–69.

58. Thompson, *Flash of the Spirit*, 134–35.

59. Georgia Writers' Project, *Drums and Shadows*, 136.

60. Ibid., 147.

61. Thompson, "African Influences on the Art of the United States," 149; Vlach, *By The Work of Their Hands*, 43–44, 110, 112; Holloway, *Africanisms in American Culture*, 175, 199–200.

62. Brent, *Incidents in the Life of a Slave Girl*, 7.

63. Thompson, *Flash of the Spirit*, 117.

64. Genovese, *Roll, Jordan, Roll*, 200.

65. Rainville, "An Investigation of an Enslaved Community."

66. Nichols, *Slave Narratives*, 27.

67. Thomas, "Some Ibo Burial Customs," contains a nineteenth-century depiction of a slave cemetery.

68. The 1831 Prohibition to Teach Slaves, Free Negroes, or Mulattoes to Read or Write, *Supplement to the Revised Code of the Laws of Virginia*, Richmond, 1833, chapter 186.

69. John Hemings was the half brother of Sally Hemings (their mother was Betty Hemings). Unlike Sally, John was freed by Thomas Jefferson in his 1826 will.

70. Stanton, *Free Some Day*, 146.

71. Garman, "Viewing the Color Line," 83.

72. The caption on the photograph (located in the Library of Congress) reads, "The tombstone of 'Uncle Joe' is a reminder of the relations between kindly master and faithful slave." Library of Congress, Portraits of African American Ex-slaves from the U.S. Works Progress Administration, Federal Writers' Project, slave narratives collections, LC-USZ62-125132, call no. LOT 13262-1, no. 8.

73. Auslander, *The Accidental Slaveowner*, 54.

74. Brent, *Incidents in the Life of a Slave Girl*, 93.

75. Puckle, *Funeral Customs*, 148–49.

76. "Scenes on a Cotton Plantation," 72–73.

77. A novel penned in 1854 by a white woman describes a slave cemetery with a fence "shaded by evergreens and shrubbery." Quoted in Henderson, *Grief and Genre in American Literature*, 81. Although the narrative is romanticized, the author had the opportunity to observe antebellum African American cemeteries firsthand.

5. The Network of Death

1. Weitzen et al., "Factors Associated with Site of Death," 323.

2. Laderman, *The Sacred Remains*, 28.

3. Diary of Thomas Palmer, father of Mary Palmer Duane, d. 13 September 1846, quoted in Wells, *Facing the "King of Terrors,"* 104.

4. *Rippons Journal,* quoted in Sobel, *The World They Made Together,* 224.

5. Gorer, *Death, Grief, and Mourning,* 171, 173, 175.

6. Smith, *To Serve the Living,* 38–45.

7. Washington, *Black Belt Diamonds,* 41.

8. Holloway, *Passed On,* 165–7.

9. Miss Gertrude White, 4 January 1919, negative no. X7251B2, Holsinger Collection, Special Collections, University of Virginia Library.

10. Tonsler Flowers, 9 March 1917, negative no. X4908B, Holsinger Collection, Special Collections, University of Virginia Library.

11. Kuyk, "The African Derivation of Black Fraternal Organizations," 577.

12. Holloway, *Passed On,* 154–55.

13. Ibid., 163.

14. *Richmond Planet,* 3 September 1892, 4.

15. Holloway, *Passed On,* 150.

16. DuBois, *The Souls of Black Folk,* 150.

17. Nichols, *Slave Narratives,* 27.

18. Smith, *To Serve the Living,* 25.

19. WPA, *The Negro in Virginia,* 162–63.

20. Records of the First Baptist Church, 16 March 1863, MS 4620, Special Collections, University of Virginia Library.

21. Ellingsen, *Reclaiming Our Roots,* 209.

22. Woodson, *The African Background Outlined,* 170.

23. Albemarle County Deed Book 68, vol. 2, pp. 443–45 (26 February 1874).

24. Historic records from Monticello prove that Robert Hughes was born in 1824 (Stanton, *Free Some Day,* 160). Incorrect birth or death dates are occasionally inscribed on gravestones.

25. Lucia Stanton and Dianne Swann-Wright, Getting Word project, accessed 14 January 2009, http://www.monticello.org/gettingword/robert-hughes.html. Also see Stanton, *Free Some Day,* 159–60.

26. Charismatic slave preachers were involved in numerous revolts, hence the suspicion and repression that they faced on plantations (Joyner, *Down by the Riverside,* 171). Specifically, preachers who did not exhort slaves to be obedient to their master often faced punishment (Blassingame, *The Slave Community,* 132).

27. Baldanzi and Schlabach, "What Remains?" 52.

6. Lost Communities of the Dead

1. Virginia state law specifies that descendants and genealogical researchers may visit cemeteries on private property once they have given "reasonable notice to the owner of record or the occupant of the property, or both." Code of Virginia §57-27.1. A separate code specifies that visits to a cemetery "for any purpose other than to visit the burial lot or grave of some member of his family shall occur during the daytime or else the trespasser is guilt of a Class 4 misdemeanor." Code of Virginia §18.2-125.

2. Based on research conducted by A. Robert Kuhlthau and Julius Barclay, with assistance from the African American Genealogy Group of Charlottesville.

3. Jed. Hotchkiss, topographical engineer, "Map of Albemarle County," Staunton, VA, 1867, Library of Congress, Geography and Map Division.

4. For example, the 1804 law passed by the Virginia assembly that stated, "All meetings of slaves at any meeting house or any other place in the night shall be considered an unlawful assembly." The punishment was up to twenty lashes. Guild, *Black Laws of Virginia,* 71.

5. Kneebone et al., *Dictionary of Virginia Biography*, 84–86.

6. U.S. Census 1920, Scottsville, Albemarle, Virginia, roll T625_1878, p. 13B, enumeration district 13, image 349, house no. 239, family no. 245.

7. Albemarle County Deed Book, vol. 66, p. 249.

8. Lay, *The Architecture of Jefferson Country*, 140–41.

9. Johnston, photographs of Redlands; Haley, "Redlands," 50.

10. These buildings are often called "Delco houses," and the batteries contained in them were designed by Charles Kettering to provide electricity to rural homes and farm buildings. The Delco-Light farm electric plant opened in 1916 and provided electricity to more than a million farms until President Roosevelt passed the Rural Electrification Act in 1936. "Delco-Light Farm Electric Plant," accessed 17 December 2012, http://www.doctordelco.com.

11. Blassingame, *The Slave Community*, 181–83; Gutman, *The Black Family*, 230.

12. Edward Carter will, 21 February 1792, accession no. 807, University of Virginia Library.

13. Budros, "Social Shocks and Slave Mobility," 556.

14. Thompson, *A Phase I Archaeological Survey at Free State*, 13.

15. Stanton, *Free Some Day*, 103–7, 112–14, 116, 124, 156; Gordon-Reed, *The Hemingses of Monticello*, 247, 482–83, 506, 656–58, 694.

16. Albemarle County Will Book 4, p. 14, cited in Thompson, *A Phase I Archaeological Survey at Free State*, 15.

17. An archaeological survey documented sites dating back ten thousand years to the Paleo-Indian period. Underwood, Lewes, and Birkett, *A Cultural Resources Reconnaissance Survey*, 7–8.

18. Thompson, *A Phase I Archaeological Survey at Free State*, 24.

19. Hauser Homes website, accessed 12 March 2009, http://www.hauserhomes.com /communities/index.cfm?community_id=81.

20. Birkett, Lewes, and Cline, *Archaeological Documentation of the Dunlora Cemetery*, 4.

21. Ibid.

22. Thompson, *Archaeological Delineation of the Brown/Carr Family Cemetery*, 8.

23. Code of Virginia §57-26.

24. "When a graveyard, wholly or partly within any county, city or town, has been abandoned, or is unused and neglected by the owners, and such graveyard is necessary, in whole or in part, for public purposes . . . such county, city or town may acquire title to such burying ground by condemnation proceedings." Code of Virginia §57-36. Also note Code of Virginia §57-38.1, which states that "the owner of any land on which is located an abandoned family graveyard . . . may file a bill . . . for the purpose of having the remains interred in such graveyard removed to some more suitable repository."

25. Interviews by Melissa Shore, ca. 2002, posted to the now defunct Ivy Depot Film Project website, accessed 20 December 2008, http://www.3notched.com/ivy_depot.

7. Gravestone Genealogies

1. Charlottesville Area Association of Realtors website, accessed 20 December 2008, http://www.caar.com.

2. "Restrictions as to location of cemeteries and quantity of land," Code of Virginia §57-26, section 1.

3. *AARP: The Magazine*, "Top 10 Healthiest Places to Retire," 2008; *Black Enterprise*, "Best Places to Retire," 2008.

4. The author's website dedicated to African American cemeteries in central Virginia contains information about this cemetery: http://www2.vcdh.virginia.edu/cem/db/cemetery/details /JKS/.

5. Jeremy Borden, "Mapping One Grave at a Time: Professor Preserves Cemeteries," *Daily Progress,* 26 February 2007, A1, A6.

6. U.S. Census 1870, Fredericksville Parish, Albemarle, Virginia, roll M593_1631, p. 402B, image 276, house no. 1665, family no. 1685.

7. U.S. Census 1900, Earlysville, Albemarle, Virginia, roll T623_1697, p. 2B, enumeration district 4, house no. 28, family no. 28.

8. Alice Cannon, personal communication with the author. Cannon lives in Bleak House and has conducted extensive historic and ethnographic research on the individuals enslaved on the plantation and their descendents.

9. U.S. Census 1880, Rivanna, Albemarle, Virginia, roll T9_1352, p. 42, enumeration district 2.

10. Alice Cannon, personal communication with the author.

11. U.S. Census 1930; Rivanna, Albemarle, Virginia, roll 2434, p. 2A, enumeration district 5. Nathaniel Evans is listed as the head of the household; his son Roscoe Evans is the other member of the household.

12. Rainville, "An Investigation of an Enslaved Community."

13. Ingham, "Building Businesses," 642.

14. Mallon, "Passing, Traveling, and Reality," 648–52; Brown, *Clotel,* 185.

15. Senna, *Caucasia.*

16. Dusinberre, *Strategies for Survival,* 28–49; Rothman, *Notorious in the Neighborhood.*

17. U.S. Census 1880, Whitehall, Albemarle, Virginia, roll T9_1352, p. 109, enumeration district 4.

18. U.S. Census 1870, Fredericksville Parish, Albemarle, Virginia, roll M593_1631, pp. 263–64, image 293.

19. Raboteau, *Slave Religion,* 229.

20. Von Briesen, *The Letters of Elijah Fletcher,* 45, 73–74, 77–78.

21. Stohlman, *The Story of Sweet Briar College,* 39, 45, 88.

22. In Virginia, the practice of hiring out began after the Revolutionary War as white farmers adapted to decreasing tobacco production (which required a large labor force) and increasing wheat production (requiring fewer hands and thus resulting in a surplus of enslaved laborers). Frey, *Water from the Rock,* 222–23.

8. Connecting Communities through Their Burial Grounds

1. Inscoe, "Carolina Slave Names," 547–49.

2. *Albemarle County,* ADC Atlas, 1996.

3. Simmons, "Conservation, Cooperation, and Controversy," 403.

4. U.S. Department of the Interior, National Park Service, National Register of Historic Places Nomination Form for Mount Fair, DHR file no. 02-97 (1990).

5. National Register of Historic Places Nomination Form, section 7, p. 5.

6. Woods, *Albemarle County in Virginia,* 150–53.

7. A variation on this system was the "double cycle," which involved crop rotation and the application of manure from livestock to fallow fields in order to increase soil fertility. Nelson, *Pharsalia,* 75–80.

8. National Register of Historic Places Nomination Form, section 8, p. 1.

9. Ibid., section 7, p. 1.

10. Foss, *From Whitehall to Bacon's Hollow,* chapter 3.

11. Puckett, *Folk Beliefs of the Southern Negro,* 36, 78, 113–16.

12. Leone and Frey, "Conjuring in the Big House Kitchen," 380–81.

13. Nicholls, "Igede Funeral Masquerades," 70–76; Noon, "Death Concepts of the Ibo," 638.

14. Gomez, *Exchanging Our Country Marks*, 213.

15. Sobel, *The World They Made Together*, 97. For examples of the contemporary practice of erecting bottle trees in Tidewater Virginia, see Thompson, "Bighearted Power," 42 and n. 31.

16. Barden, *Virginia Folk Legends*, 107.

17. Foss, *From White Hall to Bacon Hollow*, chapter 1.

18. Ibid., chapter 3.

19. A total station is an electronic theodolite used by surveyors to produce accurate maps.

20. Puckett, *Folk Beliefs of the Southern Negro*, 94.

21. Bezaleel Brown will, 1829, Brown family papers, 1745–1888, accession nos. 3513 and 3513-a, Special Collections, University of Virginia Library.

22. Ibid.

23. Ibid.

24. Lay, *The Architecture of Jefferson Country*, 53–54, 123, 129, 132, 184.

25. For an account of business taking precedence over families remaining together and the ease with which slave families could be separated, see Morgan, "Slave Life in Piedmont Virginia," 448–49.

26. Benjamin Brown Sr. will, 1726, Albemarle County Courthouse.

27. Miller, *History and Genealogies*, 696.

28. Lay, *The Architecture of Jefferson Country*, 53–54.

29. Coons, *Benjamin Brown, Sr. of Brown's Cove*, 669.

30. Franklin's last name was inscribed on the stone, but is omitted here because of the recent burial date.

31. Glassie, *Pattern in the Material Folk Culture*, 37–39, 64–67.

32. Innisfree website, http://www.innisfreevillage.org/.

33. Coons, *Benjamin Brown, Sr. of Brown's Cove*, preface.

34. "An Inventory and Appraisement of the Est. of Bezaleel G. Brown," 1826, Albemarle Will Book 8, p. 160.

35. Albemarle County Deed Book, vol. 60, p. 599.

36. U.S. Census 1870, Fredericksville Parish, Albemarle, Virginia, 304–14.

9. Commemorating and Preserving Historic Black Cemeteries

1. Solomon Court website, accessed 8 January 2009, http://www.gemc.com/solomon/solomon.htm.

2. For example, the memorial erected at the African Burial Ground in New York. LaRoche and Blakey, "Seizing Intellectual Power."

3. National Register of Historic Places website, accessed 20 December 2008, http://www.nationalregisterofhistoricplaces.com/. The National Register now has a new website, accessed 31 December 2012, http://www.nps.gov/nr/.

4. National Register of Historic Places database, http://nrhp.focus.nps.gov.

5. Calculated by searching the online database of National Register properties, updated as of 18 September 2010, at http://nrhp.focus.nps.gov. On that date the register contained 87,138 places; 1,704, or about 2 percent, were listed under the assigned significance of "black."

6. Little, "Nominating Archeological Sites," 19.

7. *UVA News*, "Discoveries Date to 19th Century," 7 June 2005.

8. Ford, *The Foster Family Venable Lane Site*.

9. Bon-Harper, Neiman, and Wheeler, *Monticello's Park Cemetery*, 9–14, 22–24.

10. Avoca Museum website, accessed 15 December 2008, http://www.avocamuseum.org/timeline.htm.

11. Faulconer, "Restoring a Gravesite Forgotten by Time," 2.

12. "Restoration and New Road Bring Visitors to Forgotten Altavista Slave Cemetery," WDBJ TV news report, 30 August 2012, accessed 19 October 2012, http://www.wdbj7.com/news /wdbj7-restoration-and-new-road-bring-visitors-to-forgotten-altavista-slave-cemetery -20120830,0,1402237.story.

13. Swedburg, " Lost: Virginia Church Built by Freed Slaves."

14. Strangstad, *A Graveyard Preservation Primer,* 62.

15. Ibid., 7.

16. The recently revised J. F. Bell Funeral Home Records database, http://www2.vcdh.virginia .edu/jfbell.

10. Cemeteries as Classrooms

1. Bacque, "Public Cemeteries Are Part of City's History," C-1, C-5.

2. Cross-White, *Charlottesville: The African American Community,* 39, 48, 49.

3. Albemarle County Deed Book 68, vol. 2, p. 444 (26 February 1874), cited in Delaney, "Daughters of Zion Cemetery Project," 3.

4. Albemarle County Deed Book 79, pp. 110–11 (25 May 1933), cited in Delaney, "Daughters of Zion Cemetery Project," 7.

5. Charlottesville Circuit Court, Clerk's Office, Deed Book 19, p. 14 (23 September 1907), cited in Delaney, "Daughters of Zion Cemetery Project," 13–14.

6. *Daily Progress,* "City Asked to Operate Cemetery," 24 July 1971, 3–3.

7. Albemarle County Deed Book 71, pp. 417–18 (28 March 1877), cited in Delaney, "Daughters of Zion Cemetery Project," 22.

8. Albemarle County Deed Book 71, pp. 417–18 (28 March 1877), cited in Delaney, "Daughters of Zion Cemetery Project," 5.

9. Charlottesville Circuit Court, Clerk's Office, Deed Book 10, p. 172 (16 November 1899), cited in Delaney, "Daughters of Zion Cemetery Project," 6.

10. Delaney, "Daughters of Zion Cemetery Project," 22.

11. Cross-White, *Charlottesville: The African American Community,* 77.

12. Delaney, "Daughters of Zion Cemetery Project," 23.

13. *Daily Progress,* 3 September 1910, 1–2.

14. U.S. Census 1880, Charlottesville, Albemarle, Virginia, roll 1352, family history film 1255352, p. 302C, enumeration district 13, family and household 71; U.S. Census 1920, Charlottesville Ward 4, Charlottesville (Independent City), Virginia, roll T625_1882, p. 1A, enumeration district 28, image 1075, house 904.

15. *Daily Progress,* 27 February 1915, 1–5.

16. *Daily Progress,* 1 March 1897, 1–3.

17. *Daily Progress,* 2 November 1931, 7–2.

18. *Daily Progress,* 1 September 1905, 1–4.

19. Duncan, *Civilizing Rituals,* 8.

Bibliography

Adjei, Ako. "Mortuary Usages of the Ga People of the Gold Coast." *American Anthropologist* 45, no. 1 (1943): 84–98.

Akin, John G. *A Digest of the Laws of the State of Alabama—1833*. Montgomery: Alabama Department of Archives and History.

Ames, Kenneth L. "Ideologies in Stone: Meanings in Victorian Gravestones." *Journal of Popular Culture* 14, no. 4 (1981): 641–55.

Auslander, Mark. *The Accidental Slaveowner: Revisiting a Myth of Race and Finding an American Family*. Athens: University of Georgia Press, 2011.

Austin, Allan D. *African Muslims in Antebellum America: A Sourcebook*. Critical Studies on Black Life and Culture 5. New York: Garland, 1984.

Bacque, Peter. "Public Cemeteries Are Part of City's History." *Daily Progress*, 25 May 1975, C-1, C-5.

Baldanzi, Jessica, and Kyle Schlabach. "What Remains? (De)Composing and (Re)Covering American Identity in *As I Lay Dying* and the Georgia Crematory Scandal." *Journal of the Midwest Modern Language Association* 36, no. 1 (2003): 38–55.

Ball, Charles. *Slavery in the United States: A Narrative of the Life and Adventures of Charles Ball, a Black Man*. 1837. Reprint, New York: Negro Universities Press, 1969.

Barden, Thomas E., ed. *Virginia Folk Legends*. Charlottesville: University Press of Virginia, 1991.

Bender, Thomas. "The 'Rural' Cemetery Movement: Urban Travail and the Appeal of Nature." *New England Quarterly* 47, no. 2 (1974): 196–211.

Birkett, Courtney, David W. Lewes, and Jason Cline. *Archaeological Documentation of the Dunlora Cemetery, Albemarle County, in Conjunction with Court-Ordered Burial Removal*. WMCAR project no. 03-18. Williamsburg, VA: William and Mary Center for Archaeological Research, 2004.

Blassingame, John W. *The Slave Community: Plantation Life in the Antebellum South*. Rev. and enl. ed. New York: Oxford University Press, 1979.

Boles, John B., ed. *Masters & Slaves in the House of the Lord: Race and Religion in the American South, 1740–1870*. Lexington: University Press of Kentucky, 1988.

Bolton, H. Carrington. "Decoration of Graves of Negroes in South Carolina." *Journal of American Folk-Lore* 4 (1891): 214.

Bon-Harper, Sara, Fraser Neiman, and Derek Wheeler. *Monticello's Park Cemetery*. Monticello Department of Archaeology Technical Report Series, no. 5, 2003.

Boxley, Mary Frances, comp. *Gravestone Inscriptions in Amherst County, Virginia*. Amherst, VA: M. F. Boxley, 1985.

Brannon, Peter A. "Central Alabama Negro Superstitions." *Birmingham News*, 18 January 1925.

Brent, Linda [Harriet A. Jacobs]. *Incidents in the Life of a Slave Girl.* Edited by Maria Little. 1861. Reprint, New York: Harcourt Brace, 1973.

Bromberg, Francine W., and Steven J. Shephard. "The Quaker Burying Ground in Alexandria, Virginia: A Study of Burial Practices of the Religious Society of Friends." *Historical Archaeology* 40, no. 1 (2006): 57–88.

Brown, William Wells. *Clotel; or, The President's Daughter: A Narrative of Slave Life in the United States.* London: Partridge and Oakey, 1853.

Budros, Art. "Social Shocks and Slave Mobility: Manumission in Brunswick County, Virginia 1782–1862." *American Journal of Sociology* 110, no. 3 (2004): 539–79.

Burns, Sarah. "Images of Slavery: George Fuller's Descriptions of the Antebellum South." *American Art Journal* 15, no. 3 (1983): 35–60.

Cassy, or Early Trials. Boston: John P. Jewett, 1855. Online at http://www.iath.virginia.edu/utc/childrn/cbcassyhp.html.

Chambers, Douglas L. *Murder at Montpelier: Igbo Africans in Virginia.* Jackson: University Press of Mississippi, 2005.

Coons, F. H. Boyd. *Benjamin Brown, Sr. of Brown's Cove, Albemarle Co., Va: A Brief Survey of Some of His Descendants and Their Buildings.* Charlottesville: Virginia Regional Architecture, 1984.

Cross-White, Agnes. *Charlottesville: The African-American Community.* Dover, NH: Arcadia, 1988.

Delaney, Ted. "Daughters of Zion Cemetery Project: Final Report." Undergraduate honors thesis, University of Virginia, 2001.

Delaney, Ted, and Phillip Wayne Rhodes. *Free Blacks of Lynchburg, Virginia, 1805–1865.* Lynchburg, VA: Southern Memorial Association, 2001.

Dethlefsen, Edwin, and James Deetz. "Death's Heads, Cherubs, and Willow Trees." *American Antiquity* 31, no. 4 (1966): 502–10.

Deutsch, Albert. "The Sick Poor in Colonial Times." *American Historical Review* 46, no. 3 (1941): 560–79.

Deyle, Steven. "The Irony of Liberty: Origins of the Domestic Slave Trade." *Journal of the Early Republic* 12 (Spring 1992): 37–62.

Dorson, Richard M. "Negro Tales of Mary Richardson." *Midwest Folklore* 6, no. 1 (1956): 5–26.

Du Bois, W. E. B. *The Souls of Black Folk.* 1903. Reprint, New York: Penguin, 1997.

Duncan, Carol. *Civilizing Rituals: Inside Public Art Museums.* New York: Routledge, 1995.

Dusinberre, William. *Strategies for Survival: Recollections of Bondage in Antebellum Virginia.* Charlottesville: University of Virginia Press, 2009.

Early, Fay (Mrs. J. E.), and Mrs. Gordon Harris. *Record of Cemeteries in Albemarle County, Virginia, Including Charlottesville.* Vol. 13. Charlottesville, VA: Jack Jouett Chapter of the Daughters of the American Revolution, 1968–70.

Ellingsen, Mark. *Reclaiming Our Roots: An Inclusive Introduction to Church History from Martin Luther to Martin Luther King, Jr.* Norcross, GA: Trinity, 2000.

Faulconer, Justin. "Restoring a Gravesite Forgotten by Time." *News and Advance,* 26 April 2010, 1–2.

Foss, George. *From Whitehall to Bacon's Hollow.* http://www.klein-shiflett.com/shiflettfamily/HHI/GeorgeFoss/.

Ford, Benjamin. *The Foster Family Venable Lane Site: Report of Archaeological Investigations.* Prepared by Rivanna Archaeological Consulting. Charlottesville: University of Virginia, 2003.

Frey, Sylvia R. *Water from the Rock: Black Resistance in a Revolutionary Age.* Princeton, NJ: Princeton University Press, 1991.

Frey, Sylvia R., and Betty Wood. *Come Shouting to Zion: African American Protestantism in the American South and British Caribbean to 1830.* Chapel Hill: University of North Carolina Press, 1998.

Galland, China. *Love Cemetery: Unburying the Secret History of Slaves.* New York: HarperCollins, 2010.

Garman, James C. "Viewing the Color Line through the Material Culture of Death." *Historical Archaeology* 28, no. 3 (1994): 74–93.

Genovese, Eugene D. *Roll, Jordan, Roll: The World the Slaves Made.* New York: Vintage, 1976.

Georgia Writers' Project, Savannah Unit, Work Projects Administration. *Drums and Shadows: Survival Studies among the Georgia Coastal Negroes.* 1940. Reprint, Athens: University of Georgia Press, 1986.

Glassie, Henry. *Pattern in the Material Folk Culture of the Eastern United States.* Philadelphia: University of Pennsylvania Press, 1969.

Gomez, Michael A. *Exchanging Our Country Marks: The Transformation of African Identities in the Colonial and Antebellum South.* Chapel Hill: University of North Carolina Press, 1998.

Gomez-Aparicio, Lorena, and Charles D. Canham. "Neighborhood Models of the Effects of Invasive Tree Species on Ecosystem Processes." *Ecological Monographs* 78, no. 1 (2008): 69–86.

Gordon-Reed, Annette. *The Hemingses of Monticello: An American Family.* New York: W. W. Norton, 2008.

Gorer, Geoffrey. *Death, Grief, and Mourning in Contemporary Britain.* London: Cresset, 1965.

Gray, Arthur, and Elizabeth Gray. "Out-of-the-Way-Tombstones." *Virginia Magazine of History and Biography* 46, no. 1 (1938): 38–43.

Guild, June Purcell. *Black Laws of Virginia: A Summary of the Legislative Acts of Virginia Concerning Negroes from Earliest Times to the Present.* New York: Negro Universities Press, 1969.

Gutman, Herbert. *The Black Family in Slavery and Freedom, 1750–1925.* New York: Vintage, 1977.

Haley, Dru Gatewood. "Redlands: The Documentation of a Carter Plantation, Albemarle County, Virginia." Masters thesis, University of Virginia, 1977.

Handler, J. S., M. D. Conner, and K. P. Jacobi. *Searching for a Slave Cemetery in Barbados, West Indies: A Bioarchaeological and Ethnohistorical Investigation.* Center for Archaeological Investigations research paper no. 59. Carbondale: Southern Illinois University, 1989.

Hare, Augustus J. C. *Epitaphs for Country Churchyards.* Oxford, 1851.

Hatcher, William E. *John Jasper: The Unmatched Negro Philosopher and Preacher.* New York: Fleming H. Revell, 1908.

Henderson, Desiree. *Grief and Genre in American Literature, 1790–1870.* Surrey, UK: Ashgate, 2011.

Hildreth, Richard. *The Slave.* Boston: John H. Eastburn, 1836.

Hollis, Susan Tower. "Otiose Deities and the Ancient Egyptian Pantheon." *Journal of the American Research Center in Egypt* 35 (1998): 61–72.

Holloway, Joseph E, ed. *Africanisms in American Culture.* Bloomington: Indiana University Press, 2005.

Holloway, Karla F. C. *Passed On: African American Mourning Stories.* Durham, NC: Duke University Press, 2002.

Hunter, Robert, Jr. *Quebec to Carolina in 1785–1786, Being the Travel Observations of Robert Hunter, Jr., a Young Merchant of London.* San Marino, CA: Huntington Library, 1943.

Hurmence, Belinda, ed. *We Lived in a Little Cabin in the Yard.* Winston-Salem, NC: John F. Blair, 1994.

Ingersoll, Ernest. "Decoration of Negro Graves." *Journal of American Folk-Lore* 5, no. 16 (1892): 68–69.

Ingham, John N. "Building Businesses, Creating Communities: Residential Segregation and the Growth of African American Business in Southern Cities, 1880–1915." *Business History Review* 77, no. 4 (2003): 639–65.

Inscoe, John C. "Carolina Slave Names: An Index to Acculturation." *Journal of South History* 49, no. 4 (1983): 527–54.

Jackson, Charles O. "American Attitudes to Death." *Journal of American Studies* 11 (1977): 297–312.

Jamieson, Ross W. "Material Culture and Social Death: African-American Burial Practices." *Historical Archaeology* 29, no. 4 (1995): 39–58.

Johnston, Frances Benjamin. Photographs of Redlands Plantation. In the Carnegie Survey of the Architecture of the South. Available through the University of Virginia Library, Virgo title control no. a2769234/5.

Joyner, Charles. *Down by the Riverside: A South Carolina Slave Community.* Urbana: University of Illinois Press, 1984.

Kelso, William M. *Jamestown: the Buried Truth.* Charlottesville: University of Virginia Press, 2006.

Kneebone, John T., et al., eds. *Dictionary of Virginia Biography.* Vol. 3. Richmond: Library of Virginia, 2006.

Kopytoff, Igor. "Ancestors as Elders in Africa." *Africa: Journal of the International African Institute* 41, no. 2 (1971): 129–42.

Kuyk, Barbara. "The African Derivation of Black Fraternal Organizations in the United States." *Comparative Studies in Society and History* 25, no. 4 (1983): 559–92.

Laderman, Gary. *The Sacred Remains: American Attitudes toward Death, 1799–1883.* New Haven, CT: Yale University Press, 1996.

LaRoche, Cheryl, and Michael Blakey. "Seizing Intellectual Power: The Dialogue at the New York African Burial Ground." *Historical Archaeology* 31, no. 3 (1997): 84–106.

Larsen, Nella. *Passing: Authoritative Text, Backgrounds and Contexts, Criticism.* Edited by Carla Kaplan. 1929. Reprint, New York: W. W. Norton, 2007.

Lay, K. Edward. *The Architecture of Jefferson Country: Charlottesville and Albemarle County, Virginia.* Charlottesville: University Press of Virginia, 2000.

Leone, Mark P., and Gladys-Marie Fry. "Conjuring in the Big House Kitchen: An Interpretation of African American Belief Systems Based on the Uses of Archaeology and Folklore Sources." *Journal of American Folklore* 112, no. 445 (1999): 372–403.

"Letters on the Productions, Industry, and Resources of the Slave States." *New York Times*, 25 February 1853.

Little, Barbara. "Nominating Archeological Sites to the National Register of Historic Places: What's the Point?" *Society for American Archaeology Bulletin* 17, no. 4 (1999): 19.

Long, Reverend John Dixon. *Pictures of Slavery in Church and State.* Philadelphia: T. K. and P. G. Collins, 1857.

Mallon, Ron. "Passing, Traveling, and Reality: Social Constructionism and the Metaphysics of Race." *Noûs* 38, no. 4 (2004): 644–73.

Mason, George Carrington. "The Colonial Churches of Norfolk County, Virginia." *William and Mary Quarterly*, 2nd ser., 21, no. 2 (1941): 139–56.

———. "The Colonial Churches of Warwick and Elizabeth City Counties." *William and Mary Quarterly*, 2nd ser., 21, no. 4 (1941): 371–96.

May, Nicholas. "Holy Rebellion: Religious Assembly Laws in Antebellum South Carolina and Virginia." *American Journal of Legal History* 49, no. 3 (2009): 237–56.

McCarthy, John P. "African-Influenced Burial Practices and Sociocultural Identity in Antebellum Philadelphia." Paper presented to the fourth World Archaeology Congress, 1999.

Miller, W. H. *History and Genealogies of the Families of Miller, Woods, Harris, Wallace, Maupin, Oldham, Kavanaugh, and Brown.* Lexington, KY: Press of Transylvania, 1907.

Morgan, Philip D. *Slave Counterpoint: Black Culture in the Eighteenth-Century Chesapeake and Lowcountry.* Chapel Hill: University of North Carolina Press, 1998.

———. "Slave Life in Piedmont Virginia, 1720–1800." In *Colonial Chesapeake Society*, edited by Lois Green Carr, Philip D. Morgan, and Jean B. Russo, 433–84. Chapel Hill: University of North Carolina Press, 1988.

Morgan, Philip D., and Michael Nicholls. "Slaves in Piedmont Virginia, 1720–1790." *William and Mary Quarterly*, 3rd ser., 46 (1989): 211–51.

Minchinton, Walter, Celia King, and Peter Waite, eds. *Virginia Slave-Trade Statistics, 1698–1775*. Richmond: Virginia State Library, 1984.

Nelson, Lynn A. *Pharsalia: An Environmental Biography of a Southern Plantation, 1780–1880*. Athens: University of Georgia Press, 2007.

Nichols, H. P., and the Works Progress Administration. *Slave Narratives: A Folk History of Slavery in the United States*. Vol. 8. Washington, DC: Library of Congress, 1941.

Nicholls, Robert W. "Igede Funeral Masquerades." *African Arts* 17, no. 3 (1984): 70–76, 92.

Noon, John A. "A Preliminary Examination of the Death Concepts of the Ibo." *American Anthropologist* 44, no. 4 (1942): 638–54.

O'Donnell, William E. "Religion and Mortality among the Ibo of Southern Nigeria." *Primitive Man* 4, no. 4 (1931): 54–60.

Olmstead, Frederick Law. *A Journey in the Seaboard Slave States; With Remarks on Their Economy*. London: Sampson Low and Son, 1856.

Parrinder, Geoffrey. *African Traditional Religion*. 1962. Reprint, Westport, CT: Greenwood, 1975.

Parsons, Elsie Clews. *Folk-Lore of the Sea Islands, South Carolina*. Memoirs of the American Folk-Lore Society 16. Cambridge, MA: American Folk-Lore Society, 1923.

Pierson, Hamilton. *In the Brush; or, Old-Time Social, Political, and Religious Life in the Southwest*. New York: D. Appleton, 1881.

Puckett, Newbell Niles. *Folk Beliefs of the Southern Negro*. Chapel Hill: University of North Carolina Press, 1926.

Puckle, Bertram S. *Funeral Customs, Their Origin and Development*. London: T. W. Laurie, 1926.

Raboteau, Albert J. *Slave Religion: The "Invisible Institution" in the Antebellum South*. New York: Oxford University Press, 1978.

Rainville, Lynn. "African American History at the Sweet Briar Plantation." *Sweet Briar Alumnae Magazine* (2004): 7–10.

———. "Home at Last: Mortuary Commemoration in Virginian Slave Cemeteries." *Markers: Annual Journal of the Association for Gravestone Studies* 26 (2009): 54–83.

———. "An Investigation of an Enslaved Community and Slave Cemetery at Mt. Fair, in Brown's Cove, Virginia." *Magazine of Albemarle County History* 61 (2003): 1–26.

———. "Saving the Remains of the Day: Recognizing the Importance of Historic Black Cemeteries." *Tribune* 59, no. 204 (1 January 2009): A1, A5.

———. "Social Memory and Plantation Burial Grounds: A Virginian Example." *African Diaspora Archaeology Newsletter*, March 2008, http://www.diaspora.uiuc.edu/newsletter.html.

Randolph, Benjamin F. Farm diary, 1852–1866. Randolph-Hubard Collection, Special Collections, University of Virginia Library, University of Virginia. Accession #2424-a.

Randolph, Peter. *Sketches of Slave Life; or, Illustrations of the "Peculiar Institution."* Boston, 1855. Online at http://docsouth.unc.edu/neh/randol55/randol55.html.

Ranlet, Philip. "The British, Slaves, and Smallpox in Revolutionary Virginia." *Journal of Negro History* 84, no. 3 (Summer 1999): 217–26.

Rathbun, Ted A. "Health and Disease at a South Carolina Plantation: 1840–1870." *American Journal of Physical Anthropology* 74 (1987): 239–53.

Rawlings, Keith. *Gone but Not Forgotten: Quinette Cemetery, a Slave Burial Ground*. St. Louis: Messenger Printing, 2003.

Regosin, Elizabeth. *Freedom's Promise: Ex-slave Families and Citizenship in the Age of Emancipation*. Charlottesville: University Press of Virginia, 2002.

Richards, T. Addison. "The Rice Lands of the South." *Harper's Monthly Magazine* 19 (1859): 731.

Roediger, David R. "And Die in Dixie: Funerals, Death, and Heaven in the Slave Community, 1700–1865." *Massachusetts Review* 22 (1981): 163–83.

Rothman, Joshua D. *Notorious in the Neighborhood: Sex and Families across the Color Line in Virginia, 1787–1861.* Chapel Hill: University of North Carolina Press, 2003.

Rundblad, Georganne. "Exhuming Women's Premarket Duties in the Care of the Dead." *Gender and Society* 9, no. 2 (1995): 173–92.

Schoolcraft, Mrs. Henry R. *The Black Gauntlet: A Tale of Plantation Life in South Carolina.* 1860. Reprint, New York: Negro Universities Press, 1969.

"Scenes on a Cotton Plantation." *Harper's Weekly,* 2 February 1867.

Seeman, Erik R. *Death in the New World: Cross-Cultural Encounters, 1892–1800.* Philadelphia: University of Pennsylvania Press, 2010.

———. "Reassessing the 'Sankofa Symbol' in New York's African Burial Ground." *William and Mary Quarterly,* 3rd ser., 67, no. 1 (2010): 101–22.

Senna, Danzy. *Caucasia.* New York: Riverhead Trade, 1999.

Simmons, Dennis E. "Conservation, Cooperation, and Controversy: The Establishment of Shenandoah National Park, 1924–1936." *Virginia Magazine of History and Biography* 89, no. 4 (1981): 387–404.

Smith, Suzanne. *To Serve the Living: Funeral Directors and the African American Way of Death.* Cambridge, MA: Belknap Press of Harvard University Press, 2010.

Sobel, Mechal. *The World They Made Together: Black and White Values in Eighteenth-Century Virginia.* Princeton, NJ: Princeton University Press, 1987.

Stannard, David. "Death and Dying in Puritan New England." *American Historical Review* 78 (1973): 1305–30.

Stanton, Lucia. *Free Some Day: The African-American Families of Monticello.* Charlottesville, VA: Thomas Jefferson Foundation, 2000.

———. *Slavery at Monticello.* Charlottesville, VA: Thomas Jefferson Foundation, 2000.

Steward, Austin. *Twenty-Two Years a Slave, and Forty Years a Freeman: Embracing a Correspondence of Several Years, While President of Wilberforce Colony, London, Canada.* West Rochester, NY: William Alling, 1857.

Stohlman, Martha Lou Lemmon. *The Story of Sweet Briar College.* Sweet Briar, VA: Alumnae Association of Sweet Briar College, 1956.

Stokes, Sherrie. "Gone but Not Forgotten: Wakulla County's Folk Graveyards." *Florida Historical Quarterly* 70, no. 2 (1991): 177–91.

Strangstad, Lynette. *A Graveyard Preservation Primer.* New York: AltaMira, 1995.

Swedburg, Helenah. "Lost: Virginia Church Built by Freed Slaves." *Preservation Magazine,* online edition, 5 February 2009. http://www.preservationnation.org/magazine/2009/todays-news/lost-virginia-church-built.html.

Thomas Jefferson Foundation. *Thomas Jefferson's Monticello.* Chapel Hill: University of North Carolina Press, 2002.

Thomas, N. W. "Some Ibo Burial Customs." *Journal of the Royal Anthropological Institute of Great Britain and Ireland* 47 (1917): 160–213.

Thompson, Robert F. "African Influences on the Art of the United States." In *Black Studies in the University,* edited by Armstead L. Robinson et al., 122–70. New Haven, CT: Yale University Press, 1969.

———. "Bighearted Power: Kongo Presence in the Landscape and Art of Black America." In *Keep Your Head to the Sky: Interpreting African American Home Ground,* edited by Grey Gundaker with the assistance of Tynes Cowan, 37–64. Charlottesville: University Press of Virginia, 1998.

———. *Flash of the Spirit: African & Afro-American Art & Philosophy.* New York: Vintage, 1983.

Thompson, Stephen M. *A Phase I Archaeological Survey at Free State: An Historical African-American Community in Albemarle County, Virginia*. Report submitted to Stonehaus Development by Rivanna Archaeological Services. Charlottesville, VA, 2005.

———. *Archaeological Delineation of the Brown/Carr Family Cemetery*. Report submitted to Stonehaus Development by Rivanna Archaeological Services. Charlottesville, VA, 2007.

Toulmin, Harry. *The Western Country in 1793: Reports on Kentucky and Virginia*. Edited by Marion Tinling and Godfrey Davis. San Marino, CA: Huntington Library, 1948.

Underwood, John R., David W. Lewes, and Courtney J. Birkett. *A Cultural Resources Reconnaissance Survey of the Proposed Belvedere Development Project, Albemarle County, Virginia*. Submitted to Stonehaus Development by the William and Mary Center for Archaeological Research. Williamsburg, VA, 2004.

Viator. "The Night Funeral of a Slave." *Commercial Review* 20 (February 1856).

Vlach, John Michael. *By the Work of Their Hands: Studies in Afro-American Folklife*. Charlottesville: University Press of Virginia, 1991.

Von Briesen, Martha, ed. *The Letters of Elijah Fletcher*. Charlottesville: University Press of Virginia, 1965.

Walsh, Lorena S. "The Chesapeake Slave Trade: Regional Patterns, African Origins, and Some Implications." *William and Mary Quarterly*, 3rd ser., 58, no. 1 (2001): 139–70.

———. *From Calabar to Carter's Grove: the History of a Virginia Slave Community*. Charlottesville: University Press of Virginia, 1997.

———. "The Transatlantic Slave Trade and Colonial Chesapeake Society." *OAH Magazine of History* 17, no 3 (2003): 11–15.

Washington, Booker T. *Black-Belt Diamonds: Gems from the Speeches, Addresses, and Talks to Students of Booker T. Washington*. New York: Negro Universities Press, 1969.

Weitzen, Sherry, Joan Teno, Mary Fennell, and Vincent Mor. "Factors Associated with Site of Death: A National Study of Where People Die." *Medical Care* 41, no. 2 (2003): 323–35.

Wells, Robert V. *Facing the "King of Terrors": Death and Society in an American Community, 1750–1990*. Cambridge: Cambridge University Press, 2000.

Wilkinson, Richard H. *The Complete Temples of Ancient Egypt*. London: Thames and Hudson, 2000.

Woods, Rev. Edgar. *Albemarle County in Virginia; Giving Some Account of What It Was by Nature, of What Is Was Made by Man, and of Some of the Men Who Made It*. Charlottesville, VA: Michie, 1901.

Woodson, Carter G. *The African Background Outlined; or, Handbook for the Study of the Negro*. Washington, DC: Association for the Study of Negro Life and History, 1936.

WPA. *The Negro in Virginia*. Compiled by workers of the Writers' Program of the Work Projects Administration in the state of Virginia. Winston-Salem, NC: John F. Blair, 1994.

Cemetery Websites with Searchable Databases

African-American Cemeteries in Albemarle and Amherst Counties, VA: http://www2.vcdh.virginia.edu/cem/.

Allegheny Cemetery, Pittsburgh, PA: http://alleghenycemetery.com/.

Hollywood Cemetery, Richmond, VA: http://webcemeteries.com/Hollywood/.

Old City Cemetery, Lynchburg, VA: http://www.gravegarden.org/.

Index

Figures, maps, and tables are indicated by italic page numbers.

gravestones and headstones, 23–50; anomalous markers, 30; gender differences in, xiii, 32–33; genealogies reconstructed from, 98–113; materials used for, 24–25, 26, 27, 39–40, *40;* multiple stones commemorating one individual, 38–39; obelisks as, 27–29, *28–29;* punctured gravestones, 27, *27;* racial differences in materials used for, 39–40, *40;* size and shape of, 25–27, *26–27;* in slave cemeteries, 31, 62–64, *63;* social status influencing location of, 50; technology influencing, 24, 27, 32; terminology of "headstone" vs. "gravestone," 23–24; types of markers, 23–24, 47; unmarked graves, 2–3, 62, 129–30; of veterans, 22, 41. *See also* cemeteries; inscriptions and epitaphs; mortuary landscapes; motifs on gravestones

graveyards. *See* cemeteries
Great Awakening, 44, 45
Green Level Plantation, 139
Grimes, Patrice, 160

Hallock, Gardiner, 160–61
Hardin, Benjamin, 95
Hardin Tavern Slave Cemetery, 95–97
hauntings, 117–19
Headquarters Plantation, 126
headstones. *See* gravestones and headstones
Hearns, Billy, 77–79, 94
Hearns Cemetery, 77–79
Hemings, John, 62–63
Herndon, Jesse, 154
Hickory Baptist Church Cemetery, 39, 46
Hildreth, Richard, 55
hilltop locations of burial grounds, 14, 16
"hiring out" practices, 110, 176n22
Historical Highway Markers program, 134, 135
Hollins, Signora, 109
Holly Memorial Gardens, 48
Hollywood Cemetery, 48
Holsinger, Rufus W., 68, *68–69*
home deaths, 66–67
hospital deaths, 66
Hughes, Robert, 74–75, 174n24
hush harbors, 72

ICA (Ivy Community Association), 95–96
Innisfree community, 128–29, *130,* 131

inscriptions and epitaphs, 33–38; biographical, 33, 34, 35–37; in churchyard cemeteries, 73; content and sources of, 33–34; in Daughters of Zion Cemetery, 36–37, 152, 154, 155; defined, 33, 34; "erected by" inscriptions, 37–38; methods of recording, 6, 165–66; racial differences in, 40–41, *41,* 46; in slave cemeteries, 62–63, *63;* uncommon examples of, 34–35; in Zion Baptist Church Cemetery, 6

Internet: virtual cemetery databases, 147–48; virtual genealogical research, 21–22
interracial relationships, 105–6
In the Brush; or, Old-Time Social, Political, and Religious Life in the Southwest (Pierson), 57, *58*
Ivy Community Association (ICA), 95–96
ivy motifs, 30–31, 41, 42, 46

Jackson, Silas, 62, 71, 98, 99
Jackson Family Cemetery, 98–100
Jacobs, Harriet, 56, 61, 64, 65
James, Phil, 131
Jamestown colony burial practices, 47
Jasper, John, 57–58
Jefferson, Calvin, 75
Jefferson, Thomas, 35, 75, 138, 169n17
J. F. Bell Funeral Home, 70–71, 74, 147–48
Jim Crow laws. *See* segregation
Johnston, Delia, 157
Johnston, Phillip, 157
Jones, Florence, 33–34
Jones, Lee, 35

Kettering, Charles, 175n10
Kitty Foster site, 13, 137–38, *138*

lamb motifs, 32, 103
landscapes. *See* mortuary landscapes
Langley, Agnes, 13
Langley, Lizzle, 13
Larsen, Nella, 105
Latham, Jennifer, 100–101, 118
Lay, K. Edward, 83–84, 85
Lee, Etta, 34
Lewis, Agnes, 82
Lewis, Jane, 61
Lewis, Katherine, *81,* 81–82
Lewis, M. T., 154–55, *155*

Shelby, Letitia, 47
shells, symbolism of, 61
Shenandoah Valley Electric Cooperative (SVEC), xii, xiii
Shore, Melissa, 96–97
shroud-covered coffins, 56
slate grave markers, 24
slave cemeteries and mortuary rituals, 51–65; coffins constructed for, 55–56; graveside offerings and ritual finality, 59–61, 122, 122–23; gravestones and markers in, 31, 62–64, 63; inscriptions in, 62–63, 63; locating, 13–16; midnight funerals, 57–59, 58–59; mortuary landscapes of, 64–65; placement of, 14–15, 61–62; on plantations, 14–15, 61–62; postbellum use of, 65; preparing bodies for burial, 54–55, 67; procession to cemetery, 56; religious beliefs concerning death, 54; second burials, 52; types of, 13; unmarked graves in, 2–3, 62, 129–30. See also slave populations; *specific names of cemeteries*
Slave Census, U.S., 1, 14
slave patrols, 59
slave populations: ancestry of, 53–54; large gatherings, laws prohibiting, 52; literacy laws for, 2, 62, 167n3; religious beliefs among, 44–45, 54; in Virginia, 44, 49, 53, 170nn48–49. See also slave cemeteries and mortuary rituals
slave trade, 44, 53, 169n24, 169n27
soapstone grave markers, 24, 26, 27
social construction of race, 105–6
social status, gravestone location influenced by, 50
software used for website, 21–22
soil sinkage, 49–50
Solomon Family Cemetery, 132–33
South Garden Baptist Church Cemetery, 10
spirit sightings, 117–19
Steppe, Wilson, 126
Steward, Austin, 56
stone grave markers, 24, 25
Stonehaus Developers, 88–89, 91–92
stump preachers, 72
supernatural sightings, 117–19
SVEC (Shenandoah Valley Electric Cooperative), xii, xiii
Sweet Briar College, xiv, 2, 3, 108, 109, 113

Sweet Briar Plantation and Burial Ground, xiv, 2, 3, 107–10, 113, *113*

table style grave markers, 47
technology, gravestones influenced by, 24, 27, 32. See also Internet
Terrell/Lewis Family Cemetery, 91–92, 95
Thomas, Mattie, 78–79
Thomas Jefferson Foundation, 138–39
Thompson Family Cemetery, 17–20, *18*
tombstones. See gravestones and headstones
Tonsler, Benjamin, 68–69, *69*, 155
Total Station mapping device, 21–22
Trans-Atlantic Slave Trade Database, 53
tree of heaven (*Ailanthus altissima*), 49, 109
trees, ring of, indicating burial ground, 14–16
twentieth-century cemeteries, 16–17
Twenty-Two Years a Slave, and Forty Years a Freeman (Steward), 56

Union Run Church and Cemetery, 74–75
University of Virginia Slave Cemetery, 136–38, *137–38*
unmarked graves, 2–3, 62, 129–30
U.S. Geological Survey, 15, 116
U.S. Slave Census, 1, 14

Vena, Napoleon, xi
Vernon, Bob, 110
veterans gravestones, 22, 41
Veterans History Project, 22
vinca, 15
Virginia: laws protecting descendant rights to cemeteries, 19, 78, 94, 174n1; literacy laws for African Americans in, 2, 62, 167n3; slave populations in, 44, 49, 53, 170nn48–49. See also Albemarle County
Virginia Bureau of Vital Statistics, 16–17
virtual cemetery databases, 147–48
virtual genealogy, 21–22

Wakefield Church Cemetery, 35
Wake Forest Church, 35
wakes, 67–68, *68*. See also funerals and funeral industry
Walker, Angieline, 7
Walker, Louise, 8
Walker, Valdrie, 109
walking tours of cemeteries, 160

Waller, Henry, 142–43
Walnut Level Plantation and Slave Cemetery, 15, 127–31, *129*
Washington, Ben, 61
Washington, Booker T., 67
Washington, Sarah, 61
water, symbolism of, 14, 61
websites. *See* Internet
West, Laurence, 70
Wheeler, Derek, 135
White, Gertrude, 68, *68*
White, Rickey, 75
white cemeteries: gravestone materials used in, 39–40, *40;* inscription types in, 40–41, *41,* 46; locating, 13, 14, 15; motif choice in, 41–43, *42,* 45–46; on plantations, 13, 14, 15
Wild Rose Cemetery, 16, 39, 45–46
Winston, Gladys Fauntleroy, 139

women, differences in gravestones for, xiii, 32–33
wooden grave markers, 25, 26, 64
Woodson, Carter G., 73–74
Works Progress Administration (WPA) interviews, 61, 71, 118
worship of ancestors, 54
Wright, Tamar, 152

yucca plants, 10–11, 25, 49, 62, 171n54

Zion Baptist Church and Cemetery, 4–8; decahedron-shaped structure of, 4–5, *5;* deceased population, characteristics of, 7–8; founding of, 6; inscriptions on gravestones at, 6; motifs on gravestones at, 6–7, *7,* 30
Zion Hill Baptist Church, 74, 75